THE
LITTLE
DINOSAURS
OF
GHOST
RANCH

THE
LITTLE
DINOSAURS
OF
GHOST
RANCH

EDWIN H. COLBERT

COLUMBIA UNIVERSITY PRESS

NEW YORK

COLUMBIA UNIVERSITY PRESS

NEW YORK   CHICHESTER, WEST SUSSEX

COPYRIGHT © 1995 COLUMBIA UNIVERSITY PRESS

A list of credits for the illustrations appears on pp. 249–50.

Library of Congress Cataloging-in-Publication Data

Colbert, Edwin Harris, 1905–
    The little dinosaurs of Ghost Ranch / Edwin H. Colbert.
       p.   cm.
    Includes bibliographical references and index.
    ISBN 0–231–08236–3
    1. Coelophysis—Arizona.   I. Title.
  QE862.S3C58   1995
  567.9'7—dc20   94–36417
                                CIP

Printed in the United States of America

c 10 9 8 7 6 5 4 3 2 1

This book is lovingly dedicated to the memory of

Arthur and Phoebe Pack,

and of

James and Ruth Hall,

whose devotion to dinosaurs

and whose generous support of dinosaur hunters

made Ghost Ranch internationally renowned

in the annals of dinosaur research.

CONTENTS

PREFACE

The story of the little dinosaurs of Ghost Ranch may be viewed as a paleontological case history, for it recounts the various aspects of discovery, excavation, preparation, and research that determine the status of fossils as valuable records of past life. The appreciation of fossils as important scientific objects is becoming increasingly crucial, not only to paleontology as a scientific discipline but also to the informed public, which has a growing and sophisticated knowledge of fossils for what they are—the valuable and often irreplaceable raw data on which is built our knowledge of past life. These remarks are made for good reason because during the past decade or two a trend has developed toward the acquisition of fossils as curiosities or trophies, or even as objects of art.

Of course, as people become more and more interested in fossils, it is understandable that they may want to own fossils. And there is no reason why paleontological buffs should not own fossils, so long as they respect the rights of scientific institutions—museums and universities—to have full access to fossils of recognized significance. Such fossils should be in institutional collections, where they will receive proper protection and care and be available for present and future generations of scholars and museum visitors for study, exhibition, and contemplation. Professional and amateur paleontologists are now engaging in cooperative efforts.

The story of the little dinosaurs of Ghost Ranch is an example of how fossils are brought to light and preserved for posterity by professional and amateur paleontologists working together for the sake of science and posterity. Their fieldwork was not easy; they suffered through the vagaries of weather, which ranged from blazing heat to unremitting rain to miserably wet snow, as well as the annoyances caused by gnats, mosquitoes, and other pests. In the laboratories they put in long hours of preparation work and study. But in the end, these workers were rewarded by seeing the specimens properly stored, imaginatively displayed, and perceptively interpreted in publications. And the work in the laboratory and the research room still goes on, as it will for years to come. Much has yet to be learned.

A successful fossil expedition almost always requires the attention of people other than paleontologists. In the case of collections made on private land, the landowner or proprietor's positive attitude and assistance are of utmost importance. At Ghost Ranch we were fortunate to have had the sympathetic help, right from the beginning, of Arthur and Phoebe Pack, the owners of the ranch. During those summers of work the Packs did everything imaginable to facilitate our efforts at the quarry. Special mention should be made of the heavy work performed by Herman Hall, the foreman, with the ranch's bulldozer. Furthermore, Arthur and Phoebe almost instantly became our true and trusted friends, as I am sure we became theirs. We spent many happy hours with the Packs, and the summers were doubly pleasant because of their gracious company.

The same was true of Jim and Ruth Hall, with whom we had close contact after the Packs had donated the ranch to the United Presbyterian Church of the United States, to be used as a conference center. Jim Hall, the director of the ranch, took an active interest in the fortunes of the dinosaur quarry, and it was through his well-directed hospitality that institutions other than the American Museum (as I sometimes refer to the American Museum of Natural History)—namely, the New Mexico Museum of Natural History (then a nascent institution), the Carnegie Museum of Pittsburgh, the Museum of Northern Arizona, and the Yale Peabody Museum—made successful excavations at the quarry during the summers of 1981 and 1982. Furthermore, Ruth Hall was for years an ardent student and protector of the fossils at Ghost Ranch. Along with her other activities, she spent countless hours teaching the children, talking to adults, and giving lectures—all about the Triassic vertebrates of Ghost Ranch.

Today the dinosaur quarry and its dinosaur, *Coelophysis* (pronounced seel-o-fise-iss) *bauri*, are very much a part of the ranch, for which the present director, Joe Keesecker, deserves much appreciation.

Several years ago a large wing was added to the Florence Hawley Ellis Museum at Ghost Ranch. This new addition—a museum in its own right—was appropriately named the Ruth Hall Paleontology Museum. It is now directed by Lynett Gillette and features many large exhibits illustrating the paleontology of Ghost Ranch, including a huge block from the quarry—the most recent block to be removed. This block contains a superb, very large articulated skeleton of *Coelophysis bauri*. The excavation and removal of the block were completed by Lynett and David Gillette (state paleontologist of Utah), ably assisted by numerous dedicated volunteers. It is the centerpiece of the exhibit room at the museum.

I wish to express here my deep sense of admiration and gratitude to the three men who worked with me during that first summer of 1947 at Ghost Ranch—namely, Carl Sorensen, George Whitaker (who discovered the bone deposit), and Thomas Ierardi. Sorenson and Whitaker continued the work the following summer (1948), and it is because of their skill and dedicated efforts that the two superb articulated skeletons (American Museum numbers 7223 and 7224) were successfully removed from the places where they had rested for more than 200 million years and prepared for exhibition and study.

Various paleontologists and their associates, representing the museums mentioned earlier, worked at the dinosaur quarry in 1981, 1982, and 1985. Particular mention should be made of Greg MacDonald and a group of volunteers representing the New Mexico Museum; David Berman, Allen McCrady, Amy Henrici, and Norman Wuerthele for the Carnegie Museum; Timothy and Liz Gordon Rowe for the Museum of Northern Arizona; Mike Fracasso for Yale University; Robert Reisz and five assistants for the University of Toronto; and David and Lynett Gillette for the Ruth Hall Paleontology Museum at Ghost Ranch. The efforts of these people would hardly have been possible without the assistance provided by Jim Shibley, the foreman at Ghost Ranch. Jim continued the work of earthmoving, lifting, and hauling that had been done years earlier by Herman Hall and the Ghost Ranch bulldozer.

As will become clear, making collections in the field is just the beginning of the story. So I wish to acknowledge here the unsung efforts of numerous scientific preparators for their extremely skilled work in the tedious preparation of the multitudinous *Coelophysis* skeletons at the several institutions where they found their eventual homes. At the American Museum of Natural History great credit is due Carl Sorensen and George Whitaker, as well as Professor John Ostrom of Yale University (at the time a graduate student at Columbia University), for so painstakingly releasing the skulls and skeletons from their rocky tombs. Among the other people who have prepared *Coelophysis* specimens, many of whose names are unknown to me, I wish to acknowledge the work done by Scott Madsen and Allen Tedrow, at the Museum of Northern Arizona, and by Alexander Downs, who prepared the magnificent block now at the Smithsonian Institution (and who more recently revealed the large skeleton in the Ghost Ranch block).

I am most grateful to the American Museum of Natural History—where I labored for forty years and under whose auspices I carried out my part of the Ghost Ranch dinosaur project. It was there that I accomplished the greater part of my studies on *Coelophysis*. I am particularly obliged to David and Lynett Gillette for all their help through the years at Ghost Ranch.

In addition, I wish to express my appreciation for courtesies extended to me by other institutions where I was able to study *Coelophysis* specimens from the Ghost Ranch Quarry: namely, the Carnegie Museum of Pittsburgh, Yale's Peabody Museum, the Museum of Comparative Zoology at Harvard, the Royal Tyrrell Museum in Drumheller, Alberta, the Ruth Hall Paleontology Museum at Ghost Ranch, and of course the Museum of Northern Arizona, where I have worked since my retirement from the American Museum in 1970. My thanks go to Mary Dawson and David Berman of the Carnegie Museum, John Ostrom of Yale, Farish Jenkins of Harvard, Phil Currie of the Royal Tyrrell Museum, and Lynett Gillette of the Ruth Hall Paleontology Museum for assistance and many courtesies. I am also deeply indebted to the Museum of Northern Arizona for the publication of my monograph on *Coelophysis* (*Museum of Northern Arizona, Bulletin Series* 57) under the editorship of Diana Lubick and to the late Lois Darling and to Louise Waller for their illustrations of bones and skeletons in that volume.

I sincerely appreciate Dr. James A. Farlow's critical reading of the manuscript of this book, and I am very grateful to Jim for his detection of various errors and for his suggestions—all of which improved the text.

And, as on former occasions, I wish to thank Anne Cole for converting an often illegible manuscript into a typescript and the editorial staff of Columbia University Press for much assistance.

Edwin H. Colbert
Museum of Northern Arizona
Flagstaff

THE
LITTLE
DINOSAURS
OF
GHOST
RANCH

ONE

THE DISCOVERY

At the beginning of the summer of 1947 I was in the Southwest to search for fossils. It was to be a continuation of the previous summer, when I had spent some months with a field assistant, Bill Fish, in Arizona—especially in the Petrified Forest, looking for the remains of ancient animals, specifically amphibians and reptiles, that had lived in what was then a tropical landscape near the equator among giant trees that are now turned to stone. I had obtained a permit for Petrified Forest work from the Department of the Interior. In those days that took some doing, because a request for a permit allowing one to search for and collect fossils in a National Park had to go all the way up the chain of command to none other than the secretary of that great federal agency, and then all the way back down again to the humble petitioner. Thus I was all set to take up where I had left off.

I should begin by mentioning that back in the summer of 1945 I had been invited to teach the summer course in paleontology at the University of California at Berkeley, an invitation I readily accepted, since the stringencies imposed by the war effort such as gasoline rationing made it well-nigh impossible for paleontologists to go out into the field to look for fossils. So there I was, teaching one course a day, mainly to a group of young ladies and a few young men who, for one reason or another, were not in uniform. And during those hours when I was not teaching or preparing lectures I was studying Triassic fossils in the university's paleontological collection.

Quite a few of the fossils that came under my purview were the skulls of long-snouted phytosaurs, these being crocodile-like reptiles that had been found in Triassic sediments at a place called Ghost Ranch, New Mexico. The very name was intriguing, and I hoped that someday I might see this place where so many phytosaurs had been found. At the time I had no idea of what Ghost Ranch was like. Two years later I was to find out.

Thus in early June 1947 I disembarked the train in Albuquerque—in those days we still traveled quite a lot by train—along with my colleague George Simpson. George and I were both on the scientific staff of the American Museum of Natural History in New York, where, early in the spring, we had planned simultaneous field programs in the Southwest. He was to work in the Eocene sediments of the San Juan Basin of northwestern New Mexico, searching for ancient mammals, while I would be working in the Triassic beds of the Petrified Forest of Arizona, looking for reptiles and amphibians even more ancient than George's mammals. We left New York separately, but found each other on the train in Kansas City. And when we arrived in Albuquerque we met the other members of our field crews. George Simpson was to be assisted by Bill Fish, who had worked with me the previous summer, while I would have as my assistant George Whitaker, who had worked with Simpson the year before. I was also joined by a neighbor and good friend, Tom Ierardi, a professor at City University of New York—out for a summer of fun and adventure.

We were then all relatively young folks, full of vigor and quite prepared to undergo a summer of rigorous climbing and probing and digging in the cliffs and badlands of the Southwest. George Simpson, my immediate superior at the American Museum and three years my elder, was a remarkable man—one of the great international figures in paleontological and evolutionary studies—a man whose accomplishments stand high in his chosen field, and who will continue to shine as a beacon to future generations of students of past life. George was not a prepossessing figure; he was smallish and of slight build. His complexion was rather fair, and his thinning hair was light yellow. In those days he had a beard that added a modicum of fullness to his narrow face. But he was tough and did not hesitate to work just as hard as his assistants in the field—climbing and shoveling and lugging large, heavy fossils from the sites where they had been found to a waiting jeep or truck—no matter how difficult the terrain or how hard the journey. One would hardly guess that beneath that far from imposing exterior resided the spirit of a true genius. Indeed, George Simpson was the one person I have known over a long lifetime whom I would, without hesitation, characterize as a genius. And this opinion is shared by the scientific community.

As for George Whitaker, who was to be my working companion during the summer, one should picture a medium-tall individual in his twenties, with unruly black hair and a thin, black mustache; an intense person of tremendous energy. George was a southerner who had grown up in Valdosta, Georgia, and who had come to the American Museum to work in the fossil laboratory only a few years before our Ghost Ranch adventure. He was dedicated to paleontological preparation and fieldwork, and he displayed concentrated purpose and much ingenuity in his efforts to get fossils out of the ground. He had a short fuse, and one could imagine him as a reincarnation of an unreconstructed Reb, ready to fight and die for his cause. He had another side: he liked to cook—so, of course, he was chosen as our chef for the summer.

Tom Ierardi was not of the paleontological persuasion, but he was widely read, interested, and out for a summer of adventure. He was a rather short person, well built and very strong. And a special thing about Tom was his willingness to do his share of all the hard work that befell our lot; he did not regard a summer in the field as a time for high jinks.

Bill Fish, like George Whitaker, was a trained preparator from the American Museum's paleontological laboratory. He was a quiet person, in a way the antithesis of Whitaker—but, nonetheless, another who worked efficiently and productively. He had served in the navy during World War II and had experienced some exciting action in the North Sea. For example, he was a member of the crew of the lead decoy ship that enticed the Nazi battleship *Bismarck* to come out of hiding in the Norwegian fjords, presumably planning to destroy an Allied convoy, only to be itself destroyed by vessels of the Royal Navy that had been lying in wait just over the horizon. Bill said it had been quite a chilling experience to see that big warship bearing down on them, its guns primed to inflict awful destruction.

We started the summer together, all of us driving up to the San Juan Basin in a couple of surplus army jeeps, each pulling a two-wheeled trailer loaded with camping gear and the various equipment and supplies that fossil hunters, especially the hunters of ancient bones, find necessary.

For a few days we camped together near the little sagebrush village of Lindreth, which is on the eastern border of the San Juan Basin in northwestern New Mexico—George Simpson's chosen collecting ground. Then one morning I suggested that before George Whitaker, Tom, and I took off for the Petrified Forest, we pay a visit to Ghost Ranch, the place where those phytosaurs I had studied at Berkeley two summers earlier had come from. The idea was seconded by all with enthusiasm, so the next day, June 14, we headed toward Ghost Ranch, some forty miles to the east, for a day of pleasant sightseeing.

During the first part of our trip we drove through cool forests of ponderosa pine, with the colorful cliffs of Mesa Prieta rising a thousand feet above the road on our left. On our right, as we drove east, the dominant form of Cerro Pedernal came into view—a lone mountain that towered into the sky, a landmark visible from afar throughout this part of New Mexico. At first it rose before us in the form of a steep-sided, seemingly flat-topped table, rising above gentle forested slopes that reached down to yellow and white cliffs like those of Mesa Prieta. But as we continued eastward we saw that the crest of Pedernal, having given at first sight from the west an impression of a high mesa or table, was not that at all. As we got closer and viewed it from the north, it proved to be a sharp, knifelike ridge, or rather a steep-sided north-to-south gable crowning the long, pine-covered slopes. Moreover, even from the distance of our road, we could see that this hard ridge forming the summit of Pedernal was composed of basalt—the remnant of a volcanic flow that had covered this particular area about eight million years ago. The processes of erosion, continuing through the millions of years until our own time, had removed vast quantities of sediment and volcanic rock, leaving the hard, protective summit of Pedernal in its present form—a beacon for ancient and modern humans over the past ten thousand years.

Further on, east of a little settlement named Youngsville, we came out on a plateau, where in some roadcuts we saw—in the finer sediments of which the plateau was formed—deposits of heavy conglomerates formed of large and small pebbles, intermingled like raisins in a pudding. Here were the signs of ancient stream action—of vigorous watercourses debouching onto a plain.

But these nearby sights were minor distractions because beyond us eight or ten miles to the east was a line of high cliffs of incredible beauty. These were the cliffs of Ghost Ranch, running from south to north beyond the Chama River, and in the cliffs we saw a record of Mesozoic history. At the base were red and tan and chocolate-colored badlands, the Chinle Formation that is so characteristic of late Triassic deposition in the Southwest. Above the Chinle beds were cliffs, white and lemon-yellow, representing the Entrada Formation of Jurassic age. And on top of these sheer cliffs was a layer of dazzling white gypsum, like meringue on a lemon pie—the Todilto Formation, also of Jurassic age. Above the Todilto was an extensive exposure of chocolate brown and light-colored cliffs and hills, receding and rising far back beyond the limits of the Entrada-Todilto barrier. This elevated hilly topography, the surface of which was extensively covered with small juniper trees, was formed by the Morrison beds, which in many parts of the West, including northern New Mexico, contain the bones of late Jurassic dinosaurian giants. Finally, on the skyline, was a crested ridge, composed of the brown Dakota sandstone of early Cretaceous age. This was Mesozoic history on a grand scale; a sight to gladden the eye of the beholder. (See figures 1 and 2.)

A brief digression from the story of our first visit to Ghost Ranch will be helpful at this point, to explain why we saw those brilliantly colored cliffs

FIGURE 1 The Mesozoic section at Ghost Ranch, New Mexico. In the valley beyond the trees in the foreground are Quaternary and Recent alluvial deposits, cut by the Arroyo del Yeso (which runs just beyond the trees and is not visible in this picture). From the level floor of the valley rise the rounded red hills of the Triassic Chinle Formation. Behind and above the Chinle badlands are the yellow cliffs of the Jurassic Entrada Formation, capped by a layer of white gypsum—the Jurassic Todilto Formation. Above the Todilto are the long slopes of the Jurassic Morrison Formation, comprising thick gray and purplish shales and clays. At the top of the sequence is a long, prominent ridge formed of the Cretaceous Dakota sediments.

FIGURE 2   The Entrada-Todilto cliffs, with the sloping Chinle beds at the base, just across the little valley of Arroyo del Yeso from the dinosaur quarry. These cliffs, formed of a massive, rather hard sandstone, are undermined by erosion of the soft Chinle beds beneath, and consequently the vertical cliff faces are maintained.

that stretched for miles to the north and south in terms of Triassic, Jurassic, and Cretaceous rocks, and why they were more individually described as belonging, for example, to the Chinle Formation or the Dakota sandstone. This necessitates some discussion of the geologic time scale, which is used all over the world.

The rocks of the earth's surface have been divided into four great time divisions known as *eras,* these, except the Proterozoic (commonly known as Precambrian time), being divided into *periods,* the periods into *epochs,* and the epochs into lesser divisions, known as *stages.*

This arrangement of geologic time is based primarily on the sequence of fossil-bearing sedimentary rocks throughout the world. By observing the positions of rock layers in relation to one another, and by analyzing the evolutionary stages of fossils contained in the individual layers, known as *formations* (which are rock units that can be mapped, whether they are exposed over many thousands of square miles, or whether they are of restricted extent), it has been possible over the years to set up a worldwide sequence of rocks and their contained fossils. From this a universal scale of geologic time has been defined.

In the geologic timescale shown in table 1 the four great eras of geologic history are shown in order, from the oldest—the Proterozoic and Paleozoic eras at the bottom of the chart—through the middle years of earth history—the Mesozoic era—and on to the youngest great division—the Cenozoic era—at the top. It is established practice to delineate the sequence of time divisions in this manner, from the oldest at the bottom to the youngest at the top, because that is the way the rocks forming the crust of the earth were deposited.

The three eras with abundant fossil records are divided into their respective periods, and the periods into epochs. The absolute ages of the epochs are indicated by figures, noting the beginning and the end of each epoch, expressed in millions of years ago (by convention denoted in the modern literature of geology by the letters MYA or MA).

Table 2 shows the late Permian, Triassic, Jurassic, and Cretaceous epochs and their constituent stages, which are the stages pertinent to the story of the Ghost Ranch dinosaurs. It should be added that the two stages intimately associated with *Coelophysis* are those constituting the end of Triassic history, namely, the Carnian and Norian stages. The Chinle Formation (see figure 3), in which *Coelophysis* is found, probably spans the Carnian-Norian sequence, at least in part.

That said, we return to our story. With such an inspiring view beckoning to us, we continued east to Federal Highway 84, and then drove a few miles north until we reached the Ghost Ranch gate, which bore a sign emblazoned with an emblematic picture of a cow skull. (The skull design, we soon found out, had been done for the ranch by Georgia O'Keeffe, a nearby neighbor.)

We drove through the gate and proceeded along a red dirt road to the ranch headquarters, a veritable oasis of trees and green lawns, which sheltered and surrounded several one-story buildings. The most prominent of these buildings occupied a raised terrace, where it seemed to command the immediate surroundings; indeed, as we were to learn, it was the headquarters for the ranch. Immediately in front of this building was a large flagstone patio. The facade of the building held large plate-glass windows that looked out across a little valley traversed by a small stream known as Arroyo del Yeso. To the west was the magnificent sweep of cliffs and

TABLE 1
Geologic Time Scale

Era	Period	Epoch	MYA (millions of years ago)
Cenozoic	Quaternary	Holocene	0.01
		Pleistocene	
			1.6
	Neogene	Pliocene	5.2
		Miocene	
			23.3
	Paleogene	Oligocene	35.4
		Eocene	
			56.5
		Paleocene	
			65.0
Mesozoic	Cretaceous	Late	97.0
		Early	
			145.6
	Jurassic	Late	157.1
		Middle	
			178.0
		Early	
			208.0
	Triassic	Late	235.0
		Middle	
			241.1
		Early	
			245.0
Paleozoic	Permian	Late	256.1
		Early	
			290.0
	Pennsylvanian[a] Carboniferous Mississippian[a]	Late	322.8
		Early	
			362.5
	Devonian	Late	377.4
		Middle	
			386.0
		Early	
			408.5
	Silurian	Late	424.0
		Early	
			439.0
	Ordovician	Late	463.9
		Middle	
			476.1
		Early	
			510.0
	Cambrian	Late	517.2
		Middle	
			536.0
		Early	
			570.0
Proterozoic	Precambrian		
			4500.0?

[a]North American geologists recognize these two periods in place of the Carboniferous.

TABLE 2
Stages of the Late Permian Period and the Mesozoic Era

Era	Period	Epoch	Stage	Events
Mesozoic	Cretaceous	Late	Maastrichtian Campanian Santonian Coniacian Turonian Cenomanian	*Extinction* Zenith of dinosaurian evolution
		Early	Albian Aptian Neocomian	Appearance of flowering plants
	Jurassic	Late	Tithonian Kimmeridgian Oxfordian	Gigantic dinosaurs
		Middle	Callovian Bathonian Bajocian Aalenian	Continued dinosaurian evolution
		Early	Toarcian Pleinsbachian Sinemurian Hettangian	Early stages of dinosaurian evolution
	Triassic	Late	Norian Carnian	Ghost Ranch dinosaurs First dinosaurs
		Middle	Ladinian Anisian	Thecodont dominance
		Early	Scythian	Early archosaurs
Paleozoic	Permian	Late	Tatarian Kazanian Ufimian	*Extinction* Mammal-like reptiles

peaks—the country we had traversed on our way from Lindreth. Quite prominent was Pedernal—the ten-thousand-foot high peak described above—formed of the sequence of Mesozoic rocks and surmounted by the thick ridge of basalt. (This heavy, igneous rock was the reason, of course, for the preservation of Pedernal as a mountain.)

Just beyond the headquarters building, and even a bit higher on the terrace, was a modern dwelling, its front consisting of large expanses of windows that also looked out across the valley landscape. This was the dwelling of Arthur Pack, the owner of the ranch, and his family (see figure 4).

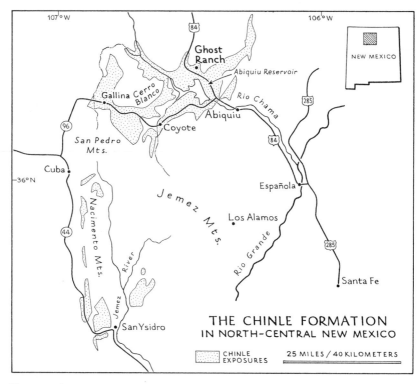

FIGURE 3   Map showing the exposures of the Triassic Chinle Formation in New Mexico. Modified, after O'Sullivan 1974, and Schwartz and Gillette 1994. Cartography by George Colbert.

Beyond these buildings were a number of small, one-story structures constructed in the southwestern adobe style—formerly the guesthouses of what had for quite a few years been a dude ranch. One of these little cottages—set against the side of a small hill where it was shaded by two enormous cottonwood trees, was "Ghost House," the first building erected on the ranch.

As we pulled up in front of the headquarters building we were greeted by a slightly built, sandy-haired man who welcomed us with a smile. He was Arthur Pack. Arthur was not in the least disconcerted by our abrupt, unannounced arrival. He identified himself, we identified ourselves, and without further ado he invited us into the headquarters for lunch.

It was a most enjoyable luncheon, served in a friendly, southwestern-style room, attended by Arthur, but presided over by Arthur's wife, Phoebe, who at the same time kept a maternal eye on the Pack children, Charles and "little" Phoebe. Herman Hall (the ranch foreman) was there, and the meal was served by Herman's wife, "Jimmy." I mentioned to Arthur that some of us would like to spend a few days poking around in the Chinle Triassic Formation on the ranch before going on to our designated summer campaign in Arizona. He said that would be just fine, so we returned to our campsite in the sagebrush near Lindreth with visions of a few interesting days at Ghost Ranch.

Before departing from Ghost Ranch that day I asked Arthur how the ranch got its name. He had an interesting story to tell, best recounted here in the words he wrote some years later.

Near the end of the nineteenth century, a Spanish American family by the name of Archuleta . . . built a stockade of cedar poles plastered with mud and straw, which we now call the Ghost House; they channeled wa-

FIGURE 4   Arthur and Phoebe Pack at Ghost Ranch.

ter out of Yeso Canyon behind the ranch headquarters; they became herders of sheep and cattle. The family were the descendants of retainers or servants of Spanish explorers, possessing a mixture of Mexican-Indian blood with Andalusian-Spanish.

The people of northern New Mexico . . . were highly superstitious, believing in witches or evil spirits called "Brujos." Their method of acquiring wealth included hard work, but they also took wealth where they found it. It is probably in this latter way that the Archuletas built up their herd of both sheep and cattle, for this little canyon offered an excellent hide-out for cattle thieves. According to a well-substantiated story, one of the Archuleta brothers managed to drive some cattle down to the settlements around Santa Fe, where he sold them for gold. When he returned, the elder Archuleta brother accused him of holding out for more than his share of the money. During the argument that followed, the elder man picked up an ax and killed his brother on the spot—virtually a re-enactment of the Biblical drama of Cain and Abel. . . .

Thereafter the "curse of Cain" seems to have fallen upon the little canyon. Cain (whose name in our story was Juan Ignacio Archuleta) suspected his dead brother's wife of knowing where the gold was hidden. He threatened her, not with her own death but with the sacrifice of her baby girl. . . . Our "Cain," as head of the family, now declared that the following day his little niece must be bound and left in the hills to propitiate [a] devilish evil spirit. So when night fell, the girl's mother stole out, haltered a burro, put the child on it, and fled to the old pueblo of San Juan in the Española Valley.

This child eventually moved with her mother to Utah and married, but she returned here sixty years later and told us her story. . . . Told by her mother that the disputed gold was hidden in a buried pot in or near the Ghost House, she had come to ask our permission to search for it. No one ever found it.

The "curse of Cain" continued even after the little girl escaped. A posse of indignant neighbors fell upon the Ghost Ranch, captured two suspected cattle thieves, and hanged them from the big cottonwood trees beside the Ghost House. [The trees are still there.] Juan Ignacio himself escaped, but more trouble was in store. The government of New Mexico had never managed to collect any taxes on the Archuleta homestead. Having no money, the Archuleta family was eventually dispossessed and the tax title fell to a Santa Fe lawyer. Juan Ignacio Archuleta and his family moved up the Arroyo Seco and built an adobe hut there.

Following the First World War, there came to northern New Mexico a young woman of Boston's bluest blood. . . . There she met a Texas cowboy and married him without waiting for the family consent. This couple made a remarkable team. The woman had the necessary social connections back East to get paying "dudes" and he had the Western know-how needed to run a ranch. They built New Mexico's most famous dude ranch at Alcalde near San Juan pueblo, which prior to Santa Fe had been the first Spanish capital of the upper Rio Grande region.

In a game of cards, he won title—according to his own story—to the old Archuleta-haunted homestead above Abiquiu. . . .

A year or so later came the 1929 stock market crash. San Gabriel Ranch [then the name of their dude ranch at Alcalde] had no guests, no income, and huge debts. Bankruptcy followed. The creditors took everything that they deemed of any value; but they allowed the lady from Boston, who was now divorced from her cowboy husband, to keep the "worthless Archuleta homestead," so far up the Chama River on a very bad road that no one wanted it. She moved into the old Ghost House and tried to pick up the pieces of her life. Because her Spanish-American neighbors so feared the place, she called it Ghost Ranch. Indeed, there were good justifications for the name. The local neighbors told hair-raising stories about an old well near the house which was supposed to conceal the bodies of murdered visitors.

One's imagination might continue to elaborate on the theory of the evil spirits or the "curse of cain." Old man Juan Ignacio suffered continued misfortune and became blind. The lady from Boston sold Ghost Ranch to me, married another cowboy who gambled the proceeds on third-rate race horses, and was harried out of the state by indignant creditors. . . . She died right after World War II in hiding and poverty just across the Colorado line.   (Pack 1960:10–12)

Such was the sad and rather gruesome story (recounted to me by Arthur more informally than in his written version) that I took back with me to our camp that night.

When we drove back from Ghost Ranch to Lindreth I did not fully appreciate our good fortune in arranging to do some paleontological exploration on land belonging to Arthur Pack. But I was soon to realize how important to the success of our summer's work our relationship with Arthur and Phoebe would be.

Arthur was a remarkable person, a man of considerable means who lived a simple life, a man with a sympathetic understanding of and a deep appreciation for the true values of Mother Earth and her creatures. His father, Charles Lathrop Pack, was a pioneer advocate of forest conservation; he founded the Charles Lathrop Pack Forestry Foundation, of which in time Arthur became president. Furthermore, Arthur and his father founded the American Nature Association, which for many years published *Nature Magazine* (not to be confused with the British scientific weekly *Nature*), Arthur being the editor of the magazine during its later years. (Eventually *Nature Magazine* was combined with *Natural History,* published by the American Museum of Natural History.) Arthur was dedicated to the conservation of all wild things, botanical and zoological, and to the advancement of knowledge about life on the earth, past and present. Consequently, he was the very person to support our activities at Ghost Ranch. How his support would be concretely expressed, during that first summer of our work at the ranch, will become apparent.

Later, in 1955, the Packs gave Ghost Ranch to the Presbyterian Church, under whose sponsorship—especially under the leadership of James Hall, for many years director of the ranch—it became (and remains) a conference center known throughout the world. Every year at Ghost Ranch numerous seminars and symposia take place on subjects of the widest variety and significance; seminars on the paleontology of northern New Mexico are held biannually or annually.

In the summer of 1947 we were making our own plans. George Simpson (later joined by his wife, Anne) and Bill Fish were to begin their summer collecting campaign in the vicinity of Lindreth, while George Whitaker, Tom, and I would go to Ghost Ranch for a week or two of prospecting before continuing to the Petrified Forest in Arizona. Simpson and I made arrangements to keep in close touch with each other through the summer.

Little did we then suspect that "keeping in touch" would be a matter of communicating across a few dozen miles rather than from one camp in New Mexico to another two hundred miles away in Arizona.

Two or three days later Tom, George Whitaker, and I were back at Ghost Ranch. There we set up our tents beneath some sheltering trees along the edge of a little stream known as Arroyo del Yeso—"Gypsum Gully" it might be called in the less sonorous and less romantic English language. The early Spanish settlers so named this little watercourse because of the presence along its banks of gypsum blocks that had fallen from the Todilto Formation crowning the nearby cliffs (see figure 5).

On the morning after establishing our camp we set out to explore a near-

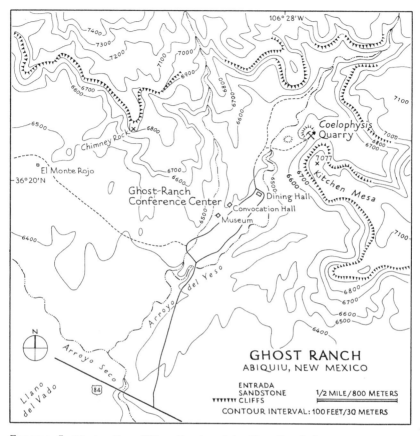

FIGURE 5   The location of Ghost Ranch and the Ghost Ranch dinosaur quarry along
Arroyo del Yeso, New Mexico. Figures indicate altitude in feet above sea level. Adapted
from the U.S. Geological Survey topographic sheet, Ghost Ranch Quadrangle, 1953, 7.5
Minute Series. Cartography by George Colbert.

by canyon that cut through the Chinle beds at the base of the cliffs. I knew
that University of California parties had previously explored and collected
on the flats between the ranch headquarters and the Chama River, where
the Chinle Formation is exposed as rounded badlands. Perhaps up the canyon something might be found, and it was. Within an hour or so after having started our fossil hunt we found a nice phytosaur skull. Our purpose
was to make a probing search of the sediments here, mainly to get some
idea of the type of fossils to be found, but here was a specimen too good to
pass up. So we set about collecting it. This required three days of effort.
    First the specimen was carefully exposed by chiseling and scratching

away the surrounding rock in which it was embedded. And as the fossil bone came to light it was treated with a preservative (in those days we used white shellac thinned with alcohol). Then, with the entire length of the skull uncovered, Japanese rice paper was applied to the bone surface and treated with soft brushes dipped in shellac. When the preservative was dry, the bone had a rather tough protective covering. A heavy bandage of burlap dipped in plaster of paris was then pressed onto the paper-covered bone in much the same fashion as a physician applies a cast to a broken limb. The idea was to immobilize the specimen. After the plaster was dry we cut under the fossil to free it from the rock, turned it over, cleaned the bottom of the specimen, and applied rice paper and plaster. Finally a straight juniper branch, cut from a nearby tree, was plastered against the specimen to give it additional strength.

By this time, what with the enclosing cast of plaster, the specimen was pretty heavy. There was only one thing left to do: devise a sling so that we could hoist and carry the specimen out of the canyon. The going was rough, but we finally made it to our jeep, and from there it was a simple matter to haul the fossil to our camp.

That is how large fossils are usually collected—one doesn't dig them out of the ground indiscriminately. If one were to try to do so the result would be a pile of fossil trash—a specimen broken into dozens or even hundreds of fragments.

Having the phytosaur skull safely on board, we resumed our exploratory probe of the Chinle Formation in this area, with an eye to future collecting. But first a few words about phytosaurs.

Known as thecodont reptiles, they are particularly characteristic of late Triassic rocks across much of the northern hemisphere. As mentioned, phytosaurs were crocodile-like in aspect; it would be more accurate to say that the crocodiles and alligators and gavials of our modern world are phytosaur-like, because the phytosaurs came first. They evolved as elongated, scaly reptiles of considerable size (some of them were twenty feet and more long) that obviously lived in lakes and rivers and streams. If one envisions a modern crocodile with its nostrils on a prominence just in front of the eyes, instead of at the tip of the snout, one has a reasonable picture of a phytosaur.

These successful reptiles lived during the late Triassic period, about 230 to 200 million years ago. They were aggressive predators that dominated late Triassic landscapes in North America and Eurasia. Then, during the

FIGURE 6 Ierardi (white cap) and Whitaker placing a plaster cap over the fossil bones initially uncovered at the quarry to protect them during subsequent quarry operations.

transition from the Triassic to the Jurassic period, the phytosaurs became extinct, and the crocodilians arose from thecodont (not phytosaur) ancestors. They imitated the phytosaurs in a most uncanny fashion and have enjoyed a remarkably successful evolutionary history for some 200 million years—in other words, from the beginning of the Jurassic to the present. This is a good illustration of evolutionary parallelism.

Why did the phytosaurs become extinct, while their imitators, the crocodilians, were so supremely successful? Here we are confronted with one of the prime puzzles of paleontology, something about which bone hunters speculate ad infinitum.

The next day, Sunday, June 22, we did some more prospecting, again with the idea of making an exploratory probe of the nature of Chinle fossils in this region, as a basis for future collecting. Tom and I went in one direction, George Whitaker in another. Shortly before noon George came running over from the hillside where he had been poking around to the hillside on which we were doing the same.

As he scrambled up the slope toward us it was evident that he was very excited. He had a right to be; in his hands he had some tiny bone fragments, including a well-preserved claw. They were the fossil remains of *Coelophysis*, a small Triassic dinosaur—at least that was my identification of these fragments, and I was pretty confident I was correct.

Why did I feel sure that these few fragments belonged to *Coelophysis?* Because I was familiar with the literature on Triassic fossil reptiles, and furthermore because I had spent many hours during the previous few years examining and studying such fossils in museum collections. It is not miraculous that paleontologists can pin down the relationships of a fragmentary fossil found in the field; it is part of the business of being a paleontologist. And yet time and again I have heard people express amazement at the assessment of a fossil, based on the examination of a small fragmentary bone or a tooth. I can claim no particular skill in this aspect of paleontological practice; in this area the palm goes to my friend, Don Baird (for many years at Princeton, now retired). Don always had an uncanny eye for the interpretation of fragmentary fossils. Indeed, on more than one occasion I have sought a second opinion from Don concerning some fossil with which I had been struggling. If Don agreed with my interpretation I would feel quite confident that I had made a correct decision.

We all scrambled down the talus slope where George had joined us, crossed an intermittent rivulet—a tributary of Arroyo del Yeso—and climbed up the opposite talus slope to the level at which George had found his bone fragments. There we found small pieces of fossil bone scattered in moderate abundance.

It seems that paleontologists often make important discoveries just at quitting time, often on the last day of the field season. George found those fragments just before lunch time. So we went back to camp, about a quarter of a mile away, for some nourishment and rest after a long morning, and particularly for some discussion of the discovery that he had made. Needless to say, we returned in short order to the discovery site.

We soon found, almost completely covered by loose talus, the stratum of rock that contained the fossils. So we cleared away the soft sand of the slope and began carefully to dig back into the hill to uncover the fossil layer, using small awls and other hand tools. It was clearly not at this stage an operation calling for picks and shovels.

The more we dug, the more fossils we found, so that before the afternoon was over we were beginning to realize that here was a most unusual concentration of dinosaur bones—not the huge bones of the giant dinosaurs of song and story, but rather the tiny bones of ancestral dinosaurs, dinosaurs that lived before the giants.

For several days we continued our probing of the deposit in order to make a proper assessment of the site. This is from my field notebook of June 26.

> Continued work in dinosaur quarry. This quarry keeps developing more and more, as we work it. Obviously it is not an isolated skeleton with associated odd bits of bone, but a comparatively extensive deposit containing a number of skeletons.

(That note was the paleontological understatement of the year: the Ghost Ranch quarry has yielded literally hundreds of articulated and partly articulated *Coelophysis* skeletons, constituting one of the richest dinosaur deposits ever discovered.)

This was a concentration of skeletons belonging to a dinosaur that hitherto had been known only from scattered bones and bone fragments, discovered in the late nineteenth century in this very region of New Mexico. By now we realized that we were faced with a problem of considerable dimensions, as well as with some hard decisions.

Here we were on our way to the Petrified Forest, where we had a permit to work for the summer, a piece of paper obtained with no little difficulty on our part, and with a remarkably long series of desks to be crossed within the Department of Interior. It seemed to us as if, after all that governmental attention, we were almost duty-bound to make an appearance in Arizona. Yet in that hillside at Ghost Ranch was a paleontological opportunity of the kind rarely experienced in the bone-hunting profession.

What to do? The answer, it seemed to me, was clear—to stay at Ghost Ranch for the summer and develop the dinosaur quarry, and apologize to the folks at Petrified Forest, hoping that the government authorities would understand the situation. But first I thought it necessary to get in touch with George Simpson as soon as possible and apprise him of our discovery and of the decision I believed was the proper one.

Consequently, on Saturday, June 28, six days after our first discovery of *Coelophysis* bones at Ghost Ranch, we drove to Española, our main base of supplies some forty miles to the southeast of Ghost Ranch. There we telephoned Simpson where he was now encamped—at the Collins Ranch near Lindreth. I told George about our discovery and gave him my opinion as to its significance. Of course he was interested, one might say excited, and without hesitation he agreed to come over to Ghost Ranch the following Monday.

So it was that on Monday, June 30, George Simpson and Bill Fish arrived at the ranch late in the morning. We all went up to the quarry site where, after examining the ground and inspecting the fossils we had already uncovered, George most generously declared that "this was the greatest find ever made in the Triassic of North America." Perhaps his statement was hyperbolic—made in the heat of the moment when we were all excited by the nature and the scope of the discovery. But he *did* say that—for I made a note of it in my fieldbook at the time.

It was indubitably a very important and exciting discovery. Therefore George and I sat down and wrote an agenda for the days ahead. Here are our decisions, as set down in my fieldbook.

1. Carl Sorensen should join us as soon as possible. (Carl was a senior preparator at the American Museum paleontological laboratory in New York. Both George and I felt that we needed additional staff to carry on our summer campaign, and Carl had the proper field experience to give us the necessary help.)
2. Carl and George Whitaker should work straight through the summer— probably through September. (They did.)
3. If necessary, we should return next year to continue the work. (Carl and George did—with their wives. That next year I was in Britain at the International Geological Congress.)
4. At the completion of this project there should be a discontinuance of Triassic collecting until preparation should catch up on the material at hand. (The halt occurred, although preparation did not catch up. It still has not caught up.)
5. Funds for this year, to come as much as possible from the Paleontology Endowment Fund. (An internal matter of American Museum bookkeeping)

After making these decisions, George Simpson and Bill Fish joined Arthur and Phoebe and the rest of us for some afternoon refreshments; they then departed for the Collins Ranch, with George making some pungent remarks about how some people have all the luck and live the life of Riley, while others (he and his party) would be suffering the privations of a comparatively primitive life on the Collins Ranch.

With George's good-natured grumblings still ringing in my ears, I immediately contacted the National Parks people, informed them of our discovery, and apologized for our failure to materialize at the Petrified Forest as planned. I think they understood the situation and forgave us—at least I hope they did. Certainly no hard feelings seemed to ensue.

The discovery of *Coelophysis* at Ghost Ranch is a good example of the role of serendipity in paleontological research. According to the Oxford English Dictionary *serendipity* is a word "coined by Horace Walpole upon the title of the fairy-tale *The Three Princes of Serendip,* the heroes of which were always making discoveries, by accidents and sagacity, of things they were not in quest of." Exactly so, at Ghost Ranch.

───────────────── ▬ ─────────────────

TWO

PLANS, PREPARATIONS, AND SOME THOUGHTS

Even before George Simpson came over to Ghost Ranch for our council of war concerning strategic plans for the summer, I was convinced that we would end up spending our time at Ghost Ranch. So there were periods for contemplation, to be indulged in at the close of those first days at our camp.

After our preliminary probings of the quarry site, after our evening meal prepared by George, after my struggles with my daily fieldbook—accomplished while sitting on a cot in the tent and fighting off the moths and other insects attracted by the bright light of the Coleman lamp that hissed away at my elbow—and after a retreat into blankets as the heat of the day gave way to the progressively cooler air of the evening and night (typical in summer in the desert and semidesert regions of the mountainous West), there came a few moments of repose before I was enveloped by sleep—moments for thinking about what was in the past and what was to come. These were moments during which to weigh whether we had done the right thing in proposing so drastic a change of plans, and to wonder what might result from the new course of action we were considering.

Would the quarry be as productive as the first few days of exploratory work seemed to indicate? Would our summer campaign be rewarded with a collection of dinosaur skeletons of such significance as to justify our abandonment of the original plans, our rejection, in a sense, of the opportunity that had been extended to us under the hard-won permit to explore in the

Petrified Forest? I suppose questions of such nature have, over the years, disturbed the dreams of many explorers in new unknown lands.

One prerequisite for success in the search for fossils is a facility for improvisation, especially a willingness to change plans and not be trapped within a rigid schedule. This is more important than one might think, particularly in these modern days of grants in aid of research, including that which involves fieldwork and fossil collecting. Granting agencies more often than not require the harried suppliant to outline his or her hoped-for results in the application for monetary assistance; so if one winds up doing something quite different from what had been envisioned in the application for the grant, one may be asked hard questions.

We were lucky in that we were working on American Museum funds and were not bound by the dictates of an outside grant. Of course before beginning the summer campaign scheduled for the Petrified Forest, we had committed to paper a plan that outlined in general what we would try to accomplish in the colorful badlands of Arizona. But within the past few days everything had changed, as is frequently the case in geological and paleontological fieldwork. Our new course of action had to be accommodated; that was necessitated by our unexpected and exciting discovery. So, as I reviewed in my mind the events of the previous few days, I felt increasingly comfortable with our decision. Serendipity had triumphed, and I could go to sleep.

That such thoughts went through my mind during those first nights at Ghost Ranch illustrates an aspect of geological and paleontological fieldwork that is frequently unrecognized or ignored, not only by those who have only peripheral or occasional exposure to the art and the practice of interpreting earth history but also by seasoned practitioners. This is the importance of thinking, and I am not being facetious. It has been said that a large part of fieldwork is thinking—of sitting quietly and contemplating what has been found, what has been seen, the significance of things accomplished, and what to do in the time ahead.

Arthur Lakes, the Oxford-educated quondam schoolmaster who spent some years during the final decades of the nineteenth century collecting dinosaurs for O. C. Marsh of Yale, enlivened his field notebooks with watercolor sketches depicting the activities of his fellow fossil hunters. One of his charming sketches, quite amateurish in execution but nonetheless authentic and appealing, shows a dinosaur quarry near Morrison, Colorado, within which are seen some huge bones fully exposed and resting on the ground, while off to one side three collectors are busy with picks and shovels. But in the center of the quarry one sees a proper Victorian scientific gent—serious, and bearded, formally dressed, his hat clapped squarely on his head—using a large dinosaur vertebra as a chair and scowling at the gigantic leg bones and vertebrae before him. The title of the drawing is "Professor Mudge contemplating bones" (Benjamin Mudge, on the faculty of the Agricultural College of Kansas, was retained by Marsh as one of his field collectors). (Colbert 1983:29 reproduces this drawing.)

It is an unconsciously amusing little picture, but nevertheless it makes its point. Fossil collecting is more than wielding a pick and a shovel; it involves the physically unstrenuous but intellectually demanding practice of "contemplating bones." Professor Mudge's contemplations were just as vital to the course and success of the paleontological project as were the physical activities of his companions on the other side of the quarry.

During that summer all of us devoted many hours to thinking and planning, which inevitably resulted in many discussions among ourselves about what we were finding and how we were to deal with the problems that confronted us. These discussions, as it developed, were enjoyed to a large extent in comfortable surroundings.

One morning Arthur Pack appeared at our camp near Arroyo Yeso as we were cleaning up our breakfast pots and pans in front of our tents. The evening before we had told him about our forthcoming decision to spend the summer at Ghost Ranch and probably to abandon our plans to go to the Petrified Forest.

"You fellows can't spend the summer here in a tent," said Arthur. "Why don't you move into the Johnson House?"

I don't know what George Whitaker and Tom thought at that moment, but Arthur's invitation was music to my ears. A pretty tough summer of digging lay ahead for us, but now it could be ameliorated by the comforts of a house. No longer would there be the alternating cycles of dust and mud inherent in tent life; no longer would I face the ordeal every night of working up field notes under the light of a hot lantern, with moths and other insects banging into my face and eyes and down my neck. No longer would we attempt to clear away the caked dust of a day in the quarry with scanty baths; no longer would we have to cook over a camp stove, enduring a necessarily limited menu, consisting largely of fried and boiled foods. Camping out is great for a summer vacation of a week or two, but as a steady thing, week in and week out, month after month, it gets to be pretty tiresome. Furthermore, living in a tent when one has a job to do wastes a lot of time.

So I accepted Arthur's invitation with inner shouts of joy, as I'm sure was the case with my two companions. We immediately made preparations for the move.

The Johnson House, as it was called then, had been built by Mr. Johnson of Band-Aid fame (by arrangement with Arthur Pack) as a vacation retreat, but at that time it was empty. Nor was it to be occupied in the foreseeable future—except by us. It was a commodious, two-story dwelling built in the southwestern adobe style, with thick walls and protruding log *vegas* (or beams) supporting the floor of the second story and the flat roof. The outside was earth-brown stucco. Of course it was pleasantly cool in the summer by virtue of the thick walls; in addition it was partially protected from the sun by a large cottonwood tree situated close to the south side of the house.

Downstairs were a large living room—decorated in the southwestern fashion with solid mission furniture—a couple of other rooms, and a modern kitchen. Upstairs were two spacious bedrooms, each with its own bath. For three bonediggers (and soon there would be four) it was unparalleled luxury. Indeed, I have never lived in such style while collecting fossils, before or since.

It may be helpful to say something about the Ghost Ranch buildings as they were then, and as they are now. As has been mentioned, some years after we had worked there Arthur Pack (in 1955) gave Ghost Ranch to the Presbyterian Church to be used as a retreat and a conference center. So the ranch as we knew it, with a dozen buildings or so, grew into a large complex, with assorted conference buildings, a huge dining hall, service buildings, a museum, and cottages and dormitories capable of accommodating four hundred plus people at a time. All through the summer, today, several weekly seminars are conducted simultaneously on subjects ranging from archeology to zoology; with sessions in between devoted to social studies, world affairs, and almost everything else pertinent to our modern world. All this development, which has made Ghost Ranch preeminent as a conference center, was accomplished largely by the late Jim Hall, with the enthusiastic assistance of his wife, Ruth (see figure 7). Jim was truly a most remarkable person; Ghost Ranch as it is today is his monument. And in memory of Ruth, who became a dedicated fossil preservationist, the ranch's Ruth Hall Paleontological Museum was created. This collection, to-

FIGURE 7   Jim and Ruth Hall.

gether with the adjacent and connected Florence Hawley Ellis Museum of Anthropology, affords to the seminar participants—as well as to the visiting public—a most excellent record of Ghost Ranch from the days of the dinosaurs and earlier, until the arrival of early man to the Southwest, and the history of the varied peoples in this region through the past thousand years.

But let us return to the Ghost Ranch of 1947, before all the developments described. We were given what might be called sumptuous quarters in the Johnson House—the building now called Cottonwood, which houses the ranch library. A stone's throw away, where today the great dining hall is situated, lay the end of a large alfalfa field.

The ranch headquarters, where we had dined with Arthur and Phoebe that first day when we arrived at the ranch on our preliminary scouting tour, was the gathering place of all then inhabiting the ranch—the center for activities. (So it is today, but as a reincarnation of the original headquarters building, which was completely destroyed by fire in March 1983.) Adjacent to it, as noted, was the house (now known as Casa Loma) of Arthur and Phoebe. It was here that an occasional late afternoon summer ritual developed while we worked at the ranch—namely, a "sundowner" with the Packs, when we enjoyed a half hour of drinks and pleasant conversation after our day in the quarry. Of course on such occasions we made ourselves presentable before appearing, and part of that process involved an after-work frolic in the swimming pool, then located about a quarter-mile or so up a ranch road from the headquarters toward our quarry. (The pool has long since vanished; its buried remains may now be faintly discerned in the area known as the Teepee Village.)

Down a slope from the headquarters and from the Packs' home, where we spent those pleasant late afternoons, were a bunkhouse, some barns, and other service buildings for people working at the ranch. A generator was located there, chugging away making electricity for the ranch. And between the Pack house and the Johnson House were several cottages, including the Ghost House (the original ranch building), these remaining from the days when the place operated as a dude ranch.

For the orientation of those acquainted with the ranch as it now exists, our first camp down by Arroyo Yeso—the camp we abandoned when Arthur invited us to live in the Johnson House, was where the building known as the Long House now stands.

Such was Ghost Ranch in 1947 when it was a quiet, idyllic backwater—

home to Arthur and Phoebe and their two children, to Herman and Jimmie Hall (no relation to Jim Hall) and their daughter, and to us, quite comfortably, for the summer. One other presence at Ghost Ranch in those days was "Blackie," more properly David Burnham, who managed the alfalfa fields. Blackie lived in a rock and adobe homestead he had built some miles to the east of the ranch headquarters, and from which he commuted to the ranch every day.

Off to the west was Georgia O'Keeffe's house, and beyond that the Bennet house (purchased by the ranch in 1956, to be for many years the home of Jim and Ruth Hall).

O'Keeffe chose to live here because of the marvelous scenery that surrounded her house on all sides. She loved the colors of the Chinle Formation that occupied the foreground around her dwelling—the banded reds and whites and purples so characteristic of the hundreds of feet of sandstones and clays and the mixture that geologists call siltstones, which formation carries within its layered deposits the fossils that had attracted us. She also was intrigued by the great vertical cliffs of the Entrada Formation, immediately above the Chinle, and the white Todilto gypsum capping above the Entrada. One of her well-known landscapes, painted in 1943, shows this sequence of Chinle, Entrada, and Todilto that rises just behind her home. For her these Mesozoic rocks of Ghost Ranch and the surrounding country were a symphony of colors, bright beyond belief for many people (including impressionist painters who had not seen them). Lacking formal training in geology, O'Keeffe, with her perceptive eye, depicted the land forms and the earth colors of the Southwest with an understanding that is a constant delight to members of the geological fraternity who have studied that country.

O'Keeffe was also intrigued by Cerro Pedernal, south of the ranch. It appears in several of her paintings—a silhouette against the sky. In "Pelvis with Moon" painted in 1934, Pedernal is a blue silhouette at the bottom of the picture, most of the canvas being occupied by the white, weathered pelvis of a cow, with the moon above. "Pedernal and Red Hills," painted in 1936, shows the Chinle badlands of Ghost Ranch in the foreground, with a blue Pedernal rising behind them. In "Pedernal," a 1945 work, Pedernal again appears as a blue silhouette, its profile the focal point of the painting (O'Keeffe 1976).

Our primary concern of course, was with the Chinle Formation, in the upper part of which the newly discovered dinosaur quarry was located.

Looking beyond Ghost Ranch the Chinle Formation is exposed in northern New Mexico as a somewhat crescent-shaped sedimentary band of varying width and thickness, extending from a northern extremity about ten miles northeast of Ghost Ranch, through the ranch, and on to the west as two great prongs, one reaching west along the Chama River for about twelve miles, the other extending about twenty miles to the south and west through Coyote and on to Gallina, from which locality there is a northward extension about five miles in length. In this area the Chinle Formation varies from about 400 to 1,300 feet (120 to 400 meters) thick.

However, the Chinle Formation is widely exposed in New Mexico and Arizona; indeed, the name of the formation is derived from Chinle, Arizona, about two hundred miles west of Ghost Ranch. The extraordinarily colorful Chinle outcrops in the eastern part of Arizona, long designated by the Spanish inhabitants of the Southwest as "El desierto pintado," and by their English-speaking neighbors, the "Anglos," as "The Painted Desert," especially those exposures contained within the Petrified Forest National Park.

Previously it was remarked that the cliffs of Ghost Ranch represent all three periods of Mesozoic history, namely the Triassic, Jurassic, and Cretaceous, thus presenting glimpses of the Age of Dinosaurs on a grand scale. It is now time to give these Mesozoic cliffs further attention. The sequence of the formations and their ages in the Ghost Ranch section is presented in table 3.

This is the simple way of looking at the cliffs, but one should realize that although all three Mesozoic periods are thus represented at Ghost Ranch, these massive cliffs and badlands actually divulge to the discerning eye only a fraction of Mesozoic history. Indeed, more of the history of Mesozoic time is missing from the Ghost Ranch section than is present. And this is the usual situation when one is trying to decipher the story of the rocks and the story of life as represented by the fossils contained within those rocks.

TABLE 3
Sequence of Formations in the Ghost Ranch Section

Cretaceous Period	Dakota Formation	175–200 ft.
Jurassic Period	Morrison Formation	175–725 ft.
	Todilto Formation	75–100 ft.
	Entrada Formation	100–300 ft.
Triassic Period	Chinle Formation	325–590 ft.

In a sense reading the book of the earth is like trying to put together a comprehensive history from a long series of volumes, each of which consists of some well-preserved pages, but is missing many pages, and contains other torn and crumpled pages that can be comprehended only with great difficulty. It is by combining the information in the many volumes, by collating and by cross-checking, that a complete and coherent story may be put together.

So it is with geologic history. Some information can be obtained concerning each Mesozoic period from the rocks in the Ghost Ranch cliffs. But this must be supplemented by information assembled from the rocks in other regions, not only in North America but also in other parts of the world.

Therefore, if we look at the Ghost Ranch section with the entire story of the Mesozoic in mind, and particularly with some concern for the ages of the rocks present (as well as the rocks that might have been present but are not), a different impression emerges of the rock sequence that forms the cliffs and badlands. But here a brief digression is needed to say something about absolute geologic time.

For many years geologists necessarily speculated about the age of the earth and the individual ages of rocks that compose the crust of the earth. For example, one classic method was to try to determine how long the oceans had taken to reach their present stage of salinity—assuming that the primordial ocean was free of salt. It was not a very satisfactory exercise in scientific speculation, nor were various other assumed criteria for determining the age of the earth.

Then the dilemma over the age of the earth and the age of the rocks forming the earth's crust was solved with the discovery of radioactivity. Here was the hoped-for clue to the absolute ages of the rocks in the earth's crust that had for so long been desired. Radioactivity is the spontaneous breakdown of certain elements, which leads to permanent changes in the atoms involved. And research during the twentieth century has proved that the rates of such breakdowns are constant. The studies have been directed to analyses of the breakdowns of uranium into lead, of potassium into argon, and of rubidium into strontium. The entire process is known as radioactive decay, and the absolute ages of such rocks can be determined by measuring the ratios of the involved elements in various rocks. The procedures and techniques involved are sophisticated and complex, and no attempt will be made to explain them here, but perhaps the brief statement set forth above gives some idea about how our knowledge of the ages of rocks has been established.

The rocks belonging to the several periods of earth history have been divided into stages, and as a result of worldwide studies the lower and upper limits of the several stages have been determined in absolute years. The three Mesozoic periods have been divided into a sequence of as many as thirty-one stages.

For example, the Dakota Formation, the topmost formation in the Ghost Ranch sequence, has been determined as belonging to the Albian stage of the Cretaceous period, the upper boundary of the Albian being dated at 97 million years ago, its lower boundary at 112 million years ago. By a simple matter of subtraction we see that the Albian had a duration of some 15 million years. But the Dakota Formation at Ghost Ranch probably does not by any means represent the full extent of Albian time; therefore one must suppose that it indicates a shorter time lapse. The same probably is true for the other formations in the Ghost Ranch sequence.

A delineation of the Mesozoic rocks at Ghost Ranch, so simply depicted in table 3, is more realistically represented in table 4.

If the several Mesozoic formations at Ghost Ranch were in each case representative of the full extent of the stage to which they belong, the Mesozoic there would be somewhat less than one-fourth present. But it is probable that, as in the case of the Dakota Formation, none of the formations occupy the full durations of the time stages to which they belong. Therefore it seems likely that the rocks exposed at Ghost Ranch represent much less than a quarter of the Mesozoic, perhaps no more than one-tenth of Mesozoic time. It is indeed a fragmentary record—but fortunately the gaps are supplied by rocks and fossils in other parts of the world. So all in all the full history of the Mesozoic era is reasonably well known, and into that long history, extending through 180 million years, the Ghost Ranch segments may be inserted.

To return to the details of the Chinle Formation, it has long been the practice of geologists to subdivide geologic formations, where such is justified, into lesser units known as members, not to be confused with stages (see table 4) which are universal *time* units. The Chinle Formation is so thick and varied that in the general Ghost Ranch region several members have been named within its vertical boundaries; these being from bottom to top, and therefore from oldest to youngest, the Agua Zarca Sandstone Member, the Salitral Shale Member, the Poleo Sandstone Member, and the

TABLE 4

Mesozoic Formations at Ghost Ranch

Period	Epoch	Stage	Formation	Intervals	Notes
Cretaceous	Upper	Maastrichtian through Cenomanian		32 MY	Absent
Cretaceous		Albian	Dakota	15 MY	Dakota at Ghost Ranch only part of this interval
Cretaceous	Lower	Aptian through Neocomian			Absent
Jurassic	Upper	Tithonian		6.5 MY	Absent
Jurassic	Upper	Kimmeridgian	Morrison	2.5 MY	
Jurassic	Upper	Oxfordian	Todilto	2.5 MY	
Jurassic	Middle	Callovian	Entrada	4.2 MY	
Jurassic	Lower	Bathonian through Hettangian		48 MY	Absent
Triassic	Upper	Norian + Carnian ?	Chinle	14 MY	Chinle at Ghost Ranch probably only part of this interval
Triassic	Middle	Carnian through Scythian		22 MY	Absent
Triassic	Lower				

Petrified Forest Member, which grades up into a very local sedimentary phase that has not been given a formal name but is known simply as the Siltstone Member. This last member, consisting of about two hundred feet or seventy meters of light brown and red-brown siltstone (a mixture of sands and shales), may be contrasted with the more highly colored red beds of the Petrified Forest Member, which constitutes the bulk of the Chinle Formation. It is in this upper siltstone that the dinosaur quarry is located.

Several geologists who have studied the Chinle Formation in northern Mexico in general, and the expression of the Chinle at Ghost Ranch in particular, have given attention to the problem of the siltstone member, within which the Ghost Ranch dinosaur quarry is located. This level of sedimentation at Ghost Ranch was recognized and designated as the siltstone member in 1972 by J. H. Stewart, F. G. Poole, and R. F. Wilson (Stewart, Poole, and Wilson 1972:12, fig. 1). Again, in 1974 and 1977, Robert O'Sullivan delineated the siltstone member as a unit above the Petrified Forest Member of the Chinle Formation in the San Juan Basin region of New Mexico, but grading *into* the Petrified Forest Member to the east. "The siltstone member is as much as 70 m. thick near Ghost Ranch and all of it grades laterally to the southwest into the Petrified Forest member near Coyote" (O'Sullivan 1977:142). In 1989 Russel Dubiel, in a paper on the depositional environment of the Chinle Formation in New Mexico, discussed the nature of the siltstone member; as he pointed out, "the siltstone member is composed of reddish-brown to brown siltstones and very fine to fine grained quartz sandstones. The member generally weathers to a steep slope without any distinguishing characteristics" (Dubiel 1989a:B13). This describes the sediments immediately below the Entrada cliff near the Canjilon Quarry at Ghost Ranch.

Dubiel sees the siltstone member as representing a lateral expression of the Owl Rock Member of the Chinle Formation, the Owl Rock being a final representation of Chinle deposition in the Four Corners region of the southwest. "The siltstone member is interpreted to have been deposited in a marginal lacustrine setting on periodically flooded and exposed lacustrine mudflats. The laterally restricted cut-and-fill features in the Siltstone Member are interpreted as deposits in times of low lake levels" (Dubiel 1989a:B15). Obviously, these conditions resulted in the remarkable Ghost Ranch cemetery of dinosaur skeletons.

In 1993 Spencer Lucas saw the sediments immediately beneath the Entrada (the siltstone member) at Ghost Ranch as belonging to the Rock Point Formation, a unit characteristically exposed in Arizona (Lucas 1993:34, 38–39). However, the Rock Point had been placed as a lower member of the Wingate Formation (now regarded as of Lower Jurassic affinities) by John Harshbarger, Charles Repenning, and J. I. Irwin in 1957. "Thus a greater depositional break may occur between the Chinle and Rock Point than can be detected where a similarity of composition masks the contact. The intertonguing relations between the Rock Point and the Wingate (Lucachukai) seem more significant than the gradational contact between the Rock Point and the Chinle" (Harshbarger, Repenning, and Irwin 1957:7).

At Ghost Ranch no erosional break is evident between the siltstone member and the underlying Petrified Forest Member, as would be expected if the strata just beneath the Entrada cliffs were recognized as a distinct unit. A supposed disconformity at the expected level in this region has been determined by Barry Goldstein to be a sedimentary break between the Petrified Forest beds beneath and Pleistocene deposits, formed by the reworking of the Chinle sediments along the supposed line of demarcation.

These differences of interpretation reflect the way in which different geologists and paleontologists view the evidence and are typical of those found throughout geological literature. Taking all the evidence into account, the position and relationships of the siltstone member is here regarded as the topmost phase of Chinle sedimentation, or of Petrified Forest sedimentation, in the Ghost Ranch region. It is so considered because the Petrified Forest Member, so prominent at Ghost Ranch, grades upwardly into the siltstone member, as has recently been determined by Schwartz and Gillette. They mention that during their extensive fieldwork at Ghost Ranch they found no evidence of an unconformity between the upper Petrified Forest Member and the siltstone member containing the *Coelophysis* quarry as an upper facies of the Petrified Forest Member. "We agree with Dubiel [1989b] that the Petrified Forest Member grades upward to the 'siltstone member' and that the two units are not separated by an unconformity" (Schwartz and Gillette 1994:1119).

Schwartz and Gillette point out that the age of the Ghost Ranch *Coelophysis* quarry has been variously assigned to the late Carnian, Carnian-Norian, and early Norian stages, all within the late Triassic period of geologic history.

Perhaps it was a bit of prescience that inspired us to go back into the canyons behind the ranch headquarters during those first days of prospecting, rather than exploring the colorful badlands toward the O'Keeffe house—the area that had been worked by the Berkeley people before World War II, the area from which they had collected the phytosaur skulls and jaws that I had studied at the university in the summer of 1945. For without knowing just what we were doing at the time, we were exploring the brown and reddish brown upper siltstone member of the Chinle rather than the lower Petrified Forest Member that formed the colorful rounded badlands so intriguing to Georgia O'Keeffe. In those days, when I was innocent of the details that we now know characterize the ascending stratigraphy of the Chinle Formation, details that have been largely revealed in the years since our first encounter with Ghost Ranch sediments, it was all Chinle to us, as it was to most of my colleagues at the time. I recall that in

1949 Charles Camp, the University of California paleontologist who back in the 1930s had been in charge of the first field parties at the ranch, collared me one day and asked what had made us go back into the canyons to prospect, rather than centering our efforts in the badlands where he and his colleagues had collected. I had no good answer; it was just a hunch, I said, and a bit of luck. Of course, as we now realize, we were at the time looking into a higher level, a higher "horizon" as geologists often say, and therefore we were encountering a slightly later stage in reptilian evolution than would have been the case had we confined our efforts at the ranch to the previously explored layers of the Chinle Formation.

This illustrates how knowledge grows through time and practice and through the experience of those trying to refine their knowledge. Perhaps the fragmentation of the Chinle Formation by geologists into a series of sequential members from bottom to top, from earlier to later, may seem to the casual observer as an undue concern with small details, yet as our knowledge of those divisions within the Chinle Formation increases, it becomes ever more evident that the details are anything but trifling. It is by paying close attention to the sequence of fossils within a formation, a sequence dependent on the succession of one rock layer above another, that it is possible to see evolution taking place during the years in which the sediments were deposited.

In many parts of the world it is possible to trace in detail the progressive evolutionary changes among certain fossil organisms as one progresses through a formation from bottom to top. At Ghost Ranch the changes among fossils within the Chinle Formation may not be so evident; nonetheless, it may be possible to see refinements developing between the phytosaurs found down in the Petrified Forest Member of the formation and those found with *Coelophysis* up in the siltstone member. Moreover, it is interesting to see that *Coelophysis*, occurring in such great abundance in the siltstone member near the top of the Chinle, has not been found at lower levels. It looks as if *Coelophysis*, one of the earliest of all dinosaurs, was a latecomer to Chinle history.

As mentioned, I only dimly perceived some, if not all, of the subtleties of Chinle deposition and the succession of Chinle fossils when we first opened the quarry at Ghost Ranch. Yet as I thought things over I began to see that careful study of the Chinle Formation, including measurements, was very much in order. So almost from the beginning I would take time off from the quarry, to hike across the Chinle as it was variously exposed—

in flats toward O'Keeffe's house, in rounded badlands as one approached the Entrada-Todilto cliffs, and even as cliffs back where we were digging in the quarry and beyond. I did take measurements, what are called sections in geological practice, in various localities, using a hand level for my surveys, and when feasible using the contact between the Petrified Forest Member and the underlying Poleo Sandstone Member as the base for the section. Each section had its uppermost termination at the contact between the Chinle and the overlying sandstone cliffs that in those days we called the Jurassic Wingate Formation. Later in 1947 it was proved on the basis of careful work by A. A. Baker, C. H. Dane, and J. B. Reeside, Jr., of the U.S. Geological Survey that what we thought was Wingate was not the Wingate at all; it was the Entrada Formation, also of Jurassic age (see figure 8). So it has remained since, and thus does geological knowledge advance, step by step (Baker, Dane, and Reeside 1947:1664–68).

When I thought about our project, about the plan for spending a summer, and possibly more, digging within a one- or two-foot thickness of sed-

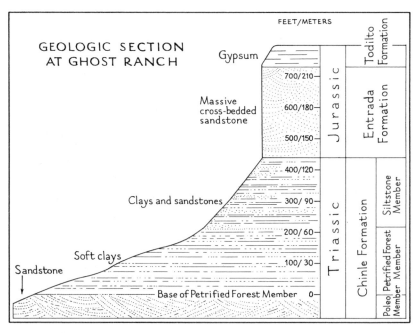

FIGURE 8   A geologic section of the Chinle Formation at Ghost Ranch. Cartography by George Colbert.

iments, selected from the hundreds of feet of the Chinle Formation exposed at Ghost Ranch—this in turn a fraction of the Mesozoic in this part of New Mexico, which in turn represents another fraction of Mesozoic history—it seemed as if our efforts might be viewed as comparatively insignificant. Yet I knew, and took comfort in the fact, that the little, individual efforts by geologists and paleontologists the world over and through the years, are the cumulative contributions that have made the grand sweep of earth history what it is. We could look at the Ghost Ranch cliffs and appreciate them as the backdrop against which we were putting forth our best efforts to unearth and decipher one small part of a stupendous story.

Considering the matter from a different angle, perhaps the excavation of numerous *Coelophysis* skeletons would not after all be a trivial matter. Here, for the first time, was an abundant record of a very early dinosaur, possibly one of the earliest. The significance of this discovery would be seen not merely as allowing the accumulation of a large sample of a single dinosaurian species (based on more specimens than almost any other species of dinosaur) but as gathering evidence about dinosaur beginnings, and about the numerous anatomical characters, here being initially expressed, that were to determine the extraordinary evolutionary success of these reptiles.

Thus a successful dig at Ghost Ranch could be more than a routine excavation—it might be, and indeed it very probably would be, a truly significant paleontological project. In my mind this made the days ahead, and what they might yield, exciting. Yet even as I thought about the possibilities accruing from the summer before us, one small (perhaps not so small) caveat was in the back of my mind. What if our quarry was a false lead? What if it "played out" instead of extending back into the hill as we assumed would be the case? Such things happen.

It should be said here that fossils do not occur throughout the extent of one level, or "horizon" within a formation. Fossils commonly occur as pockets, as small concentrations of bones or shells or whatever, within sediments that may be paleontologically barren over considerable areas. This is particularly true of the Chinle Formation, and I can think back to hours, seemingly without end, of "prospecting" in the Chinle beds, of walking and climbing, of scrambling and falling on steep slopes, all in vain. Nothing is seen. Then one day, one comes across the hoped-for discovery; perhaps a single bone or tooth, perhaps a scattering of bones, or rarely, as was the case at Ghost Ranch, a concentration of fossils almost beyond imagination.

Such a concentration signals a happening in the geologically distant past, a conjunction of conditions and events that resulted, millions of years ago, in the accumulation and preservation of animal or plant remains in a restricted area. It may have been a river bed or a pond, or in the case of marine fossils, some very special environment on the ocean floor. For the paleontologist, accumulation and preservation were the decisive factors in the ancient event, because it must be remembered that for the most part the death of an organism results in its complete effacement. Conditions in the past were seldom sufficiently favorable for the burial and preservation of bones or teeth, of shells, or of plant tissues. The same is true today. Of the millions of wildebeests that roam the African veldt each year, how many will be naturally buried in such a way as to be fossilized? Very few.

So the paleontologist is lucky (in several interpretations of the word) when he finds a fossil or a concentration of fossils. He is lucky in the first place to have stumbled across the remains. Fossils are exposed from their sedimentary resting places by erosion. If the fossil hunter comes along too early no traces of the bones are seen. If he comes along too late, they are all eroded away. If he comes along at the right time he is fortunate, not only to have been at the right place at the right time but also to have stumbled on the rare instance of burial and preservation that happened in a past age.

To return to the question that sometimes plagued me when I woke up in the stillness of the night—would our quarry develop as we hoped it would? Our whole program hinged on the assumption that the concentration of bones we had so far uncovered would continue unabated back into the hillside. Yet we had no proof that it would; we could only dig and hope for the best. So far we had extended our excavation only about two feet into the hillside, and this only over a small lateral extent.

Many a paleontologist, myself included, has followed a bony lead, becoming more and more excited as more bones are uncovered by pick and shovel, only quite suddenly to be overwhelmed by an abrupt stoppage of the fossil deposit. Charles H. Sternberg, the famous fossil hunter, who in company with his three sons, George, Charlie, and Levi, discovered and excavated numerous dinosaur skeletons, many of which can be seen in the National Museum of Canada and the Royal Ontario Museum, describes just such a happening in his book about hunting dinosaurs in Alberta, Canada.

> We were often bitterly disappointed in our finds. Take, for instance, Levi's crested dinosaur. He found some exposed tail vertebrae a little to

one side of a horse trail that came over the rocks from the open prairie above, and extended down to a branch of One Tree Creek, not far from our camp. There Levi found twenty tail vertebrae, the pelvic arch, hind limbs and many ribs. As we progressed in uncovering these, we felt confident that the entire skeleton was buried there. We were mistaken; no head, neck or front limbs were present. From the fact that some of the long pelvic bones had been snapped off, we concluded the missing parts had gone in death to gorge a living specimen of *Gorgosaurus* [now designated as *Albertosaurus*], the Tyrant of the Everglades. [In this passage Sternberg is imagining an Everglades-like environment as existing in Alberta during late Cretaceous times.] Then Charlie removed tons of rock from where he thought the tail of his *Gorgosaurus* lay, only to find it had taken another direction, and the same amount of energy was necessary there as he had wasted on a false scent.   (Sternberg 1932:71)

Such disappointments need not be the result of depredations by an ancient carnivore. Usually the villain is erosion or some other natural cause, as, for example, in a discovery made by paleontologists of the Central Asiatic Expedition of the American Museum of Natural History, in the 1920s. In Mongolia they found the four feet of a gigantic rhinoceros, properly spaced and in an upright position—but nothing more. The rest of the animal had eroded away.

So, as I thought about the weeks ahead, I could only hope that no erosional catastrophes or other natural disasters had cut off our bone deposit somewhere back within the hill. As is necessary for the paleontologist in the field and for the miner seeking gold or the driller probing for oil, we were embarking on a project that was something of a gamble. Our gamble involved the removal of many tons of rock "overburden" (the volume of rock above a particular stratum that is being investigated) in the hope that when we got down to the projected bone layer the bones would be there. We trusted that our gamble with the forces of nature would pay off.

THREE

DIGGING THEM OUT

Now for the big gamble: digging down to the bone level over an area of considerable size, hoping that the bones would be there.

As mentioned, we had at this point dug back into the hillside only about two feet, and this along a limited linear front of perhaps ten feet. Now we faced the rather daunting task of extending our quarry back into the hill as well as laterally along its slope. It was a task to be contemplated with tempered enthusiasm, for it meant days of pick and shovel work, shifting many tons of sand and rock. Such an excavation might have been accomplished with a bulldozer, and, indeed, there was a bulldozer at the ranch—one that Herman Hall, the foreman, loved to operate. But we did not think such a machine could be used safely on the steep slope that confronted us. (Later, when we had established a quarry platform and there was a horizontal surface upon which to operate, the ranch's bulldozer did come into use, but not at the beginning of our dig.)

Consequently, we began our operation by hand, shoveling away the loose talus that formed the slope of the hill, picking away at the rock laid bare by such shoveling, and heaving the loosened rock down the slope beyond our footholds. It was hard, dirty work, and sometimes frustrating, because as we disturbed the hillside the talus above us kept sliding down onto our heads and into the quarry space we were trying to create. It should be explained that the talus, the result of many years of erosion, was at the angle of repose—ready to slide down at the slightest provocation.

We had barely commenced this task when George Simpson and Bill Fish came over from their camp to inspect our prospect. And that morning, before they arrived, Herman Hall had used the bulldozer to make a road for us from the ranch to the quarry site—an admittedly primitive road, but well enough engineered to allow us access to our worksite by jeep.

So we worked for several days in the hot sun, and when we would take a break from our labors we would sit on the talus slope, drink water from our canteens, and admire the view, near and far. The nearby view was stupendous. Our dig was about forty or fifty feet above a little occasional watercourse, almost always dry, while on the other side of this intermittent rivulet was a talus slope equivalent to the one we were working in but with a surface frequently interrupted by huge blocks of sandstone and gypsum, fallen from a massive cliff of the Jurassic Entrada Formation and capped by a Todilto layer that shone white in the noonday sun. This cliff was two hundred feet or more high and was sheer—from its top down to the contact with the Chinle Formation, which formed the slope down to the stream course. At the contact between the base of the cliff and the Chinle beneath was a single young cottonwood tree, evidently nourished by water that seeped along the contact zone. In the early morning, when we would arrive at the quarry to begin our workday, the slanting rays of the sun would be reflected by the shimmering leaves of the tree to give a feeling of freshness augmented by the morning air, which still retained some of the night coolness. The massive cliff that faced us had remained a cliff because it was hard while the underlying Chinle Formation was soft. Thus erosion of the Chinle sandstone-siltstone would undermine the cliff until a portion of the cliff collapsed. Such disintegration of the cliff face evidently must have been sudden and terrifying, because from the Entrada Formation, a massive, uniform sandstone, a huge pillar of stone quite obviously had split or fallen away and had broken into the large blocks that covered the Chinle surface. And when such a column of Entrada sandstone broke away from the face of the cliff, it would often take a piece of the overlying Todilto gypsum with it. Even though we never saw such a thundering collapse take place, we could easily reconstruct the course of events from the evidence seen in some nearby Entrada cliffs. There would be exposed, by its much lighter, relatively unweathered surface, the shape of the pillar that within recent years had come down.

The fact that these massive blocks of rock were confined to the opposite slope was reassuring to us; it signified that even if a rockfall occurred, which we did not in the least expect, the descending debris would not reach us on our side of the little valley. However, a great block of sandstone protruded from the hill just above where we were digging, and we often wondered when *it* would fall on us. It is still there, but sometime in the future it surely will crash down, right into the quarry where we labored. Geological processes being what they are, that dreaded event will probably not take place for a very long time.

We did not realize how lucky we were in those early days of the quarry excavation because in our innocence we thought we had uncovered an old Chinle river channel that went right through our little hill from one side to the other. It seemed as simple as that. But recent work by Barry Goldstein, a geologist from the University of Puget Sound who specializes in Pleistocene geology, and who spent the better part of a year studying the deposits made at Ghost Ranch during the last great Ice Age, discovered that our hill is not at all a simple remnant of Chinle times. Rather, at its base and partly up its slope it is a perfectly proper Chinle deposit, but at its upper reaches it consists of Chinle sandstones and siltstones that had been cut into by a Pleistocene river system; the water of which had eroded and redeposited the Triassic beds in such a way that they look amazingly like the original sediments, accumulated more than 200 million years ago. At the very top of the hill are the unsorted rocks, sands, and silts of an Ice Age landslide. Thus the whole top of our hill consists of deposits only twenty thousand years in age—sediments that might well have washed in to replace completely the dinosaur-bearing layer, but didn't. In short, the Pleistocene river had removed most of the Chinle layers in that area, but providentially had left a little wedge of the original Triassic river bed with its contained skeletons. And providentially that is what we had stumbled onto. A cross-section diagram, adapted from Goldstein, clarifies the situation (see figure 9).

I might add that in the Entrada-Todilto cliff was a great stone face that towered above us on the other side of the draw. It was a profile with a large Roman nose jutting out from the cliff surface, and beneath that an extensive chin. That visage will be in place for a very long time to come.

When we tired of looking at "our" cliff, above which the ravens and hawks circled, we would turn some ninety degrees to the right, to look across miles of landscape, across an extensive valley known as the Piedra Lumbre; beyond this valley to the north were the miles of cliffs that formed the edge of Mesa Prieta, the cliffs along which we had driven when we

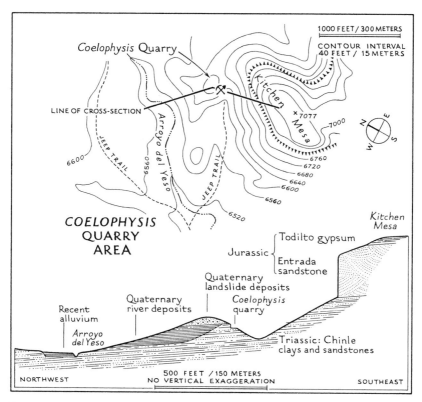

FIGURE 9   Map of the *Coelophysis* quarry area and a geologic cross section along the line indicated. The cross section is based in part on recent stratigraphic studies by Barry Goldstein. Cartography by George Colbert.

traveled from Lindreth to Ghost Ranch, while to the south were the long slopes that led to Cerro Pedernal, the isolated landmark that seemed to form an axis around which rotated our perceptions of northern New Mexico.

On July 8 George Whitaker left Tom Ierardi and me picking and shoveling away overburden, while he went to Santa Fe to pick up Carl Sorensen. Carl had immediately responded to our summons and had come out by train from New York to join us. George could not refrain from giving Carl a doleful tale about the terrible conditions under which we were living and working, and Carl swallowed George's account, hook, line, and sinker. Needless to say, Carl was overwhelmed and flabbergasted when he was introduced to our quarters at the Johnson House.

Carl was at the time a middle-aged man, a longtime member of the American Museum paleontological laboratory staff. He was a very solid citizen, a Dane by birth and originally a seaman by vocation, who had gone around the Horn of South America on a square-rigger. As a young man he gave up his seafaring career to seek employment at the American Museum, where a relative of his, Peter Kaisen, worked in the paleontological laboratory. In this manner Carl became one of the "Great Danes" who formed the backbone of the laboratory staff: Albert Thomson, a second generation Danish-American, Peter Kaisen, George Olsen, and Carl, the latter three being naturalized U.S. citizens. George and Carl, it might be added, managed to become rather fluent in English, but old Peter never became comfortable in his second language. Carl was a strong, experienced preparator and field man, a valuable addition to our little crew.

The day after joining us, Carl put on his field clothes and went with us after breakfast to the quarry, to help with the final steps of removing the overburden. Everything went well for an hour or so, and then suddenly Carl collapsed. The change in altitude (a matter of more than a mile) and the sudden exposure to the New Mexico sun were too much for him. For a few moments we were scared, but ministrations of cold water and shade brought him around; we then immediately took him to the Johnson House for a day of rest. By the next day he was fully recovered and rejoined us, to work cheerfully and efficiently through the rest of the summer.

On that same day we had dug down to a level we thought must be only a foot or less above the bone layer—having determined its probable position by surveying in from the bone layer where it was exposed at the outer edge of our projected quarry. But the crucial question was still with us: would there be a bone layer beneath us at the back quarry face, a little cliff of our own making some eight feet or so in height? (It should be kept in mind that as we extended our quarry back into the hill at a nearly horizontal aspect, the back face of the quarry increased in height, roughly on the order of a foot vertically for every horizontal foot.)

Now for the test. We made a little exploratory hole downward near the back end of our dig, wondering with the removal of each small shovelful of rock whether our test pit would be positive or negative. We had an hour or two of tense anticipation and then, finally, glory be! We saw bones—many bones within the compass of our little pit. Now the future of our quarry was clear.

The next day we went to Española, a sizable town conveniently located about thirty-five miles south of Ghost Ranch, consequently affording us a good supply base. There we purchased a thousand pounds of quick-setting plaster of paris and an assortment of lumber. The plaster was for future use; when George Simpson learned of this purchase he plaintively asked if this was not excessive. It was not; subsequently, we had to buy more plaster. The wood was for immediate use; we intended to build a roof over the quarry.

I, for one, had no desire to broil under the intense southwestern summer sun for a couple of months. And the rest of the party enthusiastically agreed with me. Perhaps I could be branded a hedonist, but it was my opinion then, as it still is, that people work best when they are comfortable. Moreover, we could justify a roof over our quarry on the grounds of paleontological security. We had been experiencing afternoon thunderstorms almost daily, for such is the southwestern weather pattern in July and August. Consequently, we had spent some hectic moments during our previous week of work, covering the quarry floor with a large canvas tarpaulin and then dashing to our jeep for protection against the wind and the rain. We had tried putting up the tarpaulin as a sort of tent over the developing quarry, but that was less than satisfactory; the tarp billowed and shook in the wind, and more often than not it came down around our ears. We wanted something more solid (see figure 10).

Therefore on July 11, we arranged several two-by-four uprights and cross beams to create supports for a roof that would slant from the back to the front of the quarry. Then we made a plank roof and covered it with the tarpaulin. This served us well for the next two months. The fossils exposed were duly protected as they needed to be, for they were remarkably fragile. And, of course, we were able to work in reasonable comfort—to expend our efforts and our thoughts on the task at hand without having to wage our personal wars against heat, sunburn, and dehydration.

A final touch to our roof-building project was to arrange a series of ten-inch-wide planks in a sort of semicircle on the talus slope above our roof. As shown in figure 11, these planks were placed on edge and held in place by pegs driven into the hillside, thereby forming a barrier against the constant dribble of loose sandy material down onto and under the roof, and eventually onto our heads. With the roof in place, we were now ready to get down to the long and at times tedious task of getting our fossils out of the ground.

It was to be a protracted operation, far more complex and difficult than

FIGURE 10   The Ghost Ranch dinosaur quarry at an early stage in its development, before the roof was in place.

our removal of the phytosaur skull during those first three days at Ghost Ranch. Here we were faced with the problem of collecting a tangled mass of skulls and skeletons, not a single specimen, and these *Coelophysis* skeletons were *exceedingly* fragile, not a robust fossil as was the phytosaur. The bones of the little skulls and jaws were very delicate, and the bones of the postcranial skeletons were also fragile, in part because the leg bones and vertebrae were hollow, like the bones of birds, and in part because the ribs and feet were remarkably slender and small. When first exposed such bones would disintegrate into tiny fragments if one were so careless as to touch them with a heavy hand. In fact, it seemed at times that merely breathing on these fossil bones would cause them to disappear before one's eyes. In such a case, as my longtime friend Al Romer of Harvard University used to say, "You don't dig them out like potatoes."

Even though we had no intention of taking the fossils out potato-fashion, neither did we intend to go to the other extreme and remove them bone by bone. The latter procedure is all very well when one is dealing with a large specimen, such as our phytosaur skull or large dinosaur bones. But when one is confronted with a concentrated assembly of skeletons and bones, such as we saw in the deposit at Ghost Ranch, the only proper and practical method is to remove large blocks of rock—each containing a skeleton, or a number of skeletons, or a concentration of bones—articulated or otherwise.

At this early stage in our operation, when we had completed most of the work of removing tons of rock overburden, and when we had the protective roof in place, we were still not quite down to the bone layer.

Why not leave the eight or ten inches of rock still above the bone layer in place, hack out a series of blocks containing the fossils, and take them back to the laboratory? It was not so simple. The bone layer, if the indications we had from the edge of the quarry and from the test pit were valid, was a continuous deposit of fossils, so that to cut out blocks, willy-nilly, would result in the destruction of fossils along the cuts; possibly or even probably fossils of great significance. Therefore a more cautious approach was necessary.

FIGURE 11 Building the roof over the quarry.

It was absolutely essential for us to expose the bone layer, not completely but enough that we could gain some idea of how the fossils were disposed and how we could best isolate blocks in the most advantageous manner from the continuous expanse of skulls, skeletons, and isolated bones, all intermingled and piled one atop another. Our task was to get down to the bone layer, make the necessary decisions, and then act accordingly.

Therefore the next step was to proceed, not with pick and shovel, but with trowels, awls, and scratching tools, with whisk brooms, soft brushes, Japanese rice paper, and preservatives. It would be slow and exacting work, but no other method would suffice. The technique was to remove handfuls of rock carefully—working down almost to the bone layer, and then to expose and identify bones, treating them with preservative and rice paper. They would then be properly hardened, so that we could work around and beyond them.

In those days we used white shellac, cut with alcohol, as the preservative; today more sophisticated preservative or hardening agents are employed, such as "B72," or, more technically, ethylmethacrylate copolymer. The point is to apply a liquid that will penetrate the fossil, not merely to make a hard coating on the outside of the bone. In addition, the preservative should be visually neutral, so that it is not readily apparent and does not lend any extraneous color to the surface of the fossil.

One of the esthetic charms of fossils is color, as determined by the presence or the lack of minerals during the process of petrification. Thus many fossils of Cenozoic mammals, the vertebrate animals that established their dominance after the extinction of the dinosaurs, are white or light in tone, so they look very much like the bleached bones of modern animals. Fossil bones of late Jurassic dinosaurs, the gigantic brontosaurs or stegosaurs, are commonly dark colored or even black. The bones of *Coelophysis* that we were excavating at Ghost Ranch are of reddish hue, contained as they are within the brown and red sediments of the Chinle Formation. It was iron oxide that established this color in the late Triassic fossils. Such colors enhance the beauty of and the interest in fossils, yet some museum directors have been known to insist on coloring the fossil bones of extinct animals white, in the mistaken impression that this would make them look more like "bones." Such are the sad and misguided efforts to improve on nature.

To return briefly to the subject of tools, paleontologists are very individualistic in their choice of "scratching tools." Some people like ice picks, while others prefer ordinary pocket knives or even large hunting knives. Perhaps the most widely used implement is a leather-worker's awl, a flattened blade, if it can be called such, about six inches long, a quarter or a half inch wide, and pointed at the end. This is heated at a forge and shaped into a hooklike curve, after which it is hafted into a wooden handle. It makes an excellent tool for working down to a delicate bone and then working around it. Whisk brooms and soft brushes are employed for clearing away the surface of fossil bones, used as vigorously or as delicately as the circumstances dictate.

Something should be said about Japanese rice paper, mentioned above. Thin sheets of this paper are placed over the bone, after it has been thoroughly hardened by the preservative agent, and are painted into place by additional applications of the preservative. When dry, the fossils are very efficiently protected by this stiffened paper coating. Rice paper is best, but expensive, so many collectors use toilet paper instead. These several techniques are employed to prepare the fossils for final excavation—the plastering that was described in connection with our removal of the phytosaur skull.

At Ghost Ranch, we spent hours almost without end, day after day, working down to the bone level, exposing such bones as we felt necessary, hardening them and applying layers of treated rice paper. Over many areas of the bone layer we put down the rice paper without exposing the bones; in other words, we hardened and papered the rock above the bones. This could be done, for example, where we would discover the first few of a string of articulated vertebrae, or the end of an articulated leg. There was no point in spending time exposing a bone or an association of bones completely—that could be done in the more settled conditions of the laboratory. Once we had established the trend of a fossil, we were able to visualize its position beneath the rock, and that was enough for our purposes in the field. It was enough to allow us to plot the specimen on the quarry map that was being developed as our work progressed.

For the purpose of making a quarry map, we established two base lines, one "horizontal" and one "vertical" as seen on the map; in reality the "horizontal" line extended from east to west, near the outer edge of the quarry and was labeled A-B, while the "vertical" line extended from north to south in the middle of the quarry, and was labeled 0-0. The A-B base line extended for twenty feet east and west, the 0-0 base line extended from the A-B line north eight feet to the quarry face that we had excavated. From these base lines a square-foot grid was established, which enabled us to locate specimens with a reasonable degree of accuracy on our quarry map. The grid was not a permanent affair—as such it would have interfered with our quarry work—but when temporarily established by the use of pegs and strings, it enabled us to mark intersections on the blocks, thereby providing reference points for locating the positions of the fossils.

Today such a grid would probably use the metric system, as it should have then. But we worked with the measuring instruments we had at hand, namely steel measuring tapes, and made our quarry map as best we could.

Our work in the quarry naturally attracted the attention of many people—at first the local folk, and subsequently visitors from afar. Georgia O'Keeffe was interested, and on July 29 she appeared at the Johnson House as we were finishing breakfast, to accompany us to the quarry. Evidently, the demonstration we provided was sufficiently interesting for her to return on August 5, this time accompanied by four jolly nuns, two from Abiquiu and two from Ohio. In spite of their long gowns they piled into the jeep along with Georgia for the trip the quarry, and a good time was had by all.

Such were my introductions to O'Keeffe. Subsequently, in 1949, I was back at Ghost Ranch to do follow-up studies on the quarry and its surroundings, and then I became better acquainted with her. That year I had a graduate student, Dick van Frank, with me, and soon after our arrival O'Keeffe invited us to accompany her and a lady companion for an evening picnic at the Echo Amphitheter, up the highway from Ghost Ranch. O'Keeffe and her friend had prepared a tasty picnic meal, and we had a campfire and much conversation. At various other times that summer I dropped by O'Keeffe's house to visit and, at her request, to look at things she had picked up in the desert—mainly bones and rocks.

Georgia O'Keeffe, internationally famous, was inevitably plagued by people who wanted to interview her. Consequently, she had erected a psychological shield around herself; she had to if she was to maintain any privacy. But she was very cordial to Dick and me. For one thing, she wanted to learn about the fossils that had been collected on the ranch; for another, I think she was friendly because I never attempted to talk about art. Indeed it would have been very presumptuous for me to have done so, and anyway I didn't know anything about the subject. So we could visit and enjoy discussions about the things that interested us, especially bones—old, sun-bleached bones for O'Keeffe, fossil bones for me.

I remember the last time I saw her at her home that summer. I stopped by, and she came out wearing an apron and looking very much like a housewife. But it happened that she was preparing a large Belgian canvas, and she talked enthusiastically about it. Since I was at hand and available, she asked me to hang up a cow skull for her in the patio, and I did, under the critical gaze of her two chow dogs.

Returning to the visitors of 1947, mention might be made of two repre-sentatives from *Life* magazine, who appeared at noon on July 16—one a writer whose name I have forgotten, the other, Bob Landry, a photogra-pher. They arrived just in time for lunch, after which they spent two hours at the quarry with us, asking questions, making notes, and taking pictures. In those days *Life* was still in its heyday as a weekly illustrated large format journal, with a circulation that numbered, I suppose, in the millions. Their visit to the quarry resulted in an article, published in the August 11 issue, including some pictures of us supposedly laboring with a block and a resto-ration of *Coelophysis* by Rudy Freund, a scientific illustrator of outstanding talent. Rudy produced an excellent portrait of the little Ghost Ranch dino-saur, particularly in view of the fact that as yet there were no prepared skel-etons or anatomical studies on which he might base his work. In view of later knowledge, his recreation of *Coelophysis* can be faulted on only two points; the neck is too short and the heel on the hind foot is too prominent (*Life* 1947:52).

One of our problems at the Ghost Ranch quarry was an "embarrassment of riches"—something that we could hardly complain about, but a prob-lem nonetheless. Here we had a layer of skeletons and bones, piled into a confusing mass and extending without interruption across the extent of the quarry floor. So how were we to divide this mass of fossils into blocks that could be handled for excavation, shipment, and preparation in the lab-oratory? Of course, it would have been nice if we could have picked up the whole fossil layer en masse and carried it back to New York, but such a no-tion was altogether fanciful. The bone deposit would have to be divided.

Our solution was to divide the quarry floor, with its contained skeletons and bones, into seven blocks: numbered I, II, IIA, III, IV, V, and VI, these occupied an area of about twenty feet from east to west, and some seven feet from south to north—that is, from the southern boundary of the quar-

ry as defined by the eroded slope, back into the hill to the quarry face that
we had exposed. This was all easier said than done. For we had to define
the lines of separation between the proposed blocks and then cut channels
more or less along these lines, keeping our cuts as narrow as possible. And
the word *narrow* is to be taken in a very restricted sense because most of our
channels were only a few inches wide. Moreover, they were tortuous in
direction because as we began to cut down we would change the direction
of the cut, or modify it, to avoid destroying an important specimen. We did
have to cut through some bones, but generally we tried not to take this
draconian measure; rather we cut carefully around a bone that traversed
the proposed channel and removed the specimen. Thus, in channeling the
quarry floor in order to isolate the blocks that were being developed, we
removed from the channels some 105 lesser blocks or individual fossils,
which were accordingly numbered.

If this description is not easily understood, perhaps referring to the
quarry map (as shown in figure 17 at the end of this chapter) will be helpful. This map shows not only the blocks we removed in 1947 and 1948
(numbered I–XIII) but also the blocks taken out by the New Mexico Museum of Natural History, the Museum of Northern Arizona, the Carnegie
Museum and the Yale Peabody Museum in 1981 and 1982, and the Ruth
Hall Museum of Paleontology at Ghost Ranch in 1985 (numbered P–1 and
C–1 to C–10.) The map clearly shows the manner in which we cut mean-
dering channels to subdivide the deposit into blocks. It also shows how
some of the channels were enlarged, in order to remove masses of fossils
that in good conscience we could not invade with a narrow cut. Such, for
example, was the channel between blocks III and IV, where number 26 was
removed—a small block in itself. A block such as this was necessarily encased in a plaster jacket, but for the most part the specimens removed from
the channels were sufficiently small that after proper treatment with shellac and rice paper, we could extract the fossil and carefully package it. And
after fossils were removed from the channel cuts, these cuts could then be
deepened to the full depth of the large blocks between which cuts were
being made.

Cutting the channels was remarkably time-consuming; days followed
days as we devoted our energies to this aspect of the quarrying operation; but it had to be done before we could proceed with the big blocks. And
it was done, with a modicum of profanity and more than a few skinned
knuckles.

Blocks I through V were our "big blocks" that summer; blocks IIA and VI were of modest proportions. Block V was the largest; on the order of eight feet long and four feet wide. Since each of the big blocks was three feet or more thick, it is evident that a block with the proportions of block V would indeed be very heavy. The volume of this block probably was about sixty cubic feet, which means that at the specific gravity of sandstone (about 2.5) the block weighed more than two tons—not counting the weight of the plaster jacket, which was considerable.

But why should we have taken such thick blocks? Because the Chinle sediments in which we were working lacked internal cohesion. If, for example, we had been dealing with a dense limestone, or a solid slate, we might have been able to remove relatively thin slabs as large as four by eight feet, but the sandstone and siltstone that comprised the Chinle Formation at Ghost Ranch were friable and not in the least self-supporting. A thin four-by-eight section of these sediments would have gone to pieces with the least amount of handling. So it was up to us to encase our big blocks with thick plaster and burlap bandages and remove them from their 200-million-year-old resting places as carefully as possible.

Consequently, after having completed the channels that we had cut to define the several blocks, we next encased the blocks, top and sides, with heavy jackets. The technique has been mentioned in chapter 1, in the description of collecting the phytosaur skull that we had discovered on our first day at Ghost Ranch. A few more details are desirable here.

This was to be a big-scale operation, as compared to our three-day removal of the phytosaur. First there was the problem of burlap, which we needed in large quantities. So during several of our trips into Española for groceries and other supplies, we visited feedstores and lumberyards, where we bought up as many empty gunny sacks as could be found in these cavernous establishments. At the ranch, odd hours were devoted to the somewhat tedious task of cutting up the sacks into strips, each strip four to six inches wide and a couple of feet long. A sack would be cut along one side and across the bottom, so that it became a flat piece of burlap, which then could be cut into the proper strips. Hundreds of strips were so prepared.

At the quarry we dipped into our supply of plaster of paris. We would fill a pan about the size of a washbasin with plaster, adding water until the mixture had the consistency of heavy cream. Then burlap strips, having been soaked in a bucket of water, were dipped into the creamy plaster, strip by strip, and each plaster-impregnated strip was applied to the top and the sides of the block, one after another. The work had to be done rapidly, so that all the plaster in the pan was used before it began to set. The best technique was for one person to dip the plaster strips and hand them in turn to a colleague who would paste them seriatim on the block. The operation would be repeated, over and over again, until a thick layer of burlap and plaster covered the block, top and sides. As can be imagined, getting the plaster strips onto the sides of the blocks within those narrow channels was not easy. As in the days when the channels were being cut, repeated remarks were addressed to the deity.

It was messy work, too. Plaster flew through the air and liberally spattered paleontologists, not to mention the immediate surroundings. Also, it was work that did not benefit the skin. After each application of burlap and plaster, the participants in the exercise had to wash their hands and arms before the plaster set. (See figure 12.)

In the end, each of the big blocks was covered, except for the bottom, with a very thick coat of burlap and plaster. It was a treatment analogous to that employed by a physician in setting a broken limb, but on a grand scale;

FIGURE 12 Carl Sorensen working on a series of blocks, the upper surfaces of which have been encased in plaster and burlap jackets.

here a mass of several tons had to be immobilized, rather than one of a few pounds.

One more procedure remained to be accomplished during this part of our work on the big blocks: to strengthen each block with "splints" in order to immobilize it as completely as possible. Again one can see a parallel with the treatment of a broken arm or leg, but again, since a two- or three-ton mass was being immobilized, the technique was applied on a large scale. Fortunately, we had splints at hand in abundance—namely, stout juniper trees from which supports of the desired shape and size could be fashioned. So we cut heavy branches, often several inches in diameter, and of the proper lengths, and plastered them on the tops of the blocks with more burlap strips. The trick was to use long strips, thoroughly impregnated with soft plaster, and then to slap each strip on the block—across the surface, over the splint, and across the surface on the other side of the splint, imitating in effect a long piece of strap-iron with a curved part in its middle for accommodation of the splint. Several of these binders were applied across the block and over the splints, so that in the end the large juniper limbs were truly integral parts of the block. We attached more than one splint to each block, frequently placing them at right angles one to another, in order to stiffen the block in every direction. So far, so good.

But what does one do with a two-ton block, thoroughly encased with plaster bandages and strengthened with heavy splints, yet still along its bottom surface an integral part of the rock that constitutes the landscape of northern New Mexico? One tries to cut the block loose underneath—the next and very big step in the quarry operation.

The tactic is to dig beneath the block as much as possible, yet leave the block supported by several "pedestals," then to protect the exposed undersurface of the block as much as possible, then to cut away the pedestals, and finally to turn the block over, for complete bandaging of its under surface, as shown in figures 13 and 14. All this is—to put it mildly—a very tricky procedure. And the trickiest part is getting the block turned over—not too difficult with a small block, but a truly breathtaking experience with a large block like the ones we were collecting. How heartbreaking it is to have a block disintegrate during this part of the operation!

Why turn the block over? In some cases it may not be necessary; for example, the big block that was placed in the museum at Ghost Ranch (C–9–82, of which more later) was slid onto a large, flatbed truck just as it came out of the ground, for the journey of a mile or so from the quarry to the

FIGURE 13   The author appraising a block as it is turned over.

museum site. But the blocks we were collecting, almost half a century ago,
were destined to be shipped two thousand miles and more, from the ranch
to New York, so that the undersurface of each had to be heavily jacketed
and reinforced.

But we are getting ahead of the story; let us go back to the jacketed, reinforced blocks, still sitting in their original positions in the quarry. The business of undercutting each of these blocks was simple pick, hammer, and
rock chisel work, performed in about the most uncomfortable way imaginable. It was something akin to miners working in a low stope, where everything had to be done lying down on one's side. Swinging a short-handled
pick or a rock hammer in such a position was tiring work, but we had no
choice but to face up to this task. Thus we spent many weary hours during
those days that the undercuts were being made.

Which reminds me of the summer when, with another field party, a big
block containing the jumbled bones and partial skeletons of Lower Mi-
ocene mammals was collected at Agate, Nebraska. At that time we tried all
sorts of dodges, all to no great avail. We even tried using a long strip of
barbed wire, pulled back and forth by two of us, one on each side of the

block. It was a dismal failure; in practically no time we stripped all the barbs off the wire, which of course negated its effectiveness as a cutting tool. Today, things have improved. Now rock saws driven by small gasoline motors can be used for undercutting work.

In our primitive way we undermined each block around its periphery, and then cut tunnels through—arranged in each instance so that the block was still supported by pedestals. Although these were time-consuming tasks, we fortunately were not constrained by fossils in our pathways; our only concern was to remove rock.

Than came the job of trying to get plaster bandages on the bottom of each block, between the pedestals. This can be a Sisyphean exercise, because one is working against gravity. The burlap bandage is dipped in plaster and then one reaches in beneath the block in an attempt to make the bandage hold against the undersurface, all the while getting liberal coatings of plaster on one's face or arms or clothes. And then, when the bandage is finally in place, and one backs away with a sigh of relief, the wretched bandage falls off, and everything has to be done all over again.

FIGURE 14 The block is completely encased in a thick, protective coat of burlap and plaster, and stout tree limbs have been incorporated into the plaster bandages to add strength to the plaster jacket. The object here being immobilized may weigh several tons.

So we devised a different approach to the problem. We cut a series of short wooden two-by-four pieces, short enough to slip sideways through each of the tunnels beneath the block that was being removed. The two-by-fours were then arranged on the ground like the ties of a railroad line and were attached to two steel cables, positioned like railroad rails, by means of large staples. This arrangement of a flexible "railroad line" was then pushed through a tunnel and up the side of the block. The parallel cables (without attached wood billets) were then brought up to the top of the block from each side and were linked by large turnbuckles. Plaster bandages were then stuffed between the bottom of the block and the wood billets within the tunnel. While the plaster was still soft the turnbuckles were tightened, thus bringing the cables with their attached billets carrying the plaster bandages firmly against the bottom of the block. With a block thus secured, the pedestals were cut away, and the block could be upended and turned over without any catastrophic disintegration. We hoped our scheme would work—and it did! Beautifully!

The turning was accomplished with a chain block and tackle, suspended from a heavy tripod that we rigged for the purpose. After the block was in its upside-down position, we removed the cables and billets, and the plaster bandages that we had stuffed into the improvised sling, trimmed the bottom of the block, and then covered it with a heavy jacket, reinforced once again by heavy splints cut from the surrounding juniper trees. Now the block was ready to be moved in any way necessary.

The blocks were undercut, prepared for turning, turned over, and given their final treatment, one at a time. To give some idea of the time involved in our quarrying activities, we worked steadily from July 12 to the end of the month exposing the top of the bone layer and treating it with preservative and rice paper. We began channeling between the blocks on August 1 and continued this work through the seventeenth of the month. Then on August 18 we began the undercutting, and on August 23 we turned the first block. By the morning of August 25, blocks I and II had been completely jacketed and reinforced and were ready for removal from the quarry. It was during this interval—on July 25, to be precise—that Tom Ierardi had to leave us because of prior commitments. We were all sorry to see him go; we would truly miss him as we labored on the blocks during the month to come.

I don't know how we would ever have taken the blocks from the quarry down to the ranch headquarters without the help of Arthur Pack. Long before the time had arrived for removing the blocks, we had discussed this problem with Arthur, and as we had hoped and expected he quite readily offered to put Herman Hall, the ranch foreman, and the big ranch bulldozer at our disposal. Herman was delighted with the prospect; he liked nothing better than to operate that huge machine, which was his mechanical darling. So on the morning of the twenty-fifth, Herman roared up the primitive road that he had carved out for us, to the base of the hill where the quarry was located. Then he began the task of carving out a road in the hill—from the little intermittent stream bed to the very edge of the quarry. The work took only an hour or so, and by the time the blade of the big machine had touched the quarry floor, the bulldozer was canted upward at an angle that was almost frightening to behold. But there it was, ready to drag the blocks down from their resting place.

Herman had provided us with a large, heavy rock sled, and we had hoisted the two blocks on the sled while he was constructing that final piece of road to the quarry. It was now a simple matter to connect the sled and its heavy burden with a log chain to the bulldozer, after which Herman backed down the steep slope, taking the blocks with him. At the foot of the hill he turned the bulldozer around, so that he could drive it to the ranch in the proper way, that is, forward instead of backward. We again hitched the sled to the bulldozer, and away went Herman with our blocks. Herman eventually hauled out our other blocks when we had them ready to be taken from the quarry to ranch headquarters.

But before then another council of war was held with George Simpson. On August 28 he came over from his camp in the San Juan Basin to appraise the progress of our work. He was accompanied by his wife, Anne, who had joined him earlier in the summer, and by Bill Fish. The blocks and the quarry were inspected and then some decisions were made. Because of schedules that had been set earlier, I was soon to leave the field, entrusting George and Carl to complete the season's work. We all wished to have everything clear and free from any misunderstandings. So we agreed that:

1. Carl Sorensen, being the most senior, would be in charge of the work after my departure.
2. Carl and George would remove all the blocks except number V, which would remain in the quarry.
3. Block V and the materials in the back of the quarry, which as yet had not been excavated to the stage of being isolated into blocks would be covered with tar paper and dirt and left until next year.

4. The blocks that were removed from the quarry were to be shipped unboxed to New York by truck.
5. The materials from the channels were to be packed in boxes and shipped with the blocks.
6. A skull that remained at the extreme southern end of the quarry would be removed if possible, for shipment to New York.
7. Our equipment would be stored at Ghost Ranch, held in readiness for another season of work in the quarry.

With our plans thus set, we enjoyed a farewell meal together at the ranch, after which Simpson and his party departed westerly for the San Juan Basin.

The following day, August 29, we set iron stakes in the quarry as more or less permanent markers for the base lines, A–B (east to west) and 0–0 (north to south) so that the quarry could continue to be mapped during the next season. Then Carl and George spent the rest of the day turning over block III, while I ranged hither and yon on the ranch, and beyond, making some final geological observations and stratigraphic notes. I was to leave the next day.

On August 30 Carl, George, and I drove to Santa Fe, where we ran into the annual fiesta—something we had not foreseen. The town was jammed with people, local celebrants, and tourists, and the noise and confusion were prodigious. Somewhere we managed to eat lunch, and then in the afternoon there were Indian dances at the Palace of the Governors (a well-kept relic of Spanish colonial times, dating from 1610). After an evening meal, also procured somehow, I said goodbye to my companions of the summer and boarded the bus for Lamy, where I was to catch the Santa Fe train bound for Chicago. As usual, the train was late, this time two hours late, and I remember as we, the passengers, waited outside, enjoying the balmy, star-lit evening, we could watch Mr. J. A. Krug, secretary of the interior, and his entourage, all of whom had been in New Mexico for some administrative or political reasons, pace up and down the platform with controlled impatience.

As I boarded the train, eastward bound, I would reflect with satisfaction on our summer at Ghost Ranch. It had been crowned with success beyond our wildest dreams, and furthermore, we knew that this success would be extended into the next field season. I had no qualms about leaving George and Carl to complete the quarry work; I knew they would wind up the season in fine fashion. Which they did.

They got all the plastered blocks turned and reinforced and down to ranch headquarters, thanks to the skillful maneuverings of Herman Hall with his bulldozer, and there the blocks were lined up on the ground, waiting for a truck to haul them east, as seen in figure 15. The truck arrived, and with the help of all available hands the blocks, with the exception of number V, were dragged into the truck. It was a large, heavy-duty vehicle, and it barely accommodated the blocks. When the driver arrived in New York with his load (I was already back at the museum) he told me that he was fined in at least one state (perhaps in more than one) for having an overweight load. Never mind, the cargo was worth the fines. As the first days

FIGURE 15 Blocks assembled for shipment to New York.

of fall came to New York we had the summer collection securely housed, waiting to be prepared, while Carl and George, now returned, were contemplating their return to Ghost Ranch for the 1948 season of work in the dinosaur quarry.

During the spring of 1948 George, Carl, and I were making plans for the summer ahead of us. This year I would not be able to participate in the Ghost Ranch dig; the International Zoological Congress was to meet in Paris in July, and during August and September the International Geological Congress was to be held in Britain. I was to attend as a delegate from the American Museum, an assignment that I was looking forward to with great anticipation. The meetings in England promised to be especially interesting because I had registered for two field conferences, one before the scientific sessions in London that would occupy a week or so devoted to the geology of the Channel coast, and the other after the London meetings, organized as a two-week bus trip from London to the very tip of Scotland. After that I had arranged to travel for more than two weeks in Scandinavia with my paleontological colleague Sam Welles of the University of California.

The European trip was delightful in all respects. Paris was Paris. The Channel coast was a delight; we had a weeklong hiking trip from Lyme Regis to Bournemouth, walking along the shore eastward every day, the sunlit waves of the Channel on our right, the cliffs of Albion on our left, where mile after mile we watched the geology unfold, from the Triassic on through the Mesozoic to the famous Upper Cretaceous chalk cliffs. Then, after the London meetings sixteen of us boarded a chartered bus, bound ever northward, to study the geology, and collect fossils. In Norway, Sweden, and Denmark Sam and I visited various museums and conferred with paleontological friends.

In spare moments that summer I would think of Carl and George, thousands of miles to the west at Ghost Ranch. They had a very good summer because they were accompanied by their wives, and all in all, the four of them enjoyed a holiday amid magnificent scenery, along with the quarry work. The ladies had a relaxing vacation; George and Carl had much work to do, but they could always look forward to meals and evenings spent with their spouses.

They picked up right where we had left off the summer before. Block V had been left at the ranch over the winter, as mentioned, so Carl and George delineated a new set of blocks, eventually numbered VII to XIIII, inclusive, and spent the summer on them. They used methods identical to those employed the previous summer, so details need not be repeated here. However, particular mention should be made of blocks VIII and IX, located at the west end of the quarry. These were the blocks that yielded two magnificent articulated skeletons of *Coelophysis*, resting side by side and eventually carrying the American Museum numbers 7223 and 7224. The skulls, necks, bodies, and limbs of both specimens are in block VIII, as was much of the tail of 7224. The tail of 7223 stretched over into block IX. Except for this intruding tail, block IX is distinguished by a mélange of fifteen skeletons and partial skeletons, entwined in the complex patterns of death and burial. Although this mixture of skeletons is impressive, it must be said that the two beautifully articulated skeletons are the jewels of the 1947–1948 seasons. More on them later.

The summer of 1948 at last came to an end, with results that would make paleontological history. It was time once again to get a truck to transport the blocks to New York. George Whitaker had this to say about getting the blocks onto the truck.

"When we loaded the truck, we thought we could get it all on. But when we started, it weighed more than we thought. We put on 18,350 lbs. There were two blocks we couldn't get on; they were VII and XI. These were chosen as the least important of the blocks. They were out on the edge and were a little weathered. These were packed down at Ghost Ranch and left until the next year for a decision about bringing them in. They were left on a sled, covered with several layers of brown tarps and some white canvas" (Whitaker and Meyers 1965:71–72).

Blocks VII and XI were given the next year to the University of New Mexico and the Museum of Northern Arizona, respectively. The fossils from block VII subsequently were transferred to the Museum of Northern Arizona; block XI proved relatively unproductive.

The story of collecting Triassic dinosaurs at Ghost Ranch has a sequel. For thirty-two years the quarry had been abandoned, and sand from the slope above the old quarry had slumped down into the dig, so that its contours were all but invisible. The ranch had been the property of the Presbyterian Church for almost three decades, and now was under the inspired direction of the Reverend James Hall—"Jim" to all of us. Hundreds of people now came to the ranch each summer to attend seminars. Since the mid-1950s, when Jim took over the direction of the ranch, it has been the policy to present a seminar every other year (and sometimes in successive years) on the paleontology of northern New Mexico, and it has been my pleasure to have participated as a leader of almost all these seminars. At the beginning, A. W. "Fuzz" Crompton of Harvard University was a leader or coleader of the seminars; Michael Morales of the Museum of Northern Arizona conducted the seminar one year, while in recent years this function has been assumed by David and Lynett Gillette, David currently state paleontologist of Utah. The seminars have been enjoyable experiences for all concerned and have almost without exception been filled to capacity, and then some. They have been popular, even though they have not been easy, for the people in the seminars have had to hike in the badlands, slip and slide down slopes, endure heat and gnats, and labor mightily while participants in other seminars at the ranch were sitting in the shade of the trees and enjoying the spectacular cliffs. And at each seminar the leaders would take groups up to the quarry site, show it to them, and give a lecture about *Coelophysis* at Ghost Ranch. On such occasions the quarry seemed to be almost a historical monument—the relic of a past chapter in the story of paleontological exploration in New Mexico.

Then in the summer of 1980 David Berman of the Carnegie Museum in Pittsburgh approached Jim Hall with the proposition that the quarry might be opened for further excavation. The purpose of the Carnegie proposal was to get a well-preserved *Coelophysis* skeleton for exhibition at the museum. There was no thought of intruding on my research efforts, which involved the *Coelophysis* skeletons that had already been collected and prepared for study. Indeed, in a letter pertaining to the proposal, Berman stated that "the Carnegie Museum's sole interest in this project is the possibility of getting an exhibit quality specimen."

Jim agreed to this proposal, but he stipulated that if the quarry were reopened, the recently founded New Mexico Museum of Natural History must participate in the dig, in accordance with a commitment that Jim had made to the Committee on Development of the New Mexico Museum. Jim also stipulated that David obtain approval from me for working the quarry again, the work to begin during the summer of 1981.

In the meantime, Tim Rowe (now at the University of Texas, but then at the Museum of Northern Arizona) had raised the possibility of participating in the reopening of the quarry in 1981. That seemed like a good idea.

So it was that David came to my home in Flagstaff, Arizona, to discuss the matter with me, and we agreed on the plan for a summer of collecting at

Ghost Ranch during the next year. Arrangements were made for the Carnegie Museum, the New Mexico Museum of Natural History, and the Museum of Northern Arizona to work cooperatively at the Ghost Ranch quarry. The plan was then extended to include Yale University Peabody Museum in the excavation.

The digging would be in a sense a continuation of the efforts of 1947–1948, but with a new cast of characters. I was by then retired, as were George Whitaker and Tom Ierardi, both by now residents of Florida. Carl Sorensen was deceased, as were Arthur Pack and Herman Hall. The new bone diggers were to be David Berman and Allen McCrady, working for the Carnegie Museum, Tim Rowe and Liz Gordon (eventually to be Mrs. Tim Rowe) excavating for the Museum of Northern Arizona, Robert Reisz of the University of Toronto with a crew of five assistants who worked for four weeks in the quarry, and Mike Fracasso, a graduate student at Yale University, who worked in the quarry for four weeks on behalf of his professor, John Ostrom. During the following summer the quarry was again the scene of intense excavation, carried on by David Berman and Allen McCrady, as well as Amy Henrici and Norman Wuerthele as representatives of the Carnegie Museum and Greg MacDonald with a group of volunteers, collecting for the New Mexico Natural History Museum.

These diggers accomplished a great deal, and many of the blocks they collected were of amazing proportions. Back in 1947–1948 we thought we had collected some large blocks, but our efforts were truly eclipsed by the bone diggers of the 1980s. Whereas the largest of our blocks may have weighed as much as four tons, these new quarry excavations yielded blocks that weighed six to ten tons each. Seldom have such large blocks of fossils been collected (see figure 16).

As had been the case a third of a century earlier, a ranch bulldozer was available, this time operated by Jim Shibley, the ranch foreman. And Jim would perform invaluable service, not only in reopening the quarry and making roads, but also in cutting down extensive overburdens.

Such a varied group of people, representing several institutions, expressed some differences of opinion as to how the blocks being excavated were to be distributed—a matter of some complexity since all the bone diggers had contributed their efforts to the several blocks. Finally, on May 25, 1984, two years after most of the work in the quarry had been completed, the interested parties held a meeting at Ghost Ranch, adjudicated by Jim Hall. Jim decided that one block that had already been taken to the muse-

FIGURE 16   The Gillette party preparing to remove the last block from the quarry in 1985. The block is the large, white object to the right of the truck and the people gathered around it. One of the largest, if not the largest, block taken from the quarry, it weighed about eight tons.

um in Albuquerque would remain there, while a very large block removed to the Museum of Northern Arizona would likewise remain at that institution. One or two blocks, at this point in Pittsburgh, eventually would be delivered to Yale University, while one block that remained in the quarry would be allocated to the new Ruth Hall wing of the museum at Ghost Ranch. The other blocks, which had been transported to Pittsburgh, eventually would be disposed of as decided by the officers of the Carnegie Museum.

As for the block that remained in the quarry, it had been outlined and plastered top and sides, in 1982, but it still remained in its original position, never having been undercut and separated from the quarry floor. There was some question as to its eventual fate until Jim's decision of 1984, which determined that it would stay at Ghost Ranch.

By that time work had begun on the Ruth Hall Paleontology Wing of the Museum at Ghost Ranch. In 1985 foundations had been built and a floor was in place, but the walls had not yet been erected. Now was the time to get the block out of the ground, moved to the museum and set in place, for the blue-prints indicated that once the walls were up, no doors would be large enough to admit the block into the building. David Gillette was the logical person to supervise this project.

It was a formidable task, successfully completed by David and a small army of volunteers during six autumnal weekends. First there was the standard plastering and undercutting and all the other tasks associated with getting such a large block ready to be moved. Then there was the move to the museum. The story, in David's words, went as follows.

The moment of truth came on the sixth weekend, in mid-November, with a chill in the air and the unspoken expectation that winter could settle in soon. Jim Shibley gently pushed the throttle as the ranch's bull-dozer eased away, pulling the block on its skids from the place where these sediments and fossils had remained undisturbed for 225 million years. The plaster held, and the block remained rigid. Over the lip of the earthen platform, and down the hill went the bulldozer with its strange cargo, the "HMS Ghost Ranch," and we still held our breath. Now down the long jeep trail, and across the stream, and up the last steep hill; the procession that followed on foot that afternoon resembled a religious cer-emony more than a scientific event, with all eyes on the bulldozer and the 8 ton plaster bandage. We had moved the impossible block, down a steep slope, across rough terrain. As the evening shadows turned to dusk we retreated to the Ghost Ranch kitchen, to celebrate the victory of the first stage and plan the second stage, for we were only half the dis-tance to our goal. . . .

Jim Hall hired a crane to lift the block, with all its supports and skids, onto the Ranch's flatbed truck. . . . Then came the short half-mile pro-cession, this time led by the truck hauling its massive white cargo that nicely complemented the falling snow, and a parade of pickups and au-tos, to the museum construction site. The bulldozer anchored the crane for balance. As the crane lifted the block off the truck we realized that we

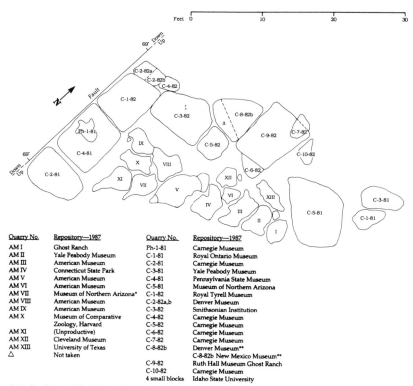

Quarry No.	Repository—1987	Quarry No.	Repository—1987
AM I	Ghost Ranch	Ph-1-81	Carnegie Museum
AM II	Yale Peabody Museum	C-1-81	Royal Ontario Museum
AM III	American Museum	C-2-81	Carnegie Museum
AM IV	Connecticut State Park	C-3-81	Yale Peabody Museum
AM V	American Museum	C-4-81	Pennsylvania State Museum
AM VI	American Museum	C-5-81	Museum of Northern Arizona
AM VII	Museum of Northern Arizona*	C-1-82	Royal Tyrrell Museum
AM VIII	American Museum	C-2-82a,b	Denver Museum
AM IX	American Museum	C-3-82	Smithsonian Institution
AM X	Museum of Comparative	C-4-82	Carnegie Museum
	Zoology, Harvard	C-5-82	Carnegie Museum
AM XI	(Unproductive)	C-6-82	Carnegie Museum
AM XII	Cleveland Museum	C-7-82	Carnegie Museum
AM XIII	University of Texas	C-8-82b	Denver Museum**
Δ	Not taken		C-8-82b New Mexico Museum**
		C-9-82	Ruth Hall Museum Ghost Ranch
		C-10-82	Carnegie Museum
		4 small blocks	Idaho State University

*Originally at University of New Mexico; fossils transferred to the Museum of Northern Arizona.
**Block C-8-82b was divided, the two halves going to Denver and Albuquerque.

FIGURE 17   Map of the Ghost Ranch blocks, collected in 1947, 1948, 1981, 1982, and 1985. Their present locations are indicated. Some of the blocks no longer exist as blocks, but the skeletons and bones discovered within them have been removed.

would have one chance only to set the block into correct position on the concrete pad. . . . In the soft gray light created by the snowfall, the block loomed high in the sky, before it was set into perfect position, an awesome package delivered on schedule, a holiday gift that visitors to Ghost Ranch can enjoy for years to come.   (Gillette 1986:3–4)

Gillette later remarked that lifting that block was a near thing for the crane, because the load was almost beyond the crane's capacity.

Over the years some thirty blocks have been removed from the Ghost Ranch quarry, thirteen in 1947–1948, sixteen during the 1981–1982 seasons, and the final block that David Gillette and has assistants removed in

1985. Consequently, it may be said that through the years the quarry has been exceedingly productive—so much so that some years ago Jim Hall and I decided that no more quarrying should be done in the foreseeable future. There was no point, we felt, in continuing excavations in the quarry, when so many blocks, a considerable proportion of them as yet unopened, were resting in museum laboratories, waiting to be prepared and studied. Perhaps the Ghost Ranch quarry should be regarded as a paleontological treasure house, to be further explored in some distant future, if at all. Furthermore, in 1977 the U.S. government had declared Ghost Ranch in general and the quarry in particular national natural landmarks, places to be preserved and protected in the years to come. Therefore the quarry may best be considered a unique place that has yielded fossil treasures in abundance, the study of which benefits science, particularly the disciplines of earth history and evolution. It is now a site to be honored rather than exploited.

What are the fates of the blocks that have been taken from the quarry? Specifically what does one institution owning a large holding of blocks do with them—a question that can be addressed to the American Museum of Natural History and to the Carnegie Museum. The answer is to be found in the practice of "open exchange" as employed by natural history museums throughout the world—in effect, a sort of scientific barter. Open exchanges are just that; collections are evaluated, and specimens are sent from one museum to another, with the understanding that sometime in the future a receiving museum will reciprocate by sending desirable specimens to a donating museum. It is a system for building up and diversifying collections without the need to spend large amounts of money.

In accordance with this practice, the American Museum of Natural History has retained just five of the blocks originally collected at Ghost Ranch. The other eight blocks have gone to institutions as shown in figure 17. Likewise, of eleven blocks that went to Pittsburgh, some have been transferred to other institutions, while others await such transfer in future years. Thus the collections made at Ghost Ranch eventually will be distributed far and wide; they will have cosmopolitan rather than local impacts within museums, throughout the science of paleontology, and for the public across the extent of North America—perhaps at some future date on other continents as well.

FOUR

BRINGING THEM TO LIGHT

Autumn at hand, and the blocks resting safely in the museum's storeroom.

This short statement of fact describes the situation in New York in 1947 and again in 1948, as well as the situations in Pittsburgh, Flagstaff, New Haven, and other places with paleontologically oriented museums a third of a century later. So far as this narrative is concerned, I will restrict my descriptions and comments to the preparation program at the American Museum of Natural History, where I was present at the time, and where I had, of course, firsthand acquaintance and involvement with the plans and the accomplishments for bringing to light the Ghost Ranch fossils, resting in their displaced Triassic graveyards, all hidden by thick, encompassing plaster bandages.

What does one do with a five-ton block of silty sandstone, wrapped in burlap and plaster, containing perhaps hundreds of fossilized bones? It is a daunting question, one that has faced many a paleontologist through the years. For the paleontologist realizes that the expenditure of so much time and labor in the field in collecting and bandaging the blocks represents but the beginnings of the very long and exacting process of preparation—the process of bringing the fossils to light and fixing them so that they will withstand scrutiny and much manipulation.

Most people who are casually familiar with the techniques of paleontology have read published accounts of expeditions to near and far corners of the earth in search of fossils, or perhaps have visited paleontological "digs" where one may observe the exhumation of the remains of extinct animals and plants.

Paleontological fieldwork is so interesting, even at times so thrilling, that for the average observer this may seem to be the sine qua non of a paleontologist's life. It is difficult for the person who has not encountered the various other aspects of paleontological research to visualize, or even be aware of, the great amount of effort and time that goes into the preparation and study of fossils *after* they have been brought into the laboratory, for work in the laboratory is generally unseen and unsung.

Here and there, at a few of the recently established museums, this hiatus in the public's knowledge of what is involved in making fossils available for study and possible display is being corrected. For example, within the Royal Tyrrell Museum in Drumheller, Alberta (a very large museum dominated by extensive displays of dinosaur skeletons), a large internal window overlooks the preparation laboratory. Here visitors may watch the technicians working on fossils. This innovation in museum construction is without doubt a valuable educational adjunct for the general public, but it is not always appreciated by the people on the other side of the window. They may not find it particularly desirable to be in the public eye throughout their working day; it's like living in a goldfish bowl. Most fossil laboratories, it should be pointed out, are generally in the bowels of the museum, where preparators may carry on their labors without feeling that they are being supervised or gawked at by strangers.

Whether done in private or in public, the preparation of fossils is long and tedious, probably comprising the major outlay of expense and labor in transforming fossils from vaguely seen objects, partially or completely enclosed in rocks, to objects of scientific and educational value that can be studied and evaluated. It is probably safe to estimate that, as a rule of thumb, the laboratory preparation in time and labor on a fossil takes more than ten times the work expended in the field. In the case of *Coelophysis*, the ratio may be on the order of twenty to one.

That is why there is a time lag, often very long, between the collecting of a fossil and the study of that same fossil—which is one reason why the paleontologist often looks with envy at the student of modern mammals or birds or insects. Research for those scientists can follow the work in the field almost immediately. The mammalogist, the ornithologist, or the entomologist prepares his or her specimens as soon as they are collected; when such folks return to the museum with their specimens they have only to get out the skins and skeletons they have collected and start right in on the study. True enough, if they have brought in skulls and skeletons, some additional cleaning may be required. The entomologist may have to do some additional preparation work in the laboratory, as does the botanist; even so they do not usually encounter a significant time lag between acquisition and research.

Thus the student of modern animals and plants can be a more self-contained individual than can the student of fossils, especially vertebrate fossils. The paleontologist needs help from laboratory technicians in order to carry out his or her research expeditiously. Indeed, it is desirable for a paleontologist to have at least one, frequently two, or even more preparators as part of his or her research team. Of course some research paleontologist do their own preparation, but at a high cost in terms of lost research time. Furthermore, after the fossils are prepared and studied, the skills of highly trained technicians often are essential in the development of exhibits. Mounting a fossil skeleton can be an exacting task. These are some of the paleontologist's considerations when examining the blocks in from the field and contemplating the work to be done.

The two summers of quarry work at Ghost Ranch had produced thirteen blocks, of which eleven were transported to New York. As has been noted, two blocks, numbers VII and XI, were transferred to the University of New Mexico and to the Museum of Northern Arizona, respectively. Some years later block I was returned to Ghost Ranch, where it was prepared by John Ostrom for exhibition in the museum that was established by Arthur Pack by the side of the highway adjacent to Ghost Ranch property. Eventually that museum was taken over by the Forest Service, and subsequently the block was returned to Ghost Ranch.

At the American Museum of Natural History, after the first summer of quarry work, preparation was devoted to blocks II and III. The following year, after the second summer in the quarry, we were especially interested in blocks V, VIII, and IX. This interest continued, so that for several years these blocks were fixtures in the preparation laboratory, where they were worked on by several preparators, notably Bill Fish and Carl Sorensen of the museum paleontological laboratory and by John Ostrom, at that time a graduate student at Columbia University, today a retired professor at Yale University and a scholar highly respected throughout the world for his research on dinosaurs. The choice of these three blocks for development was fortunate; each yielded a harvest of skeletons, skulls, and partial skeletons.

Thirteen catalogued specimens were removed from block V, seven (including the two beautiful articulated skeletons that rested side by side) were exposed in block VIII, while eighteen specimens were exposed in block IX. Specimens from these last two blocks were not removed but, rather, were cleaned and left in place—both blocks being destined for exhibition.

But we are getting ahead of the story. Let us go back to the time when the blocks, having been moved from the storeroom to the laboratory, rested on strong supports, awaiting release from the plaster jackets. At this stage in the process of preparing the blocks, the jackets were not completely removed; only the tops and the upper parts of the sides of the jackets were taken away, the bottoms and lower sides being retained to give much-needed support to the heavy blocks. Removing the jackets in those days was a messy job, performed with handsaws and knives to cut through the thick jackets and pincers to tear away the bandages, piecemeal, as they were loosened from their contacts with the rock. Today the technique is much improved by the use of electric surgical saws, of the type used in hospitals to cut casts from healed limbs. One cuts around the block with the saw, and if things go well, the top of the jacket may be removed, preferably in one large piece.

And what is seen when the top of the block is thus exposed? A broad surface covered with hardened paper, through which, here and there, the amorphous shapes of bones may be discerned. At first sight it may not appear very promising, but once the paper is softened and removed, the nature of things becomes apparent. Back in those days the rice paper was softened with alcohol; today, with the modern sophisticated agents being used to harden fossil bones, the softening process is achieved by using those solvents that carry the hardener.

Then exposed bones are immediately hardened again, so that they will not be damaged as work is carried on around them in the block. It cannot be overemphasized how very fragile the bones of *Coelophysis* are. Without proper treatment and extreme care they may go to pieces before one's eyes.

As we began the preparation of the blocks we thought we would experiment to see if there was some way to facilitate the exposing of the bones, beyond the tedious picking away at the specimens with dental tools and needles. Perhaps acid treatment might work, we thought, so we tried several reagents. Hydrochloric acid had no effect whatsoever; in fact, as soon as the liquid came in contact with the bones it penetrated the tiny cracks that crossed the bones in all directions, so that within moments any bones so treated fell apart. Hydrofluoric acid was ineffective. The matrix in which the bones were enclosed was remarkably inert.

Then there was the possibility of using a small, electric vibrating tool— something that would deliver hundreds of strokes a minute. But the vibration of such a device quickly reduced the fossil bones to powder. In the end we went back to the slow but sure technique of hand work, of careful digging with a light jeweler's hammer and a small chisel, supplemented by picking away at the rock with the aforementioned dental tools and needles. And as bone surfaces were exposed they were treated with hardener. The work was extremely slow and exacting. It was a fact of *Coelophysis* preparation that we had to face, that allowed no other option—a situation to which we necessarily became resigned.

But being resigned to a technique of preparation that might be considered the very model of unhurried caution did not mean that we were in the least unhappy about or discouraged by the long prospect that loomed ahead. Just the opposite; we, particularly John Ostrom and Bill Fish, felt elated at the opportunity to work on these blocks, uncovering their treasures bit by bit. Indeed, John has recently commented on how exciting it was for him in those long ago days to be chiseling and picking and scraping at *Coelophysis,* each day with the anticipation of seeing something new. And he did find something new almost every day.

Three preparation processes were involved in the daily work on the blocks; one was to remove rock that covered the bones, a second was to harden and delineate the bones without removing them from the enclosing matrix, and a third was to cut down the rock between bones so that individual bones stood out in clear definition. All of this demanded a steady hand and a light touch, for the fragility of the *Coelophysis* bones dictated our every move. The birdlike bones of this little dinosaur were, as has been noted, generally hollow; consequently, the actual bone surfaces were commonly quite thin and sensitive before hardening, to the touch of a careless finger.

So the work progressed, day after day, with the two skeletons in block VIII and the jackstraw pile of skulls and partial skeletons in block IX progressively coming to light. We experienced an esthetic pleasure in seeing these bones and skeletons emerge from the rock, showing their individual forms and proportions, yet always maintaining the interrelationships that made them the integrated, dynamic frames that had once supported active animals.

Often when blocks are prepared the bones are removed, one by one, to obtain individual elements that can be handled, turned over in all directions, and compared to homologous elements of related animals. We thus removed skulls and other bones from block V, but for blocks VIII and IX the only proper procedure was to expose yet leave the bones in the rocky matrix. The two completely articulated skeletons of block VIII were far too valuable scientifically and too pleasing esthetically to be dismantled. The same was true for the conglomeration of skulls and partial skeletons that were contained in block IX.

It was also advantageous to retain the skeletons and skulls and other bones in their original resting places within blocks VIII and IX simply to protect them against damage. These very fragile fossils would withstand the vicissitudes of museum life much better within their matrices than completely separated from the rock. Of course this procedure had one disadvantage; unlike free bones, bones in the rock cannot be seen from all sides and in every aspect. But with all the fossils at hand, this was no great problem; for example, what might not be apparent in one skull the left side only of which was visible, would be supplemented by another whose top could be seen, or another, exposed in palatal view.

Perhaps at this point, with the preparation of blocks VIII and IX well under way, it may be useful to take a closer look at the *Coelophysis* project, a project that we had stumbled into and had grown beyond anything that might have been anticipated. Such is the nature of paleontology. A prearranged research program is all well and good to have (and for paleontologists research involves collecting in the field just as much as preparing in the laboratory and analyzing in the study), but it is the nature of this scientific discipline to have plans blown sky-high by some unexpected development—such as the discovery of the *Coelophysis* bone bed.

As was previously mentioned, we were at Ghost Ranch as part of a comprehensive research program devoted to expanding our knowledge of Triassic amphibians and reptiles in the Southwest. Now that we had this unplanned bonanza of dinosaur skeletons, what was to become of the program? Was I to abandon it completely and concentrate on *Coelophysis*, or was I to try to integrate a study of *Coelophysis* into my Triassic program? Many paleontologists have faced a similar dilemma, and the solution has usually involved a compromise. My compromise was to carry on the Triassic studies while becoming involved in research on *Coelophysis*. Subsequent to the work at the Ghost Ranch quarry I still went into the field to study Triassic formations; indeed activities of this sort involved fieldwork in many places—Europe, South America, India, South Africa, Australia, and, eventually, Antarctica. I was trying to learn something about the history of life on Triassic continents.

All of which illustrates that paleontologists do not collect fossils merely to mount a show in a museum. Indeed, the exhibition of fossils—of any natural history objects, for that matter—is secondary to research that lends significance to such objects. Research is basic; the publication of what is learned from fossils establishes the true value of the fossils. Publications can offer explanation of the fossils to other paleontologists, to students of all ages, and to the general public. Publications on collections give authority to the institution in which collections are housed, whether a museum, a university, or a college. Without published research performed under its auspices, a museum is not truly a museum; rather it is a sideshow.

Furthermore, publications endure. In centuries to come, the walls of an institution such as the American Museum of Natural History may come tumbling down, the collections may be lost (perish the thought), but the descriptions and analyses published in the Bulletins and Novitates of the museum will endure. Nothing is so permanent as the written word. Consider the Roman empire, crumbled to dust, but Caesar's Commentaries remain a living, gripping account of the conquest of Gaul.

In a museum like the one in New York where I spent much of my adult life exhibition is important. And as we worked on the Ghost Ranch blocks we were aware that the fossil halls were destined for renovation. Therefore, the two prize blocks, VIII and IX, were being prepared not only for study but also for display in one of the new, refurbished halls.

The old adage that paleontological discoveries are made in the laboratory as well as in the field was confirmed during the preparation of the *Coelophysis* blocks. One day Bill Fish and John Ostrom, as they were digging between the ribs of the two skeletons of block VIII, began to find little bones within the rib cages. The more they explored, the more bones they found. Here was something exciting—seemingly the stomach contents of a carnivorous dinosaur! Only one other such case was known to us at that time: that of a very small European Jurassic dinosaur, *Compsognathus*, within whose rib cage are the bony remnants of a lizard, obviously the final meal eaten by this small dinosaur. Interestingly, the bones within the rib cages of the two block VIII *Coelophysis* specimens were clearly the bones of young dinosaurs of the same species, as seen in figures 18 and 19. So it

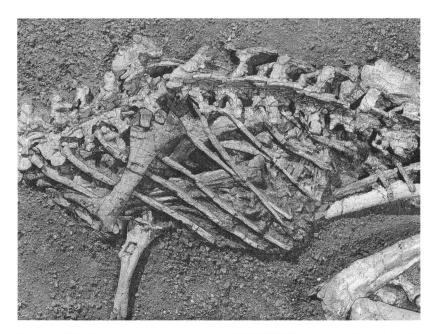

FIGURE 18   The body cavity of *Coelophysis* (AMNH 7223) containing the bones of a young *Coelophysis*—clear evidence of cannibalism in this dinosaur. Especially noticeable is the long, straight tibia-fibula of the devoured prey.

would seem that *Coelophysis* was at times cannibalistic. Or were these the skeletons perhaps of embryos? All the evidence favors the theory of cannibalism in *Coelophysis*—an idea that will be explored in more detail below. Suffice it to say here that cannibalism is well known among modern reptiles, especially crocodiles and alligators.

Other discoveries have been made in other blocks from Ghost Ranch. In block II, which went to Yale, a choice skull and skeleton of a thecodont reptile, one of the contemporaries of *Coelophysis,* emerged from among the melange of *Coelophysis* skeletons. In block C–5–81, collected by the Museum of Northern Arizona team in 1981, not only the hind limbs of a reptile, perhaps identical with the Yale specimen, appeared, but also the tiny bones, unfortunately without a skull, of a diminutive long-legged, long-armed reptile, perhaps related to other very small, attenuated reptiles found in the Triassic deposits of Europe and South America. Also in this block are numerous enamel-like scales of chondrostean fishes, such as the freshwater gars and their relatives. And during the collecting of block

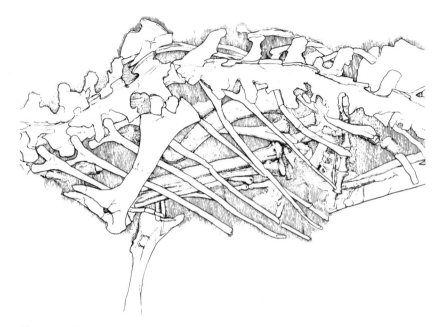

FIGURE 19   An artist's rendering of the body cavity seen in figure 18.

C–9–82, now at Ghost Ranch, some intriguing scales of a little armored reptile were found. Surprises continue to come to light as the *Coelophysis* blocks are prepared at various museums.

From the blocks prepared at different museums, *Coelophysis* skulls and skeletons of different sizes have emerged, quite obviously a record of growth stages in this little dinosaur. This valuable record, showing the changes within the skeleton as *Coelophysis* progressed from almost newly hatched infants to full-grown adults, will be discussed below. Mention might be made of a beautifully articulated skeleton that has come to light in the block at Ghost Ranch. This skeleton, ten or eleven feet long, represents a "giant" *Coelophysis*. It raises a question: what was the ultimate size limit of *Coelophysis?*

One very interesting fact became evident as initial preparation of the *Coelophysis* blocks progressed—as well as during the work on blocks at other institutions. In almost all the specimens the lower jaws are tightly locked in place against the skull. One would hardly expect this situation to be so prevalent among the many skulls and jaws of *Coelphysis* that have been uncovered in the various Ghost Ranch blocks, for it is quite common to find skulls and jaws of fossil tetrapods (the primarily land-living vertebrates) separated as a natural result of postmortem decay. As the connecting muscles and ligaments decay after death but before burial, the articulations between lower jaws and skulls give way, so that the jaws are frequently dropped down from their natural position, or as frequently are displaced. Quite often skulls and jaws are widely separated in fossil-bearing sediments. Why is this not so in the case of *Coelophysis?*

It seems obvious that the skeletons at Ghost Ranch were buried so soon after death that the muscles held the lower jaws tightly in place—so soon that skeletons were not disarticulated and scattered, but rather retained their death poses. For the paleontologist this is one of the fortunate aspects of the Ghost Ranch dinosaur mausoleum. (See figure 20.)

Furthermore, the skulls of *Coelophysis* are almost always intact. Here again we see the probable effect of quick burial after death. Reptilian skulls,

FIGURE 20   A well-preserved skull and lower jaw of *Coelophysis*, as exposed in a block from Ghost Ranch, at the Yale Peabody Museum laboratory of paleontology (specimen 41196). A part of a leg bone had to be removed in order to expose the skull completely, since having the skull entirely visible was deemed more important than keeping the leg bone intact.

unlike the solid, tightly fused skulls of mammals, are composed of discrete bones that do not fuse to any great degree during the life of the animal. Therefore it is common to find reptile skulls disintegrated in the fossil state, with the numerous bones originally composing the skull separated from their primary contacts, and frequently scattered over wide areas or even lost as a result of erosion and stream transportation before burial. The skulls of dinosaurs are particularly vulnerable in this respect; indeed it is almost legendary that the largest of the dinosaurs, the huge sauropods, are more often than not known from headless skeletons. Not so with *Coelophysis*. Usually the skulls with their interlocked jaws are still in place in each specimen, right at the front end of a vertebral column (as seen in figure 21).

Dinosaur skulls not only consist of numerous articulated but unfused bones but also may be comparatively fragile. This is not true for some of the large horned dinosaurs or the big carnivorous giants. But for many of the other dinosaurs such is the case, so that during fossilization their skulls become distorted, even if the bones retain their original relationships. Cer-

FIGURE 21 A partially prepared skull, pointed to the right, in the Ghost Ranch block. Alex Downs holds his needle-sharp instrument against the skull roof, above the long antorbital opening in front of the eye.

tainly this has been true for *Coelophysis*. In spite of the considerable number of skulls now known, none, so far as I know, are preserved in their natural, unaltered shapes.

Coelophysis skulls have been compressed and distorted by the weight of the sediments within which they are contained. Some are compressed from side to side, others from top to bottom, still others are skewed. Some are as flat as pancakes. All of this makes the interpretation of *Coelophysis* skulls an exercise in knowledgeable and imaginative restoration on paper, or perhaps in the three-dimensional medium of sculptor's clay. Yet the many skulls available have made it possible to obtain a reasonably accurate reconstruction of the skull of this little dinosaur.

It should be added that to a lesser degree compression and distortion has been the fate of some other bones in the *Coelophysis* skeleton, especially the hollow leg bones. On the other hand, most of the bones of the post-cranial skeleton in various skeletons are preserved in their natural form, so that one can see them for what they once were.

As the skeletons of *Coelophysis* were first being prepared in their respective blocks it was interesting to see that in some of the specimens the long neck had been curved back over the body, so that the skull might occupy a position above the back of the vertebral column. This was no surprise to us as we uncovered the skeletons in the blocks; this same situation has been seen for years in other long-necked dinosaurs. It is obviously the result of drying of the ligaments and muscles in the neck, shortening them and thus pulling the head back to its unnatural position above the back. Not all *Coelophysis* specimens show this, but a sufficient number do indicate that even though time may have been limited some desiccation of the cadavers occurred before they were buried (see figure 22).

As is evident, much can be learned as fossils are prepared, and we certainly learned many things as the work on the blocks proceeded. Surprises we came across included the little skeletons within the rib cages of the two large specimens, as well as the distortions of the skulls and the recurved necks in certain specimens. Information like this, revealed by the nature of the skeletons and the bones within the blocks, is part of a rather new discipline within the bounds of paleontology known as taphonomy. It is the study and interpretation of burial conditions and events that make the fossils what they are and give much more meaning to the fossils than before. More detailed attention will be given to the taphonomy of the Ghost Ranch dinosaurs in a later chapter.

As for our preparation of the Ghost Ranch dinosaurs, the time finally

FIGURE 22   Two adult skeletons (AMNH 7223 and 7224) in the final stages of preparation. The bones have been cleaned, but kept in their original death-pose positions, together in a single block. (The tails are in adjacent blocks.)

came when the exposure and cleaning and delineation of the skeletons and
bones in certain blocks were completed. Nothing more could be done to improve the appearance of blocks VIII and IX (see figure 23). John Ostrom and
Bill Fish were like the artist who has finally completed a large painting. Any
further fussing or picking on the top of the block would only have confused
things, just as in the case of the artist and his painting; additional touching
up will only spoil the final result. One must know when to stop.

The prepared surfaces of the two blocks with their contained fossils
were in every sense truly esthetic objects. Yet the sides of the blocks left
something to be desired. They were still encased by the remains of the
plaster jacket, which covered the bottoms of the blocks as well. More work
had to be done to make the blocks proper objects for exhibition. So the
plaster was cleaned from their sides, a complicated procedure was used to
remove excess plaster from the bottoms of the blocks, and steel supporting

bars were set into the undersides of the blocks, to give the necessary strength. Finally, the two blocks were ready to be placed in the exhibition hall, where they were displayed in vertical positions, attached to the backs of the exhibit cases. With appropriate labels and pictorial materials, the exhibition of blocks VIII and IX at the American Museum of Natural History

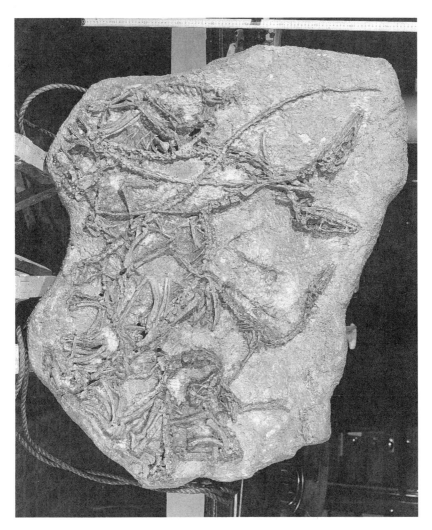

FIGURE 23 A close-up view of AMNH block IX from Ghost Ranch, with its interlaced skeletons.

was a joy to behold. Here could be seen the skeletons of some of the earliest dinosaurs as they had never been seen before.

(This is how blocks VIII and IX were displayed from 1954 until recently. At present the entire display of fossil vertebrates at the American Museum is being completely revised and rearranged. When this massive exhibition schedule is completed *Coelophysis* will be seen in new surroundings and in a new context.)

The foregoing discussion of preparation and exhibition describes one particular effort to bring the fossils of *Coelophysis* to light and to exhibit them in a meaningful way. Of course other blocks have been prepared at other museums and are still being prepared. Certainly the exhibition of such blocks will be different from the one in New York.

A few final remarks on my own *Coelophysis* research. My timetable became delayed beyond anything that had been contemplated in the beginning, the delay being caused partly of my own making, partly by things beyond my control. Many aspects of my Triassic research program had to be completed, including the journeys far and wide that have already been mentioned. Among these journeys was the epochal fieldwork in Antarctica, where my colleagues and I collected Triassic amphibians and reptiles in the Transantarctic Mountains—a bare four hundred miles from the South Pole. That was a first in many respects—one being the first truly ancient fossil tetrapods to be collected ever from a continent in which such fossils were heretofore unknown. As one result I became involved for a decade or more in the study and description of these fossils, which among other things clearly demonstrated the unity of Antarctica and Africa during the Triassic period. (That work inevitably released a spate of subsequent fossil-hunting expeditions to Antarctica, which have begun to reveal in detail the vertebrate life on that continent during Mesozoic and Cenozoic times.)

But before and beyond the Antarctic research, there were multitudinous projects and duties—research, teaching, exhibition, publishing—that occupied the days and years of my life. Then I retired from the American Museum of Natural History and moved to Flagstaff, Arizona, to become affiliated with the Museum of Northern Arizona. And it was in this new environment that I became involved with the reopening of the Ghost Ranch quarry, which of course resulted in much new material of *Coelophysis*, some of which I felt must be included in my long-delayed final work on the dinosaur. Thus my comprehensive publication of *Coelophysis* finally appeared under the aegis of the Museum of Northern Arizona some forty-two years after the discovery of the *Coelophysis* bone bed at Ghost Ranch, an overly lengthy hiatus between discovery and publication. The publication was still not as comprehensive as I might have wished, but I felt that the thing to do was to get it out, even though new materials and new information were still being extracted from Ghost Ranch blocks at various institutions. Consequently, much must still be done to complete the story of *Coelophysis* at Ghost Ranch—if it is ever completed.

BONES AND HISTORY

With all the skeletons of *Coelophysis* now at hand in museums across North America, it is sometimes easy to forget that this dinosaur, certainly one of the most abundantly documented of all dinosaurs, was, for more than half its recorded existence, a dinosaurian species with very fragmentary evidence attesting to its tenure on earth. Until the discovery of the Ghost Ranch quarry a literal handful of fragments constituted the evidence upon which our knowledge of *Coelophysis bauri* was founded. Yet this dinosaur, even though small and for many years poorly recorded, has long loomed large in the writings about dinosaurs in part because of its stratigraphic position. *Coelophysis* is on this basis one of the earliest dinosaurs—which has made it important in the eyes of those tracing the evolutionary history of the ruling reptiles of Mesozoic time.

It is therefore appropriate at this point that—having given considerable attention to the events making *Coelophysis* an abundantly known dinosaur and before entering into some fairly detailed descriptions of its anatomy, how and where it lived, and how it died—we review the circumstances of the discovery and the fate of those first fragmentary bones that came to be called *Coelophysis bauri*. The early history of the bones involves three men—David Baldwin of Abiquiu, New Mexico, who found the original fragments of *Coelophysis*; Edward Drinker Cope of Philadelphia, who first described them; and Professor Othniel Charles Marsh of Yale University, who in the late nineteenth century had something to say about dinosaurs, in general, and about those found in North America, in particular. Baldwin was a rough mountain man of the Old West, Cope was the scion of a wealthy Philadelphia Quaker family, and Marsh was a powerful, often unscrupulous figure, and a domineering presence in American science.

To begin the account, who was David Baldwin? David Baldwin has been described as a fossil collector of whom little is known—a rather shadowy figure who would disappear into the Western badlands for weeks or months at a time, subsequently to emerge with loads of fossils for his employers, principally the above-mentioned Cope, as well as Cope's bitter scientific rival, the above-mentioned Marsh.

We get a first glimpse of Baldwin in 1875, when he served on the "Wheeler Survey" (one of the famous post–Civil War geological surveys of the Western territories) under Lieutenant William L. Carpenter. When Carpenter first met Baldwin he described the mountain man as "equipped like a Mexican with a burro, some corn meal, and pickaxe. Those were his worldly possessions" (Schuchert and LeVene 1940:179).

Baldwin and his burro were well known in northern New Mexico during the 1880s, when he roamed this region in search of fossils. He liked to work in the wintertime, because even though he had to brave the cold, he had at hand a plentiful supply of snow on the ground, which furnished a source of water for the fossil hunter and his long-eared companion. Perhaps the cold was for him less disadvantageous than the summer heat and the scarcity of water. Certainly, such was his strategy of field collecting, for which he was famous in paleontological circles.

After his service on the Wheeler Survey, Baldwin worked at different times during the late 1870s and the 1880s for both Marsh and Cope.

Marsh was a man of unbounded ambition with considerable connections. A lifelong bachelor, he was a nephew of George Peabody, a famous financier and philanthropist who spent his adult life (he, too, was a bachelor) in Britain and, among other things, was a personal friend of Queen Victoria. As a young man Marsh persuaded his powerful uncle to set him up as a professor at Yale and to endow a museum there of which he would be the director. This was the Peabody Museum, today an important world center of natural history, particularly paleontology and geology. Marsh employed various men, scientifically trained and otherwise, to collect fossils for him, but treating them insensitively and paying them as little as he could get away with.

Baldwin knew very little of geology (his experience was gained first-hand in the field), but he was an astute observer and a careful collector. He was not a man to be ignored.

Yet he was ignored by Marsh, particularly after he had made a collection of Permian fossils—amphibians and reptiles—near Coyote, about fifteen miles west of Abiquiu, which Marsh never examined. Then in 1877 Baldwin informed Marsh of large dinosaur bones at Canyon City, Colorado, and Marsh paid no attention to Baldwin's letter, that is, not until Cope began to collect there, at which point Marsh sent two of his collectors, Samuel Wendell Williston and Benjamin Mudge, to the locality to reap some fossiliferous rewards.

Such outrageous behavior on the part of Marsh, who was well known as a cold and calculating person—often referred to as "the Great Dismal Swamp"—proved too much for Baldwin's sensibilities. So he transferred his full allegiance to Cope. But not before he had quarreled with Marsh over the conditions of his employment, particularly about a considerable sum of money Marsh owed him for collections that had been sent to New Haven. The disagreement eventually was adjudicated by Lieutenant Carpenter, who censured both parties for behaving with "an absence of proper business terms" (Schuchert and LeVene 1940:180).

Baldwin began working for Cope in 1880. There is no need to go into the Cope-Marsh feud, one of the most bitter controversies in the history of science, for it is largely incidental to the story being told here. Suffice it to say that both Cope and Marsh were men of independent means, both were excessively strong minded, and each hated the other with such zeal that North America was hardly large enough to contain the two of them at the same time.

Having said this, it should be noted that Cope was the antithesis of Marsh in almost every respect. Where Marsh was cold and calculating, Cope was warm and friendly; where Marsh was dead serious about everything he did, Cope was merry and often impetuous; where Marsh succeeded by hard application and by almost inhuman exploitation of his many assistants, Cope succeeded by virtue of his brilliant intellect and his own personal application to his studies (see figure 24). He was very much a loner.

The son of a wealthy Philadelphia Quaker merchant and shipowner, he had all the advantages of a privileged boyhood spent under the protection of a loving family. In his adult years he operated largely as an independent

FIGURE 24 A photograph of Edward Drinker Cope, taken in his Philadelphia study, that captures the essence of his personality.

scholar, free from any close institutional connections (something that was possible in those days but virtually impossible today) although he did maintain ties with the Philadelphia Academy of Natural Science. Although he frequently went out into the field under the most primitive conditions, he also spent considerable amounts of his personal fortune employing field assistants like Baldwin to collect fossils. In short, he was generally well-liked by those who worked for him and with him. Such was the man for whom David Baldwin was exploring and collecting in New Mexico in the 1880s.

While collecting fossils for Marsh and for Cope Baldwin lived in Abiquiu, a little town that a hundred years ago was remote and self-contained. He made it his home because he found it a convenient place from which to explore the cliffs and canyons and badlands exposures of northwestern New Mexico.

To visit Abiquiu today is in a sense to travel back through time, when the Spanish people of the Southwest were very Spanish indeed. Abiquiu, one of the oldest towns in New Mexico, is today located on a rise of ground above the Chama River, and just off Federal Highway 84, the road that runs from Española some twenty miles to the south, to Chama near the northern border of the state, and on to Pagosa Springs, Colorado. The occasional motorist who drives up the steep hill from the highway into Abiquiu is almost immediately transported in time from the black, paved road characteristic of the late twentieth century, with its attendant gasoline stations and small stores, to an uneven plaza, bordered by a few local commercial buildings as well as by dwellings, and dominated by a lovely adobe church of the type established by the Spanish fathers during the centuries when this region was a part of New Spain.

It might be said that the church exemplifies the character of Abiquiu, which has not changed radically during the past century even though its inhabitants are bilingual and drive around in the latest model cars.

A vignette of Abiquiu from almost a century and a half ago has been provided by William H. Richardson, a private soldier in the famous Doniphan Brigade, which marched from Missouri through the Southwest and into Mexico, to participate in the Mexican War, a conflict that separated Texas and the Southwest, as well as California, from Old Mexico, and added this vast area to the United States. During their famous march, which has been compared to the Anabasis of Xenophon, some elements of the

Doniphan force were quartered for several months in the vicinity of Abi-quiu. Private Richardson tells in his journal about a visit to Abiquiu, which he spelled Abique, on the evening of November 11, 1846.

> When we arrived at Abique, an old man invited us to partake of his hospitality;—an invitation we gladly accepted. We went in accordingly, and after all were seated on the floor in the posture of a tailor, a large earthen vessel was placed before us containing pepper sauce and soup, and a few tortillas (a thin paste made of corn rubbed between flat stones). The sauce caused my mouth to burn to a blister. The people are very fond of condiments, and become so accustomed to them that what will burn a stranger's mouth has no effect upon theirs. After all was over, we went across the street to attend the fandango. From the crowd, I should judge it was in high favor with all classes of the community. Some of the per-formers were dressed in the most fantastic style, and some scarcely dressed at all. The ladies and gentlemen whirled around with a rapidity quite painful to behold, and the music pealed in deafening sounds . . . I left the place about 10 o'clock and returned to our quarters. (Richardson 1849:34)

In February 1881, a third of a century after Private Richardson had sam-pled the fiery Mexican food of Abiquiu, Baldwin, accompanied by his bur-ro, was exploring rock exposures along the Chama River a few miles to the north of that town, at a locality near Arroyo Seco, which is a tributary of the Chama, and there he found some delicate little fossil bones. He collected these and put them in a sack that subsequently was sent to Cope, with an included label that read as follows.

> Label sack 2   Box 1   Prof E. D. Cope
>
> Contains Triassic or Jurassic bones all small and tender—Those marked little bones are many of them ^almost^ microscopic   All in this sack found to-gether in same place   About four hundred feet below gypsum stratum Arroyo Seco   Rio Arriba Co   New Mexico February 1881. No feet—no head—only one tooth.
>
> D. Baldwin—Abiquiu

This locality must have been in the general vicinity of present-day Ghost Ranch, New Mexico, where Arroyo Seco traverses the ranch property to join, not far beyond, the Chama River, and where Arroyo Yeso, a small tributary to Arroyo Seco, extends through the ranch to terminate against the spectacular cliffs that rise behind the ranch. (Perhaps it was in the near vicinity of, or even at, our quarry site.)

David Baldwin also collected some small bones of the same kind, that same year, near the small trading post of Gallina, about twenty-five miles as the crow flies to the west of Ghost Ranch and Arroyo Seco. The fossils were found in an exposure between a colorful hogback known as Cerro Blanco on the west and Capulin Mesa on the east.

In the list of fossils that Baldwin sent to Cope there is the following statement:

> Box 2   Contains sack 3.   Part of fossil dug out Gallina Canyon April 12—May 1. Three reptile teeth. Triassic or Jurassic. 400 feet below gypsum horizon.   180 feet above grey sandstone.

Those figures—400 feet below the gypsum horizon and 180 feet above the gray sandstone—should be kept in mind. They are diagnostic levels, referred to in later discussions.

Baldwin sent the little bones from Arroyo Seco and from Gallina to Cope in Philadelphia, along with other fossils that he had collected in northern New Mexico. Cope, unlike Marsh, was not a person to ignore the materials that were sent in by his collectors; consequently he studied and then described the fossils in two publications that appeared in 1887.

The first description of the handful of fossil fragments that Cope had received from David Baldwin was published on May 4, 1887, in the *American Naturalist*, in an article entitled "The Dinosaurian Genus *Coelurus*." The genus *Coelurus* had been established by O. C. Marsh in 1879, based on a fossil of late Jurassic age, which Marsh had named *Coelurus fragilis*. Cope's description was quite brief and without illustrations. In this short paper he named two species, which he designated as *Coelurus longicollis* (a reference to the apparent long neck, as revealed by several cervical vertebrae) and *Coelurus bauri* (in honor of Marsh's assistant, George Baur) (Cope 1887a).

As Cope devoted additional attention to the fossils from New Mexico, he decided that the little dinosaurs could *not* be placed within the Jurassic genus *Coelurus*; consequently, he moved them into the Triassic genus *Tanystrophaeus*, a reptile from Europe noted for its very long neck. In so doing he recognized a third species, which he named *Tanystrophaeus willistoni*, in honor of Marsh's then assistant, Samuel Wendell Williston (Cope 1887b:221,226,227).

It was probably no accident that Cope named two of these dinosaurian species after two of Marsh's assistants; it was a good opportunity for the combative Quaker paleontologist to express something of his contempt for the gelid scholar at Yale. Cope knew, as did most of his contemporaries, that much of the nitty-gritty detailed research published by Marsh was done by his assistants; perhaps Cope thought it would be amusing to go over Marsh's head and honor these long-suffering young men.

Two years later Cope realized that the three species he described could not possibly belong to *Tanystrophaeus*, and so with a brief paragraph in his own journal he created a new genus to contain them. Thus was the genus *Coelophysis* established, its name being based upon two Greek roots, *koilos*, meaning "hollow," and *physis*, meaning "form, nature." This name was created by Cope to indicate the very hollow bones, similar to the bones of birds, that so characterize *Coelophysis*.

Cope's creation of the genus *Coelophysis*, as published in 1889 in the *American Naturalist*, is here presented in an unabridged quotation:

> *On a New Genus of Triassic Dinosauria*,—In this journal for April, 1887. I described two species of Goniopodous Dinosauria, under the names of *Coelurus longicollis* and *C. bauri*, from the Triassic formation of New Mexico. I subsequently discovered that they could not be referred to the genus Coelurus, and placed them provisionally (Proceeds, Amer. Philos. Society, 1887, p. 221) in the Tanystrophaeus of Von Meyer. I have recently learned that the reputed vertebrae of the latter genus possesses no complete neural canal, so that the position in the skeleton of these elements, on which the genus was founded, becomes problematical. It becomes evident that the Triassic species in question must be referred to a genus distinct from any hitherto known, differing from Coelurus in the biconcave cervical vertebrae, and from Megadactylus in the simple femoral condyles, as well as in other points. I propose that it be called Coelophysis, and the three species, *C. longicollis*, *C. bauri*, and *C. willistoni* respectively. —E. D. Cope   (Cope 1889)

For more than twenty years after the creation of *Coelophysis* the bones of this early dinosaur, such as they were, remained in quiet oblivion. And during that interval they were transferred from Cope's home in Philadelphia to the American Museum of Natural History, the result of the museum's purchase of the Cope Collection in 1895. The purchase of the Cope Collection owed to the munificence of J. P. Morgan, who was persuaded to do this by his nephew, Henry Fairfield Osborn, a "disciple" of Cope and a man destined to loom large in the history of vertebrate paleontology in North America.

Enter in the year 1911 Baron Freiherr Professor Friedrich von Huene (see figure 25), a German paleontologist of great distinction, who came to the United States to gain some acquaintance with North American Triassic reptiles. Von Huene, who occupied a chair at Tübingen University, an ancient institution set in a lovely little city among the hills and valleys of Württemberg, was a well-versed student of Triassic vertebrates, especially reptiles, and had an impressive series of publications in this field to his credit. Yet despite the spate of scientific writings that had issued from his pen through the years, von Huene was no closet naturalist, confined to his desk and his laboratory. In fact he was very definitely a field man who in those early years of his life had spent many summers in the Triassic sediments of southern Germany, where he had excavated many fossils, to be taken back to Tübingen for study and often for exhibition at the university museum.

He was a long, lean, red-headed, ascetic, aristocratic individual, famous for his ability to walk mile after mile across the countryside in search of

FIGURE 25 Friedrich von Huene of Tübingen University, at the time of his trip to the United States to join Williston, Case, and Paul Miller in New Mexico.

fossils, or for other reasons. One tale is told of how von Huene, then an old man in his eighties, hiked more than one hundred miles across southern Germany to attend some scientific meetings. And at nights during this rustic journey, he slept out under the stars.

So with such a background, von Huene, by 1911 middle-aged, was quite prepared to come to northern New Mexico and join an expedition being led by Marsh's former assistant, Samuel Wendell Williston, now professor at the University of Chicago, together with Williston's son Sam, and Paul Miller, Williston's faithful assistant and laboratory technician, as well as with Professor Ermin C. Case of the University of Michigan, one of Williston's former students.

They were camped at the foot of a spectacular, red-banded cliff at the very bottom of the Arroyo de Agua, a few miles west of the village of Coyote, and north of Abiquiu. Here they were working in the Permian sediments of that locality, for Williston and Case were primarily "Permian men." But one day they visited the cliffs near Gallina, about ten miles west of their camp site, one of the places from which David Baldwin had obtained some of the *Coelophysis* bones that he sent to Cope. It is to be assumed that this visit had a particular significance for von Huene; not only was he primarily a "Triassic man," but also he had in 1906 listed *Coelophysis* among the Triassic dinosaurs found outside Europe, in his paper entitled "Ueber die Dinosaurier der Aussereuropaischen Trias." He was no stranger to *Coelophysis* (von Huene 1906:118, pl. V—fig. 5.2–10, pl. XI—figs. 1–4, pl. XII—fig. 1, text figs. 11–20).

Back in New York after his summer in New Mexico, von Huene examined the Triassic fossils that Baldwin had collected so many years before. At the suggestion of Henry Fairfield Osborn and William Diller Matthew, the eminent paleontologists at the American Museum, he agreed to redescribe the specimens. The fossils were shipped to Tübingen, and von Huene, who was given to prompt action, wrote new descriptions of the specimens. His manuscript and illustrations, together with the fossils, were returned to New York before the outbreak of World War I, with the result that his paper, entitled "On Reptiles of the New Mexico Trias in the Cope Collection," was published in 1915 in the *Bulletin* of the museum (von Huene 1915).

In this paper von Huene devoted eight pages to describing and illustrating *Coelophysis*, which he believed to contain the three species originally described by Cope (von Huene 1915:500–507). His descriptions, which supplemented and expanded the account published by Cope in the *Proceedings of the American Philosophical Society*, depicted for the first time the bones of *Coelophysis*, the illustrations consisting of thirty-seven pen and ink line drawings, accurately reproduced at half natural size. Von Huene's text and these thirty-seven illustrations provided a reasonably good, albeit incomplete, idea of what the bones of the little Triassic dinosaur were like.

Then came the discovery at Ghost Ranch in 1947. Within a few years, after some of the skeletons at the American Museum of Natural History had been sufficiently exposed and cleaned to give a reasonably clear idea of *Coelophysis*'s general anatomy and proportions, this dinosaur began to appear in publications throughout the world, principally as artists' reconstructions, but occasionally with brief descriptions as well. Therefore, within a couple of decades, while work continued in laboratories on the blocks from Ghost Ranch, *Coelophysis* became well established in the literature as a prototypical ancestral theropod dinosaur. It became so well known to the public that the Legislature of New Mexico had declared it the "official" fossil of the state. And of course it became familiar to museum visitors in New York and elsewhere.

During those years, as blocks were cleaned and skeletons were exposed, I was busy making notes and supervising the drawing of illustrations, with a view to the publication of a monograph on *Coelophysis*, a publication that would set forth the anatomical details and other facts about this dinosaur. The work went slowly, in part because of the time required for preparation of the fossils, and in part because I was sandwiching these studies in between other museum duties and projects, including my trip to Antarctica, described earlier. The research on Antarctic fossils relegated *Coelophysis* to the sidelines.

Twenty-two years after the discovery of *Coelophysis* at Ghost Ranch I retired from the museum in New York and settled in Arizona. I took my notes and illustrations with me, in the hope that I could continue and complete, in one way or another, the study of *Coelophysis*. Eventually I did this with the publication of "The Triassic Dinosaur *Coelophysis*," which appeared in a 1989 issue of the *Bulletin of the Museum of Northern Arizona*. I had originally hoped that the study of *Coelophysis* would be published by the American Museum of Natural History, but since this little dinosaur had become the property, so to speak, of several museums, it was appropriate for it to be published in the publication in which it appeared. The period of time between discovery and publication had been far longer than I had ever anticipated, but I was at last happy to have my interpretation of the Ghost Ranch dinosaur published in a scientific forum.

One might suppose that, having seen *Coelophysis* through the mill, from the first tentative discoveries out on that talus slope at Ghost Ranch, followed by the months of digging and plastering and handling of large, recalcitrant blocks, then the years of preparation work in the laboratory, the additional years of research involving measurements and interpretation, comparisons with related dinosaurs, not only in New York but at other museums, and subsequently the supervision of illustrations, the writing of manuscript, and seeing that manuscript through to publication, I would finally end my association with the little dinosaurs of Ghost Ranch. Far from it. Now that *Coelophysis* has been so completely revealed, 200 million years after its sojourn in what is now New Mexico, it would seem to have a life of its own.

Blocks are being prepared in various museums throughout North America, new fossils are being exposed, and new information about this

FIGURE 26   A skeleton of *Coelophysis bauri*, displayed as an "open mount" at the Denver Museum of Natural History under the direction of Dr. Kenneth Carpenter.

interesting dinosaur is constantly being brought to light. For example, a very large skeleton of *Coelophysis* now is emerging from the huge block at Ghost Ranch. New details concerning the anatomy of this dinosaur are being found, as the delicate work with fine tools continues at the museums where *Coelophysis* blocks are housed. Fossils associated with *Coelophysis*—fish, small reptiles, and the like—are being discovered. Indeed, much has yet to be learned.

And much remains to be seen as the result of labors carried on in laboratories across the country. In this respect particular mention should be made of the stunning new "open mount" of a *Coelophysis* skeleton set up at the Denver Museum. Here, for the first time, one can see a skeleton completely removed from its stony resting place, in full three-dimensional aspect, as a skeleton properly should be seen (see figure 26).

Furthermore, papers and books dealing with *Coelophysis* and with the world in which it lived continue to be published. *Coelophysis* is far from being a forgotten dinosaur; rather it continues to be a dinosaur that is widely regarded and widely discussed.

Needless to say, I am one of the people caught up in the ongoing discussions and arguments concerning *Coelophysis* and perhaps will be until my dying day. It all boils down to this: when George Whitaker found those first tiny fragments at Ghost Ranch, circumstances were set in motion that affected the lives of many people, including me. *Coelophysis* has most decidedly had a large impact on my life, and in this respect I have had an experience similar to that of many paleontologists.

We fossil hunters are a small but fortunate group of people.

THE QUARRY REVEALED;

OR, WHAT KILLED THE DINOSAURS?

Much can be learned from a fossil quarry. The fossils, of course, are eventually removed from the quarry to be prepared in the laboratory and studied; they are self-evident. But after the fossils have been removed there remain the rocks, the abandoned sedimentary layers that during those active, sometimes frenetic, days of digging were an integral part of the fossil story. These remains of the excavation, now a vertical rock face incised into the long, steep slope of the hill, preserve a record accessory to the fossils, a record waiting to be studied and interpreted.

When we first worked at the Ghost Ranch Quarry we were quite aware of this record in the rocks, and I, for one, was anxious that a study be made, to learn something about how the sediments had been deposited and what they had to show about the immediate environment and the climate that prevailed when *Coelophysis* roamed this land. It was a study that was needed to lend a valuable dimension to the Ghost Ranch story, but which I was not qualified to carry out. The quarry needed the scrutinizing attention of a sedimentary geologist, who was able to find the hidden meanings in the attitude of rock layers, in the significance attached to the arrangements of grains of sands and the presence of mud balls, in the import of bumps and depressions that might be virtually invisible to the untrained eye. All this was beyond me.

This was why, at an early stage of the Ghost Ranch dinosaur story, I had some conversations with John Harshbarger of the U.S. Geological Survey, and we mutually agreed that he would make a study of the quarry. He was keen to do the work, and I was confident he would carry out a comprehensive and meaningful survey.

At that time John, along with Geological Survey colleagues, had been conducting important studies of the Triassic and Jurassic rocks of the Southwest, the results of which were published in several Geological Survey Professional Papers. He had a solid knowledge of Southwest geology, based on quite a few years of fieldwork across the deserts and badlands and mountains of the Navajo country and adjacent regions.

John was a large man in every way, surely weighing more than two hundred pounds. But he could get over the ground with no trouble, and a hike of many miles in search of geological information did not in the least intimidate him. I will always remember his expressive brown eyes and his ready smile. So I was looking forward to cooperating with him on the quarry study, perhaps even assisting him a little, and I was certainly anticipating the results of his efforts. Alas, it was not to be. John became involved in other geological projects and then he died. That was years ago.

I had long given up hope that a detailed quarry survey would ever be made; indeed I had largely forgotten the matter for years when much to my delight just such a study was undertaken by two of my friends, David Gillette, a paleontologist with much experience in other aspects of geology, and Hilde Schwartz, a woman who knows a great deal about sediments— about their mineralogy, about how they are deposited, and so on. Hilde was a logical person to do such a study.

So Schwartz and Gillette made their study, the manuscript of which they gave me to read and which has just been published. It is the basis of much of what is to be said in this chapter. The study has been supplemented by conversations with them as well as Lynett Gillette, who is in charge of the Ghost Ranch Museum of geology and paleontology, and who has devoted much time and thought to the natural history of Ghost Ranch.

The earlier description of the quarry mentioned that our dig was in the side of a small hill, located just above a little occasional rivulet, a tributary to Arroyo del Yeso, the "gypsum gulch" that in turn is tributary to Arroyo Seco, near which David Baldwin had made some of his collections of *Coelophysis* back in 1881. This little hill is overshadowed by the huge bulk of what is now known as "Kitchen Mesa," which rises massively above the buildings of Ghost Ranch, its steep cliffs of Jurassic Entrada sandstone, hundreds of feet high resting on the soft slopes of the Chinle Formation, and capped with a thick layer of Todilto gypsum. "Our hill" with its quarry seemed to us at the time quite evidently a remnant of Chinle sediments that once had been of broad, lateral extent, capped by Entrada and Todilto rocks—rocks that long since have disappeared because of the inexorable processes of erosion.

After the final block was removed from the Ghost Ranch quarry, the rather unprepossessing quarry face remained as a solid reminder of work that had been done here over the course of several field seasons. The face, a vertical cut about eleven meters or thirty-five feet wide and some five meters or fifteen feet high, was at the time clear and available for study and interpretation—a condition that did not last for very long because of the slumping of sediments from the slope above the quarry. Soon the forces of weather and gravity took over, and loose talus on the hill slope above the quarry dribbled and slid down to cover the quarry face, so that today the visitor to this former excavation sees little as a reward for the hike from the ranch up to the quarry. One might say that nature has healed a scar that was made by several parties of inquisitive paleontologists.

But when Schwartz and Gillette turned their attentions to the study of the quarry face, it still stood out boldly, if not in very large dimensions, with the requisite information locked within its rocky surface. They proceeded to unlock this information. When viewing the quarry face, the first and most striking thing they saw was a fault at its western end. This fault had been visible even at the beginning of excavations, years earlier, and it had served through the years as a reference line of sorts—an abrupt termination of the fossil graveyard in that direction. The fault reveals that the cliff to the west of the break, which is almost vertical, is on what geologists call the downthrown side of the fault; that is, it has dropped down relative to the quarry block.

If one looks eastward from this fault, the quarry face when carefully analyzed appears to consist of rather wavy strata or bands of varying thickness, extending to the eastern limits of the quarry. Schwartz and Gillette mapped these strata from bottom to top (as seen in figure 27), labeling them, also from bottom to top, with the letters D through Q. The bands D through L they considered as constituting the lower quarry, while M through Q comprise the upper quarry. The lower quarry is contained in about five meters of the upper siltstone member of the Chinle Formation, the base of the quarry being some fifteen or sixteen meters (or about 50 feet) above the approximate base of the siltstone member—in other words,

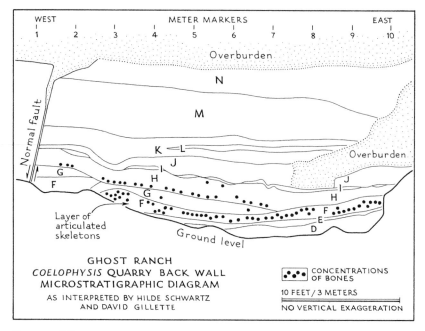

FIGURE 27   An interpretation of the Ghost Ranch quarry face, beds D through N, as modifed from Schwartz and Gillette 1994. Cartography by George Colbert.

above the zone of gradation between this member and the underlying Petrified Forest member. There are about thirty-three meters (approximately 108 feet) of sediments belonging to the siltstone member between the top of the quarry face and the base of the overlying massive Entrada Sandstone. The siltstone member of the Chinle Formation at Ghost Ranch is about fifty-five meters (or 180 feet) thick.

The fine-grained nature of the siltstone deposits, and their lateral continuity, show that they were stream deposits subject to periodic flooding and marginal to mud flats bordering a pond or lake. There is evidence of much cutting and filling, as would be expected in such stream deposits. It would seem that the climate was wet and subtropical; the presence of numerous lungfish burrows indicate seasonal conditions of alternating wet and dry seasons, very similar to the climatic regimen that one finds in northern Australia, where today lungfish closely related to their Triassic forebears still live in a sort of Triassic life-style.

The bones of *Coelophysis* occur in the lower quarry, particularly in the lower siltstones that have been labeled E through J, but band F is the main source for *Coelophysis* remains, and only in layer F are complete skeletons found. It is interesting to note that mud cracks associated with band F indicate that this layer was exposed briefly to the elements before being covered by the sediments comprising layer G. Yet in spite of this evidence of exposure to the weather as band F was being deposited, the bone surfaces themselves show no indication of significant weathering—which is an indication that the exposure of band F was quite brief.

Layers F and G together form a broad U-shaped deposit, indicating that they were channel-fill sediments. Layer G, immediately above layer F with its mass of tangled skeletons, contains mud clasts and disarticulated skeletal elements, while fragmentary associations of bones continue to be present through layer J. Such occurrences suggest that most of the bones to be found above the main bone layer (F) are reworked; in other words these fossils were plucked by river currents from the *Coelophysis* graveyard that constitutes layer F, rolled around, and redeposited in the layers above F. As one proceeds up through layer G and on into I and J the abundance of bones decreases at a remarkably rapid rate, as would be expected in a situation where river currents were being progressively isolated from the "bone layer" by the constant accumulation of sediments over that layer.

The bones of *Coelophysis* in layer F were obviously buried soon after the collective deaths of the dinosaurs; perhaps it would be better to say that the carcasses were rather quickly buried. However, the manner in which the necks of many *Coelophysis* skeletons are recurved backward, so that the skulls in these individuals are just above the pelvic region in each case, demonstrates that even though exposure before burial was brief, it was long enough for the carcasses to dry out, causing the muscles and ligaments of the neck to contract, thereby pulling the long neck back to its unnatural position over the back. Yet the lack of any evidence of scavenging by other carnivores, such as tooth marks, punctures, cracked bones, or bones with the ends chewed off, reinforces the conjecture that burial must have taken place soon after death. Likewise, the lack of any evidence of trampling, in the form of broken and damaged bones, would again seem to be evidence of rather quick burial.

In this regard, it should be mentioned that some of the layers above the F layer with its freight of *Coelophysis* skeletons, especially in the contact between layers H and J, show some indication, because of the irregular nature of this contact as well as small depressions within it, of trampling by various backboned animals. And a well-worn trough in layer J may be evidence of a "game trail," a path that was followed by many Triassic vertebrates. All this is, of course, well above, and therefore later, than the presence of *Coelophysis* at the site.

Not all the *Coelophysis* remains in layer F of the quarry are those of complete skeletons. In fact, Schwartz and Gillette indicate that only about 25 percent of the articulated materials are contained within complete skeletons. But use of the word "only" may be misleading, for 25 percent is a very high figure when one considers the incredible numbers of complete skeletons in the Ghost Ranch quarry as compared with the number of preserved tetrapod skeletons in most fossil quarries. So in spite of the comparatively high ratio of complete skeletons of *Coelophysis* at Ghost Ranch, approximately 75 percent of partial skeletons and numerous single bones remain —all indications that some sort of disturbance occurred before the carcasses became covered by sediments, perhaps in some instances even after burial. Such disarticulations may have taken place during the brief time of exposure: between the death of the animals and the washing in of sediments to cover their bodies. And some may have occurred while the carcasses were being transported by streams to their final resting places. Also some disarrangement of skeletons may have resulted from the compaction of the sediments after burial—an outcome at least in part of the weight of overlying sediments bearing down on the sands and silts in which the *Coelophysis* carcasses had become interred. In addition it was always possible that plant roots had extended down from overlying sedimentary beds to penetrate the burial places of the dinosaurs. Such dynamic activities by growing plants might have caused considerable dislocations of bones disturbed or enveloped by plant roots.

This mention of plant roots invading the *Coelophysis* burial ground from above introduces us to what Schwartz and Gillette call the upper quarry, the part of the quarry face containing beds M through Q: sediments that were deposited after the time of *Coelophysis* at the Ghost Ranch locale. This upper part of the quarry is characterized by abundant burrows and by traces of roots. As is the case with most of the siltstone member, the sediments above the quarry are composed primarily of well-sorted siltstones, of rather fine texture. But above bed O are two sandstones that show the development of extensive channel deposits.

Such is the testimony of the rocks contained within the siltstone member of the Chinle Formation at Ghost Ranch. It is a complex sequence of sediments that tell a continuing story of deposition and erosion, during the course of which the exceedingly numerous remains of *Coelophysis* were caught up by the flooding waters and deposited in small channels, where they formed a dinosaurian "logjam," or more properly, a "dinosaur jam" of carcasses.

The sequence of events, extending over some years at least, as may be interpreted from the stratigraphy of the quarry face, may be summarized as follows.

1. During an initial period, as may be seen at the bottom of the quarry, sediments, as recorded by beds D and E of the quarry face, were washed across the margins of a tropical river that flowed through a lowland dotted by ponds and mudflats.

2. Then, as a result of a periodic interval of heavy rains, the lowlands flooded, accompanied not only by the deposition of fine sands and silts across the flats but also by the cutting of small secondary channels, the result of action by strong, localized stream currents. This cutting and filling caused the numerous carcasses of the little dinosaur, *Coelophysis,* to be transported by the river currents a short distance from the place where the dinosaurs had died, to be piled up in a confused, tangled jam of bodies within one of the smaller, secondary channels that had been cut during this episode of river action.

3. Flooding continued, and the channel or channels containing the mass of carcasses filled with sediments, thus burying the bodies of the dinosaurs, which became skeletonized during this process. The accumulation of sediments over the dinosaurs as the carcasses lost flesh and other soft parts, was so gentle that a large proportion of the skeletons maintained the articulations between vertebrae, ribs, and limb bones. However, the actions of stream currents allowed parallel orientation among some skeletons, but such arrangements of the articulated skeletons and partial skeletons are not very pronounced. The record of this phase of sedimentation is seen particularly in layer F. As sedimentation continued layer G was deposited, containing, among other things, reworked bones, derived from the dinosaur graveyard because of aquatic turbulence.

4. During a postflooding interval sediments continued to be deposited, while vegetation became established on the broad flatlands. Roots from many of the plants probed their way downward, often enveloping or displacing bones, thus causing some minor rearrangements among the articulated or partly articulated skeletons. At this time there may have been considerable traffic as various reptiles comprising the Chinle fauna crossed the mudflats,

thereby churning up the soft, muddy areas at the edges of streams and ponds. Evidence of this is seen at the contact of layers H and J.

5. More sediments were deposited, partly because of minor flooding. At this time, as recorded in bed J, a "game trail" would seem to have developed where Chinle reptiles followed a path across the flats.

6. From this point on the sediments forming the upper part of the siltstone member accumulated, as seen in beds K through L in the lower quarry and M through Q in the upper quarry. These accumulations, which took place long after the days of *Coelophysis*, carried the siltstone member to its upper extremity, there to be covered by the heavy, massive sands of the Jurassic Entrada Formation.

This is the story of the siltstone member of the Chinle Formation, as it accumulated through the years of the late Triassic period, the years that are formally designated as the Carnian and Norian ages of Triassic history. And within this expanse of earth history the Ghost Ranch dinosaur grave-yard is located at a rather low position in the sequence—its base about fif-teen meters (or about 48 feet) above the contact of the siltstone member with the Petrified Forest Member below, and about forty meters below the contact between the siltstone member and the overlying Entrada Forma-tion.

We have seen the details of sedimentation within the siltstone member, just below, at, and just above the layer of dinosaur bones. And we have seen how they are accumulated, evidently as a "carcass jam" or "dinosaur jam" within a secondary stream channel that was developed during a peri-od of flooding. But as yet nothing has been said about what killed the dino-saurs, the question that especially piques our curiosity. What might have brought about the end of so many dinosaurs that their bodies piled up in an incredible concentration of skulls, vertebrae, and limbs?

The Ghost Ranch dinosaurs evidently died because of a catastrophe. The concentration of such a mass of bodies and the contents of the burial site—consisting of creatures of all ages, from very small dinosaurs not far beyond the hatchling stage to full adults—speak of the sudden death of a local population. There is no selection here according to age (or probably to sex) that might in some way explain the accumulation of skeletons seen at Ghost Ranch. Something happened; in popular parlance it would seem that a large gathering of *Coelophysis* was somehow "caught off guard"—to be killed and to be buried.

I used to think that perhaps the dinosaurs were killed by a volcanic eruption, a Triassic event to compare to the eruption of Mount St. Helens in Washington state in 1980. This conclusion was based on the fact that bentonite, an altered volcanic ash, is so abundant in the Petrified Forest Member of the Chinle Formation that geologists have frequently described these sediments as bentonitic claystone or sandstone. For instance, Stewart, Poole, and Wilson stated, "Much of the claystone in the [Petrified Forest Member] unit is believed to have been formed by alteration of volcanic debris" (Stewart, Poole, and Wilson 1972;35). Therefore, would not the same be true for the siltstone member?

But Hilde Schwartz disabused me of that idea, for while studying the Ghost Ranch Quarry, she discovered that bentonite is conspicuously absent in the siltstone member. As Schwartz and Gillette have said, "We have not found bentonite or other volcanic indicators at this stratigraphic level in the Chinle Formation or near the quarry" (Schwartz and Gillette 1994: 1126). To which I respond, *Damnation!* It was such a neat idea, a tidy theoretical bundle that explained the great concentration of *Coelophysis* skeletons without further ado. So now it is necessary to look to other possible causes for what killed the dinosaurs.

One idea that has been proposed suggests that poisoning, or perhaps disease, may have caused the tragedy so effectively documented by the dinosaur skeletons at Ghost Ranch. According to this theory the dinosaurs brought about their own demise by drinking water from a highly alkaline pond. It is difficult to either prove or disprove such a possibility. However, it should be said that petrographic analyses of the dinosaur bones—a technique that involves detailed examinations using special microscopes, which by employing polarized light can identify the mineralogical contents of the fossils—show no internal conditions within the fossil bones that would suggest disease or poisoning as factors in the deaths of the dinosaurs. Furthermore, the nature of the sediments in which the bones are contained, and the attitudes of the skeletons and partial skeletons, clearly indicate that the carcasses of *Coelphysis* were deposited and buried by stream currents, as has already been described, and not within the still waters of a lake or pond, as might be expected if these Triassic reptiles had been fatally affected by drinking the poisoned waters that might occur in such a source.

Another theory is that the dinosaurs became mired in a sticky mud bog, but this seems highly unlikely. Here the sediments and the attitudes of the buried skeletons may be invoked to refute such a notion. The sediments

are not of the disturbed nature that would be expected in a muddy quag-
mire; rather they are the typical siltstones, the mixture of fine sands and
clays laid down by river currents that so characterize this upper member of
the Chinle Formation. And the skeletons do not show evidence of extreme
struggles to escape from such a muddy trap.

Robert Bakker, who specializes in unconventional and often stimulating
ideas, has suggested that the accumulation of *Coelophysis* skeletons at
Ghost Ranch represents the remains of a "predator trap" comparable to the
famous tar pits of Rancho la Brea in California. At Rancho la Brea, which is
of late Pleistocene age, dating back only a few tens of thousands of years,
large herbivorous mammals, such as elephants, ground sloths, horses,
and bison, became entrapped in the sticky tar seeping out of the ground at
this locality. The entrapped animals, struggling to release themselves from
the viscous tar, attracted various carnivores—saber-toothed cats and
wolves in particular—who thought they saw easy meals to be had with
little effort. But then the carnivores became entrapped, like flies in fly-
paper. So Bakker rather diffidently suggested that Ghost Ranch was a
predator trap.

> Could Ghost Ranch have been such a flypaper trap? The site hasn't
> yet been analyzed sufficiently to yield any conclusions. [This was written
> before the study of the quarry by Schwartz and Gillette.] The mudstone
> at Ghost Ranch did not yield the slightest trace of asphalt. But it's not
> impossible that sticky mud might have served to have the same effect,
> trapping dinosaur feet in a viscous, inescapable mire.   (Bakker 1986:259)

The evidence against such a predator trap has been convincingly advanced by the Schwartz-Gillette study. These authors note that Chester
Stock, who thoroughly analyzed Rancho la Brea in 1956, showed that the la
Brea predator trap was characterized by certain definite features, none of
which are present at the Ghost Ranch quarry. Thus, at Rancho la Brea the
accumulation of bones includes "inordinate numbers of young, elderly,
and maimed individuals . . . ; a diverse fauna . . . ; and randomly oriented and disarticulated skeletal remains" (Schwartz and Gillette
1994:1126). And as we have seen, just the opposite conditions hold at
Ghost Ranch. The dinosaur skeletons are evenly distributed among age
groups, there are few if any maimed individuals, the fauna is not diverse
but remarkably dominated by the single species of *Coelophysis,* and the
skeletons are not randomly arranged and disarticulated, but rather show

some orientation and very little disarticulation. So much for the predator trap theory.

These days it is very popular to invoke collisions between the earth and comets or meteors to explain past extinctions. But the dinosaur graveyard at ghost Ranch hardly qualifies for such a Wagnerian twilight; it was quite obviously a local event. In this connection, Schwartz and Gillette have stated that neutron activation analysis of siltstones by Carl Orth of the Los Alamos National Laboratory, including samples from within, above, below, and lateral to the quarry, show normal iridium levels, making it improbable that the dinosaurs suffered asteroidal annihilation.

After all possibilities have been reviewed, it seems very probable that *Coelophysis* at Ghost Ranch suffered an unspectacular and mundane end. Schwartz and Gillette suggest that the dinosaurs might have died from hunger or thirst (the result of a drought), or perhaps they drowned in the flood by which the carcasses were transported (not very far) to their final resting place. This seems a reasonable explanation.

The idea of their having drowned in great numbers has considerable merit. Some years ago, a great herd of caribou in Canada drowned while attempting to cross a flooding river. Thousands of caribou carcasses were left along the banks of the river. Could not this be a modern parallel to what might have happened to a congregation of *Coelophysis* more than 200 million years ago?

Perhaps—yet it must be kept in mind that a comparison is here being made between herbivorous mammals (caribou) and carnivorous reptiles (*Coelophysis*). In our modern world *herds* of animals, notably large mammals, are typically plant-eaters like the caribou that drowned in Canada. But carnivorous animals, again speaking of mammals, typically occur in small bands, such as packs of wolves or prides of lions, or singly, such as most of the cats, or foxes, or various other meat-eaters. It may be more valid to compare ancient reptiles with modern ones.

Walter Auffenberg, in his classic study of the giant Komodo lizard, or ora, *Varanus komodoensis*, learned that these aggressive reptilian predators—animals that frequently hide along game trails to ambush their prey, which may be mammals as large as wild pigs, or deer, or even the small wild buffalo, or anoa of the East Indies—may operate singly or in small groups, in which respect they parallel modern mammalian carnivores (Auffenberg 1981:257–58). It is obvious that if these modern large predators, either mammalian or reptilian, were to gather in numbers comparable to those of the dinosaurs of the Ghost Ranch Quarry, the prey species would have to be present in prodigious quantities.

A better comparison may be between modern crocodilians and *Coelophysis*. The fact is that crocodiles and alligators, which are the largest modern reptilian carnivores, may congregate in large concentrations along river banks. These are not in any real sense herds of reptilian carnivores; rather they are aggregations possibly brought together by the presence of prey in huge numbers. Thus William Bartram, the eighteenth-century naturalist, described (if he is to be believed) an almost unbelievable concentration of alligators along a Florida river, attracted to the spot by a huge run of fishes. (This example will be cited in more detail in chapter 8.) And C. Wiman in 1913 described a mass death of crocodilians near the mouth of the Amazon River during a severe drought, resulting in the accumulation of eight thousand and four thousand carcasses at two locations (Wiman 1913).

One can suppose that situations similar to the modern examples reported for Florida and Brazil may have prevailed in late Triassic time, to cause an almost unprecedented gathering of *Coelophysis* at a locality where eventually they died, perhaps by drowning, perhaps by starvation, to be washed into restricted stream channels, there to be buried and fossilized.

One final comment. The mass death and burial of *Coelophysis* was almost certainly a local catastrophe and was *not* a part of a broad extinction of reptiles that marked the transition from Triassic to Jurassic history.

SEVEN

THE ELEGANT ANCESTOR

It is time to become better acquainted with *Coelophysis*. Much has been said already about the discovery of the dinosaur quarry at Ghost Ranch, about the activities of various paleontologists at the quarry and in the laboratories as they collected and exposed the intricate tangle of skeletons and partial skeletons from the first days of discovery to today. Yet the object of these attentions has so far remained not much more than a name, vaguely defined as a "little dinosaur." Let us now look at *Coelophysis* in detail in order to become familiar with this most interesting dinosaur in the many aspects of its anatomy: the structural relationships of its bones, the reconstructed workings of its muscles, and the implied nature of its internal organs and its physiological regimen, all of which made it such a dynamic inhabitant of the late Triassic landscape of North America (see figures 28 and 29).

Before going into the details of *Coelophysis* anatomy, and the significance of the numerous anatomical structures that distinguish *Coelophysis* within the hierarchy of dinosaurian evolution, it may be pertinent to say something in general about dinosaurs. What are the dinosaurs—those ancient reptiles so widely popular today throughout the world that they have become the subject of countless books written in diverse languages that comprise a United Nations of literature? To answer this question, we must go back to the early years of the nineteenth century.

Two Englishmen, an eccentric clergyman and professor named William Buckland and an eccentric physician named Gideon Algernon Mantell, were paleontological pioneers (before the profession of paleontology existed) who discovered and named the first two dinosaurs without knowing that they were dinosaurs. Buckland described *Megalosaurus* in 1824 on the basis of a partial lower jaw and other remains that had been discovered in southern England, while Mantell described *Iguanodon* in 1825 on the basis of teeth and various bones discovered near the Channel Coast (Buckland 1824; Mantell 1825). Both men realized that they were dealing with extinct gigantic reptiles, but both Buckland and Mantell evidently mentally pictured the fossils as oversize "lizards," for the concept of dinosaurs had not yet been born. Indeed, the idea of *Megalosaurus* as a huge "lizard" persisted for some time after its discovery and description, for we find in the opening pages of Charles Dickens's *Bleak House*, published in 1852, the following description.

> . . . implacable November weather. As much mud in the streets as if the waters had but newly retired from the face of the earth, and it would not be wonderful to meet a *Megalosaurus*, forty feet long or so, waddling like an elephantine lizard up Holborn Hill.   (Dickens 1989:1)

The concept of dinosaurs came into being in 1841 and 1842, when Richard Owen, the great English comparative anatomist, proposed that a new category of reptiles should be recognized, these to be designated as the Dinosauria. (*Dinos*, terrible; *sauros*, lizard. But Owen probably was not thinking specifically of lizards when he created the name; rather the word *sauros* connotes reptile.) "The combination of such characters, . . . all manifested by creatures far surpassing in size the largest of existing reptiles, will, it is presumed, be sufficient ground for establishing a distinct tribe or suborder of Saurian Reptiles, for which I would propose the name of Dinosauria" (Owen 1842:103).

Having thus been formally named by Owen, the dinosaurs became well established through the next few decades, and on through the present century, in the literature of fossils and in the minds of men, so that today they are known to literally millions of people throughout the world.

Then in 1887 still another Englishman, Harry Govier Seeley, published a paper entitled "On the Classification of Fossil Animals Commonly Named Dinosauria," in which he made the following statement.

> The considerations adduced appear, however, to show that the Dinosauria has no existence as a natural group of animals, but includes two distinct types of animal structure and technical characters in common,

which show their descent from a common ancestry rather than their close affinity. These two orders of animals may be conveniently named the Ornithischia and the Saurischia. (Seeley 1887:170)

Seeley's perceptive division of the dinosaurs into two groups, generally accorded the rank of orders, has survived through the years and is universally recognized and followed, although some modern authorities place the two groups of dinosaurs into a comprehensive supergroup, Dinosauria.

Numerous characters throughout the anatomy distinguish the Saurischia from the Ornithischia, but the basic character, the one on which the names of the two groups are founded, has to do with the structure of the pelvis. In the Saurischia (*sauros*, lizard, or reptile; *ischion*, hip joint) the pelvis is of reptilian design, with the three constituent bones on each side (ilium, pubis, ischium) arranged in a tripartite pattern, the ilium being the uppermost element, attached to the vertebral column, while the pubis, attached to the ilium in the region of the articulation for the femur, is directed down and forwardly, and the ischium, also attached to the ilium and the pubis in the same location as well as to the pubis, is directed down and to the rear. In the Ornithischia (*ornithos*, bird; *ischion*, hip joint) the arrangement of the three bones is generally similar to that of bones in the bird pelvis, with the pubis occupying a position parallel and beneath the ischium; a result, it would seem, of the pubis's having rotated back to this position from a forebear in which the pubis occupied the ancestral forward relationship. (In spite of names, the birds evolved from saurischian dinosaurs.)

Coelophysis, the relationships of which will be detailed in chapter 8, is a saurischian dinosaur. A quick, overall view of the adult *Coelophysis* skeleton shows us a reptile about six to eight feet, or two meters and more, long from the tip of the nose to the tip of the tail (see figures 28 and 29). (Recent work on the quarry block [C–9–82] housed in the Ruth Hall Paleontology Museum at Ghost Ranch has revealed a beautifully articulated skeleton, the length of which, when fully exposed, will probably exceed ten feet. Obviously, not all the little dinosaurs of Ghost Ranch are "little.") This length is almost equally divided between that portion of the backbone in front of the hip joint and that part behind the hip. The hip is thus the focal point of the skeleton, for it is the point of articulation for the long, strong, birdlike hind limbs, which constituted the sole support for this dinosaur. The forelimbs are relatively small and terminate in fingers that were obviously adapted for grasping, not locomotion. And at the front of the skeleton is

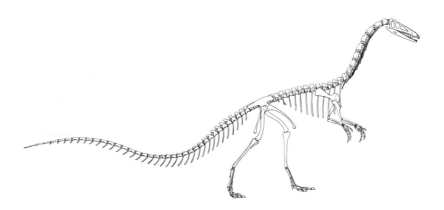

FIGURE 28   The skeleton of *Coelophysis bauri*, reconstructed in a drawing by Lois Darling under the supervision of the author.

the lightly built skull, the jaws of which are armed with numerous sharp, bladelike teeth.

This is a snapshot view of *Coelophysis,* as revealed by its skeleton. Now for the details.

Analysis of the skull is a logical place to begin, for the head is the most important part of any backboned animal—the command center for life activities. That is why our knowledge of extinct vertebrates is so often based primarily on the study of skulls and teeth; other parts of the skeleton, when present, offer the supplementary information that completes the picture.

In this respect dinosaur skulls can cause problems for the paleontologist, in part because they are often indifferently preserved and not infrequently because they are missing from the record. Many a fossil hunter has been frustrated in the field, when (having discovered a skeleton in a reasonable state of preservation, with most of the bones present) he or she realizes that even much hard digging may yield only part of the skull, if any. This is because dinosaur skulls, especially those of theropods and sauropods, can be fragile and were easily separated from the skeleton during burial and preservation. Such was the case with *Coelophysis.*

The original fossils, collected by David Baldwin, included no remains or even traces of skulls. And the skull is lacking in the most recent *Coelophysis* specimen to be discovered and studied, a partial skeleton from the Petri-

fied Forest of Arizona described by Kevin Padian in 1986. But in the Ghost
Ranch quarry numerous skulls were found—not as many skulls as skeletons by a large margin, but nonetheless enough to provide the information
necessary for a detailed understanding of the skull and lower jaws. The
information has been forthcoming only by the study of numerous skulls,
because sadly enough every skull of *Coelophysis* from the quarry is distorted in one way or another. Some skulls are squashed flat from side to
side, others from top to bottom, and some are skewed. (One very large
skull, for example, is as flattened from side to side as the proverbial pan-
cake.) But by combining information from the various skulls available it is
possible to come up with a good three-dimensional restoration of the *Coelophysis* skull, as shown in figure 30.

In an adult *Coelophysis* the skull is elongated and low, its greatest height
from the articulation with the lower jaw to the skull roof being about one-
fourth as long as the skull from its articulation with the vertebral column to
the tip of the snout. In young individuals the skull is proportionately not so
long, as would be expected: in one small skull from the quarry—about half
as long as an adult skull—the skull height is about half its length, in large
part because of the comparatively large size of the eye, as is common in
young backboned animals. This is but one of the changes that took place
during ontogenetic growth, from young to adult (see figure 31).

On each side of the *Coelophysis* skull are five openings: A very large

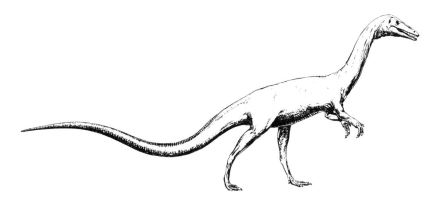

FIGURE 29   Life restoration of *Coelophysis bauri* by Lois Darling, based on her reconstruction of the skeleton.

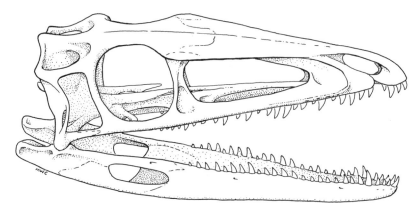

FIGURE 30   A reconstruction of the skull and lower jaw of *Coelophysis bauri* by Matthew Colbert in consultation with the author. This interpretation of the skull and jaws brings out the open nature of the skull, dominated by the large orbit and antorbital opening. Some of the bones of the palate can be seen through these openings, while the brain case is partially visible through the postorbital or temporal openings. Note the prominent notch between the premaxilla and maxilla, at the front of the skull, an indication that there was some movement between these bones—evidence of the kinetic skull that is frequent among carnivorous reptiles. ($\times$ 1/3)

opening for the orbit, the housing of the eye; an even larger opening in front of the eye, known as the antorbital fenestra; in front of that is the opening for the nostril; and, at the back of the skull, the upper and lateral temporal fenestrae that are so characteristic of archosaurian skulls. Of course the number of openings is doubled when the entire skull is considered, which gives the impression that the skull of *Coelophysis* consists of more open spaces than bone (see figures 30 and 32).

The lower jaws of *Coelophysis* are long and slender, matching the proportions of the skull, and on each side near the back of the ramus (as each half of the lower jaw is called) is an elongated opening, penetrating both the outside and the inside of the bony complex comprising the ramus.

Why are there all these vacuities in the skull and jaws of *Coelophysis?* Of course some of them are obvious: almost all vertebrate skulls necessarily have openings for the eyes and the nostrils. As for the eight other openings—the temporal fenestrae on each side of the skull behind the eyes, the fenestrae in front of the eyes, and the two openings in the lower jaw—less obvious functions must be sought.

It does seem likely that the very open skull of *Coelophysis* and its relatives was in part a development to cut down the weight of bone in the skull. In these reptiles the skull is strikingly composed of a series of bony arches (or struts, if you will) along lines of force—where such struts are needed—and of openings in areas where bone is not essential. It is a matter of organic engineering, in a sense paralleling the beams and struts one sees in a modern steel structure. (Or, one might say that modern engineers have paralleled the dinosaurs, which came along millions of years before people ever

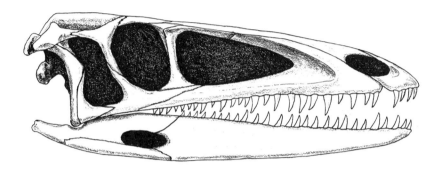

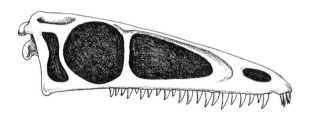

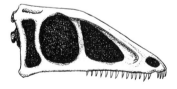

FIGURE 31   Restorations of three skulls (one with lower jaw) of AMNH 7242 (*bottom*), 7241 (*middle*), and 7224 (*top*), showing the changes in proportions during growth from juvenile to adult. Note the proportionately great enlargement of the skull in front of the eye during growth from young individual to adult, thereby establishing in the adult *Coelophysis* the enlarged jaws necessary for predation. (× 1/3)

FIGURE 32   A skull and lower jaw of *Coelophysis bauri* (AMNH 7224), side view.

entered the evolutionary scene. It is interesting to see that in the later dinosaurian giants the principles of beams and struts are widely developed in
the skeleton, especially in the vertebral column.)

Beyond decreasing the weight in the skulls and jaws, the various openings were probably adaptations to allow for the attachment of large, strong
muscles around their rims, as well as providing space to allow for the bulging of the muscles. Thus the antorbital opening on each side gave room for
a large pterygoid muscle that occupied the inner part of the front of the
skull, running down between palatal bones to attach around the mandibu-
lar opening. The principal muscle for closing the jaws, it was very powerful. The temporal fenestrae behind the eyes provided the necessary space
for the attachments and working of a large muscle complex, the capiti-
mandibularis muscle that acted in forceful concert with the pterygoid
muscle to make the closing of these dinosaur jaws an act of remarkable
speed and power. By contrast, the jaws in the dinosaurs, as in all reptiles,
were opened by using a single muscle of modest size on each side, stretch-
ing between the back of the skull and a backward extension of the lower
jaw. This is the depressor mandibulae muscle, which is so comparatively
weak that a man, if reckless and daring, can grasp the snout and jaws of a
large crocodile or alligator and hold them shut.

It should be added that within the orbit or eye socket of *Coelophysis* have been found sclerotic ossicles—small thin bones arranged as a ring of overlapping plates. In birds these plates, within the sclera of the eyeball, help resist deformation of the eye and, according to some authorities, play an important part in the mechanism of accommodation. This ring of plates, located within the very large orbit of *Coelophysis*, may indicate a keen sense of sight in that dinosaur.

When the temporal openings were first mentioned it was stated that these two openings are separated from each other by a bar composed of the postorbital and squamosal bones of the skull. This illustrates a fact about the skull of *Coelophysis*, about the skull of all archosaurs, and about the skull of reptiles in general, namely that the skull bones are well defined and separate. In mammals, humans included, the bones of the skull become largely integrated in the adult so that the skull is one solid structure, but in reptiles the bones of the skull remain separate. In *Coelophysis*, as in other theropod dinosaurs, some of the bones of the skull, and of the lower jaw, may not have been strongly bound to one another, therefore they might have slipped back and forth along the sutures between the bones. This is true among modern lizards and snakes that are characterized by a mobile skull and lower jaws—a skull that is commonly called kinetic. Thus a lizard, and especially a snake, can expand the skull and jaws along the margins of the bones, allowing the reptile to engulf a prey animal that may be larger than the normal opening of the jaw.

Various paleontologists believe perhaps this was the case with the carnivorous dinosaurs, particularly dinosaurs similar to *Coelophysis*. Was there movement, for example, between the bones forming the front of the braincase and those forming the top of the tooth-bearing section of the skull? Or between the tooth-bearing bones—the maxillae—on each side and the roof of the snout? Or between the front and the back of the lower jaw rami on each side? The question has been long debated as to how kinetic the skull of *Coelophysis* and other theropod dinosaurs may have been.

Evidently there was movement between the tooth-bearing premaxillary bones, forming the tip of the skull, and the tooth-bearing maxillary bones behind them, as well as between the two halves of the lower jaws at their forward extremities. The evidence for such movement seems clear. The borders between the premaxillary and maxillary bones on each side show a well-defined notch, while the defining sutures between these bones appear to have been loose. Furthermore the joint between the two tooth-bearing bones of the lower jaw, known as the dentary bones, is quite loose, indicating that the halves of the lower jaw in front were attached to each other only by ligaments. Perhaps *Coelophysis* was partly able to adjust the tooth-bearing bones of the skull and lower jaw to the size of the prey it was trying to devour.

The teeth are numerous and sharp (see figure 33). The premaxillary bones have four teeth on each side, which are rounded in cross-section and pointed. Obviously these were teeth for nipping, for grabbing prey and holding it. As many as twenty-six teeth are in the maxillary bone on each side, all of them recurved and flattened in cross-section, with strong keels on the front and back edges. In other words, they are knifelike blades, nicely shaped for slicing flesh. Furthermore, all but the first two maxillary teeth have serrations along the keels like those found on modern steak knives, making the teeth even more effective for slicing flesh. The first tooth in the maxilla, the one immediately behind the notch, lacks serrations on its keels; the second has no serrations on the front keel, but the posterior keel is well serrated. The dentaries of the lower jaw hold twenty-five to twenty-seven recurved teeth on each side, of which the first seven lack serrations. The eighth tooth, like the second maxillary tooth, has serrations only on its posterior keel, while all the rest have serrations on both keels. It is apparent that the anterior teeth of *Coelophysis*, both above and below, were primarily for nipping or grasping, while the majority of the teeth, those following the four premaxillary and the first two maxillary teeth, as well as the first seven dentary teeth in the lower jaw, were for cutting and slashing. It should be added that the posterior-most teeth in both the skull and the lower jaw are relatively small.

Associated with several of the *Coelophysis* skulls from the Ghost Ranch quarry are in each case two long, rodlike bones situated between the two halves of the lower jaw. These are the hyoid bones, which in combination with certain other elements that evidently were cartilaginous and therefore not preserved formed the hyoid apparatus that supported the tongue and was the base for the attachments of several muscles. In humans the hyoid is a single, U-shaped bone, but in reptiles and birds the situation is much more complex, there being several hyoid elements, some bony, some cartilaginous. Angus Bellairs, a noted authority on recent reptiles, stated that the hyoid apparatus "forms a kind of scaffolding for the soft tissues of the throat as they move in the act of swallowing; it also forms part of the throat-pump mechanism which enables air or water to be drawn in and out of the

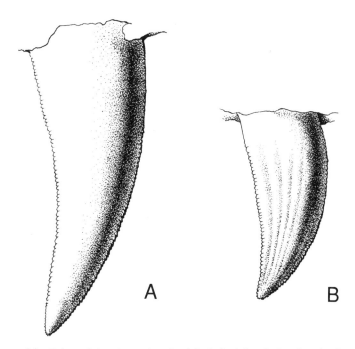

FIGURE 33   Enlarged drawings of teeth of *Coelophysis bauri*, showing the fine serrations along the front and back edges of the teeth—an adaptation for slicing meat that evolved among carnivorous vertebrates. A: eighth right maxillary tooth; B: second right maxillary tooth. (× 11)

mouth, and so assists in the pharyngeal breathing of lizards and turtles. . . . Furthermore the hyoid skeleton provides the basis of attachment of some of the muscles which bring about protrusion and retraction of the tongue" (Bellairs 1969:129).

Interestingly, the preserved hyoid bones of *Coelophysis* resemble the comparable bones in birds, more so than those of reptiles (which is just one of the many lines of evidence indicating a basic relationship between the theropod dinosaurs and birds). In birds the hyoid apparatus is involved especially with the protrusion of the tongue; perhaps such was the case with *Coelophysis*.

Finally we consider the braincase of *Coelophysis*, a matter that perhaps should have been discussed at the beginning of this anatomical account, since the brain is the most crucial of vertebrate organs; without a brain an animal cannot survive. The problem is that because of the crushing of all

Coelophysis skulls, as discussed earlier, our knowledge of the braincase in this dinosaur is not easily obtained. By studying the crushed cranial regions in the various skulls at hand, and by comparisons with other theropod dinosaurs, we can reconstruct fairly accurately what the braincase was like.

It was in essence a small box at the back of the skull behind the eyes, and within this small box was the primitive reptilian brain. It may be difficult for one who has not studied dinosaurs in detail to comprehend how very small the brain was in these reptiles, in relation to body size. Yet even in those dinosaurs with proportionately the largest brains, such as the various coelurosaurian dinosaurs including *Coelophysis* and especially the Cretaceous genus *Stenonychosaurus,* this organ is remarkably small. Even so, the size of the brain in relation to body size in *Stenonychosaurus* falls within the range typical of some birds and mammals. In other words, *Coelophysis* and some of its relatives probably were the more intelligent of the dinosaurs—if we can judge intelligence by the relative size of the brain.

(Brain size must be considered relative to body size. Thus, the relative brain size is smaller in a large intelligent animal, such as an elephant, than in a small animal, such as a mouse. But the actual brain size of the elephant is of course very large as compared with that of the mouse, and the intelligence of the elephant is obviously far greater than that of the little rodent.)

Naturally we have not found dinosaur brains, since such soft tissue was rarely fossilized. But we can get an idea of the nature of the brain in dinosaurs by studying endocranial casts made of the inside of the braincase. Such casts are not exact replicas because the brain did not occupy the full space within the braincase, but they are useful approximations. Moreover, the information provided by an endocranial cast can be supplemented by comparison with the brain in crocodiles and alligators, the nearest reptilian relatives of the dinosaurs.

It is evident that *Coelophysis,* like other theropod dinosaurs, had a primitive, reptilian brain, small in size and elongated along a gentle, horizontal S-like flexure as seen in side view. The cerebrum, the "thinking" part of the brain, was not enlarged to the degree that it enfolded the rest of the brain, as in mammals (including humans) but rather consisted of smooth cerebral hemispheres situated between rather large olfactory lobes in front and the large optic lobes, cerebellum, and medulla in the rear. Yet in spite of its deficiencies from our point of view, the dinosaurian brain was obviously sufficient for the needs of these reptiles, particularly for the small theropods such as *Coelophysis*, in which the brain was relatively large compared with body size. *Coelophysis* and its cousins were anything but clumsy lumbering animals; *Coelophysis* probably was one of the most active, well-oriented animals living in Triassic North America.

To summarize this discourse on the skull and jaws of *Coelophysis*, five points may be made:

1. The skull is lightly but strongly constructed, with bony arches along lines of force and with large openings in front of and back of the eyes.
2. Two of these openings, the orbits or eye sockets, housed large and perceptive eyes; the others except for the nostril openings, were adaptations for strong jaw muscles.
3. The jaws are armed with numerous, scimitar-like teeth, adapted for grasping prey and for inflicting slashing cuts.
4. The skull and lower jaws may have been to some degree kinetic—that is, there may have been movement between individual bones.
5. The braincase is small, at the very back of the skull, and contained a characteristic reptilian brain, yet a brain of relatively large size compared with the brains of many other dinosaurs.

The neck of *Coelophysis* is long, not only because the individual vertebrae are elongated (all except the atlas next to the skull) but also because there are so many of them. The neck contains ten vertebrae, two or three of which had been appropriated from the back of an ancestral thecodont, which probably had twenty-five or twenty-six vertebrae between skull and pelvis, seven or eight comprising the neck. The neck is as long as or longer than the back from the base of the neck to the pelvis. Figure 34 shows the bones that joined the head and neck.

Each cervical vertebra is notable not only for its length but also for its pneumaticity, because on each side of the vertebra is an elongated tunnel, enclosed on the outside by a deep flange of bone. Similar features are seen in the small Jurassic dinosaur *Coelurus,* and in the Cretaceous "ostrich-dinosaur" *Ornithomimus.* In the gigantic sauropod dinosaurs of Jurassic and Cretaceous age the cervical vertebrae are strongly excavated on their sides by deep hollows, known as pleurocoels, which are thought to have been adaptations for reducing the weight of the bone in the neck. But *Coelophysis* and the other small to medium-size dinosaurs named did not have excessive bone weight. However, the many close anatomical resemblances

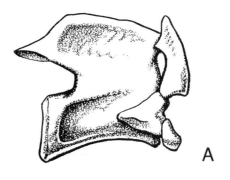

FIGURE 34   The atlas-axis complex of *Coelophysis bauri*. These were the crucial bones forming the attachment between the head and the neck; it was in the socketlike structure (*on the right*) formed by the atlas and axis that the head moved up and down and from side to side. A: right side view; B: dorsal (top) view. (× 1)

between *Coelophysis* and birds raises the possibility that the pneumatic vertebrae of *Coelophysis* as well as of *Coelurus* and *Struthiomimus* may have been for the accommodation of air sacs, such as are seen in modern birds. In birds the air sacs are accessory respiratory organs, forcing air rapidly through the small avian lungs, while at the same time they function in part as temperature control devices. As Tracy Storer has observed, "The air sacs are the principal means of dissipating the heat resulting from muscular contractions and other metabolic activities" (Storer 1943:643). Question: Do we see here some evidence that *Coelophysis* might have enjoyed a certain level of "warm-bloodedness"? Certainly, *Coelophysis* was a very active dinosaur; perhaps it was so strenuously active that some method of cooling the body was necessary. It is something to think about.

The long neck of *Coelophysis* was obviously quite flexible, allowing the head to dart this way and that in the pursuit of prey (see figure 35). Cervical flexibility in this dinosaur is proved by some of the Ghost Ranch skeletons, especially the two remarkable skeletons AMNH 7223 and AMNH 7224 that are preserved side by side. In each the neck is strongly bent, in the former laterally, in the latter vertically, the head in this skeleton being pulled back by the extreme curvature of the neck so that the skull is above the back, near the pelvis. Several other specimens show this same kind of curvature in the neck, the result of the drying and shrinkage of ligaments after death. Indeed, this particular pose is seen time and again in dinosaur skeletons.

Yet an anatomical paradox is associated with such evidence of cervical flexibility in *Coelophysis,* because in this dinosaur the cervical ribs (separate in reptiles, but fused to become integral parts of the cervical vertebrae in mammals) are incredibly long posteriorly, so that each rib extends back beneath not only the vertebra to which it is attached, but also beneath the following two vertebrae, as well as the forward part of the third vertebra in the succession. Since each cervical rib, on each side of the neck, traverses three or more vertebrae, the result is that there are "bundles" of at least three slender ribs beneath each neck vertebra on both the right and left sides. And since these fasces of ribs cross the articulations between the vertebrae, one would think that they would have made the neck stiff. How-

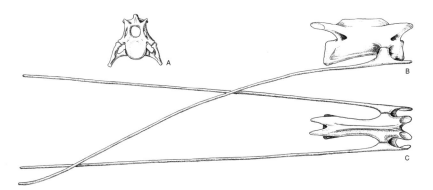

FIGURE 35 An anterior cervical vertebra and the corresponding ribs of *Coelophysis bauri.* Not only is the neck vertebra elongated, the ribs are also especially long, spanning the combined lengths of the following four vertebrae. Since similarly lengthened ribs are present on the other cervical vertebrae, the effect within the neck was that of vertebral rib "bundles" extending along each side of the neck. These ribs presumably strengthened the neck, but they must have been very flexible. A: anterior view; B: lateral view; C: dorsal view. (about × 1/3)

ever, the individual ribs are small in diameter, and one must suppose that they were quite flexible. Evidently they added strength to the neck without impairing its flexibility—a strange development, indeed!

Michael Raath, who discovered and described *Syntarsus* from South Africa, a dinosaur remarkably close to *Coelophysis* in its anatomy and certainly in its relationships, found the same situation in the South African dinosaur. In *Syntarsus* "some cervical ribs are so long that they would have reached back over the length of four or even five cervical vertebrae! In one of the blocks containing *Syntarsus* that I have here in Johannesburg with me, there are two almost perfectly preserved cervical ribs lying adjacent to each other. Both are in excess of 125 mm long and yet in both cases the average diameter of the rib shaft distal to the articular end is about 1 or 2 mm at the most! Presumably these ribs must have been particularly flexible to allow for neck movements" (M. Raath, personal communication).

It is reassuring to see confirmation of this anatomical character in the neck appearing in related theropod dinosaurs on opposite sides of the earth. Obviously it was a natural evolutionary development in *Coelophysis* and *Syntarsus*. Yet even though such ribs were extremely small in diameter, one is still puzzled as to how bone could have been so flexible. (*Syntarsus* is discussed further in chapter 9.)

The thirteen vertebrae of the back, the dorsal vertebrae, are elongated, but not to the degree seen in the vertebrae of the neck (see figure 36). These vertebrae have stout processes rising from their upper surfaces—the spines—for the attachment of strong back muscles. And from each side of each vertebra there is a broad lateral process, the transverse process, which served in part for muscle attachments and in part for the articulation of the double-headed ribs. All in all the dorsal vertebrae of *Coelophysis* indicate a strong, well-articulated back—a horizontally postured back that in a sense was cantilevered from the hip, without any support in front. An interesting feature of the dorsal vertebrae is a pair of bony bars, on each side of each vertebra, extending up obliquely from the side of the vertebra, almost to join at the base of each transverse process. These are the forerunners of a strong system of struts seen in many gigantic dinosaurs of Jurassic and Cretaceous age—struts that may be compared to the design seen in steel girders.

These thirteen vertebrae support thirteen pairs of ribs, the first pair being the longest, the succeeding ribs being progressively shorter, with the thirteenth of the series, located immediately in front of the ilium, being very short indeed. In *Coelophysis*, as in most reptiles, the ribs form a continuous

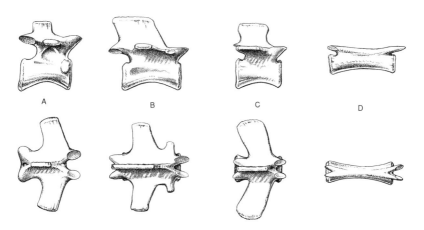

FIGURE 36   Four vertebrae of *Coelophysis bauri*, from (A) the anterior part of the back; (B) immediately in front of the pelvis; (C) the anterior part of the tail; and (D) the midportion of the tail. Each vertebra is shown facing to the right, and a lateral and dorsal view of each is shown. Note in (A) the "struts" on the side of the vertebra, beneath the broad transverse process that extends laterally, as seen in the dorsal view. Such struts become prominent and essential features of the gigantic theropod dinosaurs: like the girders of a steel bridge, they provide needed strength. ($\times$ 1/2)

series throughout the length of the presacral segment of the vertebral column. There is no distinct lumbar region, devoid of ribs, as is the case in mammals, and in some of the advanced mammal-like reptiles. It should be added that whereas in many reptiles it is difficult to differentiate the neck or cervical region with its ribs from the body or dorsal region, with its full complement of ribs, *Coelophysis* has a sharp break in the structure of the ribs between the neck and body. The most posterior pair of the cervical ribs is much shorter than the first pair of dorsal ribs.

The ribs attaching to the dorsal vertebrae are double-headed; in the more anterior vertebrae there is an articulation, the parapophysis, on the side of the vertebral centrum, to which the head of the rib, or capitulum, is articulated, while at the end of the transverse process there is another articulation, the diapophysis, for the reception of the lesser rib articulation, the tuberculum. Proceeding posteriorly, the parapophysis migrates up onto a secondary transverse process, in front of the primary process, so that both rib articulations are established on the transverse processes of the posterior vertebrae. These are minor points but are emphasized here to show that the skeleton of *Coelophysis* was a highly evolved structure.

We now come to a very particular segment of the vertebral column of

Coelophysis—the sacrum, the series of vertebrae that bind the backbone to the pelvis (see figure 37). In *Coelophysis* and its theropod dinosaurian cousins, some of them of massive weight, the articulation between the sacrum and the iliac blade of the pelvis was subjected to the strain of resisting the downward pull of the body in front of, and the tail behind the pelvis, without the compensation of forelimbs to ease that strain. As we have seen, the body and the tail of this dinosaur—of all the carnivorous theropod

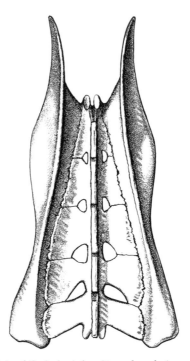

FIGURE 37 The pelvis of *Coelophysis bauri* in a dorsal view, showing the extraordinarily strong sacroiliac connection, as well as the extended, immobile sacrum. Visible here are five sacral vertebrae, the first four of which are coalesced into what amounts to a single structure, while the fifth, although still distinct, is nonetheless an integral part of the sacrum. Such a strong connection between the pelvis and the vertebral column was essential in *Coelophysis* (as it was in other bipedal dinosaurs) because the entire weight of the body pivoted at this point. Note the "bulging" of the two ilia opposite the first and second sacral vertebrae; these enlargements are the upper surfaces of strong shelves that form the upper margins of the acetabuli—the sockets for the articulation of the upper end of the femora. The heavy, overhanging upper border of the acetabular joint received the upward thrust of the femur, or, to put it another way, the downward pressure of the weight of the body against the head of the femur. Such were the adaptations for a bipedal mode of walking and running. ($\times$ 1/2)

dinosaurs—acted after a fashion like a see-saw, pivoted at the articulation between the pelvis and the hind limbs, and this of course took care of the lack of support from forelimbs. But when we consider that the weight and the proper functioning of the entire animal was centered on the sacroiliac joint, we can understand why the articulation between the sacrum and the ilium was necessarily remarkably strong.

The primitive reptiles of Paleozoic age had just two sacral vertebrae to connect the backbone and pelvis, these early reptiles having descended from amphibian ancestors possessed of a single sacral vertebra. Obviously such a limited junction between sacrum and pelvis could never have been viable among reptiles that had become very active running animals, especially reptiles such as the theropod dinosaurs that ran on their hind legs. Consequently, the sacroiliac joint was expanded and strengthened in *Coelophysis* and its relatives by the incorporation of additional vertebrae into the structure. This was accomplished in *Coelophysis* by "stealing" some vertebrae from adjacent parts of the column, to lengthen and strengthen the sacrum.

It would seem that the immediate thecodont ancestors of *Coelophysis* had already added one vertebra from the back to the basic reptilian sacrum of two vertebrae, thus developing a three-vertebrae sacrum. Just as several vertebrae were taken over from the front end of the back to provide *Coelophysis* with a long neck consisting of ten vertebrae, so an additional vertebra was taken over from the posterior end of the back, to add another vertebra to the sacrum. The total number of vertebrae in front of the pelvis, the neck and back vertebrae combined in what are known as the presacral vertebrae, was thus reduced from a probable original count of twenty-five to twenty-three (ten neck vertebrae plus thirteen back vertebrae).

Then one vertebra that had originally been part of the base of the tail was taken into the sacrum. The first four of the five vertebrae that constitute the sacrum of *Coelophysis* were eventually coalesced into a solid structure, in which their separate identities have been all but lost—this by an expansion and fusion of the sacral ribs to form a sort of "roof," the outer extremities of which are attached on each side to the ilium. The fifth vertebra of the sacrum (the one "stolen" from the tail) retains much of its original form, yet even so it is firmly a part of the elongated sacrum. All in all, the sacrum of *Coelophysis* is well designed to have served its function as a strong anchor between the backbone and the pelvis.

An interesting individual variation is to be seen in the sacrum of the two adult skeletons that are preserved side by side within a block from the Ghost Ranch quarry. In one of these, American Museum of Natural History number 7224, the dorsal spines of the sacral vertebrae are quite distinct; in the other, number 7223, they are fused into a single, solid structure. Perhaps this difference owes to age, or possibly to sex. Who knows?

The tail of *Coelophysis* consists of about forty vertebrae (not counting the vertebra lost to the tail by it having been shifted into the sacrum) and in their combined length these caudal vertebrae, as they are properly termed, often exceed the length of the presacral vertebrae. The first dozen or so caudal vertebrae are very much like the vertebrae that comprise the posterior part of the back (in front of the pelvis) but from that point on, the caudal vertebrae become progressively more slender and elongated to the last two members of the series. Furthermore, the dorsal spines of the vertebrae progressively decrease in height so that from about the twentieth vertebra to the tip of the tail there are no spines.

On the undersides of the caudal vertebrae are the chevrons, which are elongated, Y-shaped bones that articulate in each instance at the joint between two caudal vertebrae. These chevrons, quite characteristic of the tail in reptiles, begin at the junction between the first two caudal vertebrae, and continue, with decreasing length almost to the end of the tail, the last four caudal vertebrae being free of chevron bones. The chevrons provide the bases for a complex web of tail muscles.

One should envisage the tail of *Coelophysis* as having been a remarkably mobile part of the animal, a long, narrow tail, rather deep at its base and diminishing in depth from the base to the end. The base of the tail was the origin of a large muscle, the caudofemoralis, that ran forward to the upper leg bone, the femur, and provided force for the back stroke of the leg, the muscle pull that was essential for the dinosaur's long strides and rapid running. The more slender middle and end of the tail probably were essential for balance during locomotion. Perhaps one may visualize this very mobile part of the tail as whipping back and forth in opposition to the movements of the hind limbs, thereby helping to maintain the dinosaur's posture as it walked and ran across the landscape. In other words, the flexible tail of *Coelophysis* helped keep the dinosaur on course as it ran and probably aided the animal in sudden changes of direction. And, as already pointed out, the tail counterbalanced the body, making possible its sophisticated bipedal posture.

In following the backbone of *Coelophysis* from the base of the skull to the tip of the tail, we paid particular attention to the sacrum, that part of the spinal column by which it is attached on each side to the upper element of the pelvis, the ilium. Now it is proper to look at the pelvis in some detail, because this structure was of crucial importance to *Coelophysis* and to all the other dinosaurs, for that matter. The pelvis was literally the pivot on which the skeleton was suspended.

Figure 38 pictures the right side of the saurischian pelvis of *Coelophysis* (with the femur in articulation), showing the large upper ilium to which the

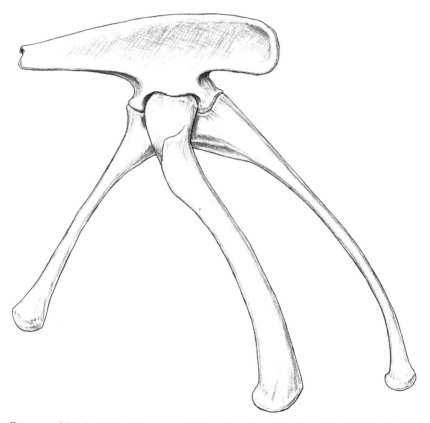

FIGURE 38   The pelvis and right femur of *Coelophysis bauri*, in right side view. Striking features of the pelvis are the elongated ilium, providing the long sacroiliac joint that was needed for an animal in which the stresses of body weight and locomotor movements were concentrated at the connection between the body and the hind limb. This figure shows the articulation of the head of the femur into the acetabulum. The *Coelophysis* pelvis has a greatly elongated pubic bone (on the right) that is fully as long as the femur. (× 1/2)

sacrum is attached, and below the ilium the forwardly directed pubis and the backwardly directed ischium. Thus the complete saurischian pelvis is made up of six distinct bones, unlike that of mammals, including humans, in which the bones of the pelvis are fused into a single large structure, designated by early anatomists as the os *innominatum*, the innominate bone, the unnamed or anonymous bone.

In many of the early saurischian dinosaurs the ilium is rather short and deep, reflecting its origin from thecodont ancestors, but in *Coelophysis* it became elongated both forwardly and at the back, in conjunction with the addition of vertebrae to the sacrum. The final result was a long and solid attachment between the fused sacrum and the two ilia, one on each side. But more was involved with the elongation of the ilium, fore and aft, than the development of an elongated and thereby a strengthened attachment between the backbone and the pelvis because this expansion of the ilium furnished enlarged attachments for powerful muscles that moved the hind limbs back and forth. Such muscles were of particular importance to a bipedal runner, as was *Coelophysis.* This development of the ilium, not only for strength within the skeleton but also for strength of the muscles attached to the skeleton, demonstrates that evolutionary refinements, even in the details of skeletal structure, may have multiple origins.

The two pubes of *Coelophysis* are very long, in fact, they are approximately of the same length as the femur (see figure 39). When seen from a front view the two bones are joined for about three-fourths of their length to form a narrow plate, but for a short distance from their ends they are again separate, and terminate in small knobs. Here we see an adumbration of pubic development in the large carnivorous dinosaurs of Jurassic and Cretaceous age, in which the conjoined pubes terminate in a large, expanded "foot" that may have been some sort of structural support for such giant dinosaurs. As for *Coelophysis,* the long pubis served in part as the origin for strong muscles that pulled the leg forward.

The two ischia of *Coelophysis,* as in the case of the pubes, are joined for about half their lengths, the junction confined to the farther (or distal) parts of the bones. The ischia are not platelike, as is the case of the pubes, but rather are in the form of rods. Furthermore they are shorter than the pubes. These bones, in their upper ends, also provide areas for the origins of muscles that activate the upper leg bone, or femur.

The three bones of the pelvis on each side have been described as coming together at the acetabulum, at the point of articulation with the head of

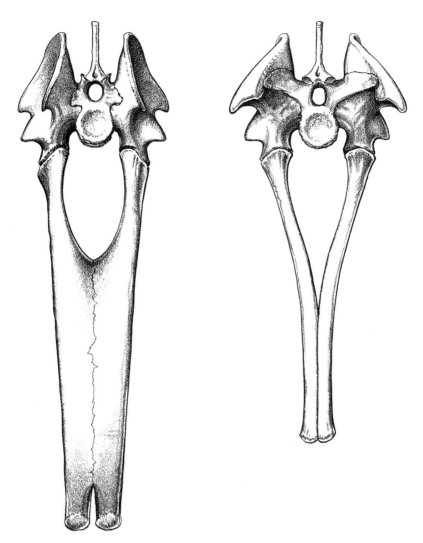

FIGURE 39 The pelvic girdle of *Coelophysis bauri*, as seen in the front view (*left*) and the back view (*right*). In both views the strong shelf on each side at the top of the acetabulum is seen just above the articulation of the ilium with the pubis and ischium, respectively. The great length of the pubic bones as well as the long symphysis that connects them is dramatically evident. The combined pubes, in this view, form an elongated forward-facing plate. The ischia, on the other hand, are rodlike bones. The large concave surfaces on each ilium, facing laterally on each side, which provided strong bases for heavy muscles that powered the hind limb, are prominent. The space between the pubes and the ischia was sufficient only for the passage of a small egg. (× 1/2)

the femur. In the thecodont ancestors of *Coelophysis* this area is a cuplike depression, but in *Coelophysis* and other dinosaurs it has opened up, to be perforated by a large fenestra, a character typical of the saurischian dinosaurs.

An interesting feature of the *Coelophysis* pelvis is the development of a large, projecting "shelf" formed on the ilium above the acetabular articulation for the femur. This shelf obviously furnished a surface to take the upward thrust of the femur (or the downward thrust of the pelvis) and is an archosaurian specialization related particularly to the bipedal mode of locomotion.

One more detail. When seen in front (anterior) and back (posterior) views, the pubes and the ischia of *Coelophysis* below their articulations with the two ilia form rather narrow openings that served for the passage of eggs. It seems pretty evident that *Coelophysis* reproduced by laying birdlike eggs; certainly the pelvis does not appear to have been engineered to accommodate live births.

The hind limbs of *Coelophysis* are remarkably similar to the legs of birds, a point that has already been made and one of various reasons for seeing a basic relationship between the theropod dinosaurs and birds. The femur, the upper leg bone, is hollow, as are all the long bones of *Coelophysis,* and is gently bowed in an anterior direction, while its upper end, or the head of the femur, is offset medially, that is, toward the pelvis with which it articulates, at a sharp angle. Thus when the femur is in place, with the head nested within the socket of the pelvis, the acetabulum that has already been described, the shaft of the femur is brought into a position closely parallel to the lower bones of the pelvis. This swings the leg into such a position that the lower leg bones, the tibia and fibula, are essentially vertical in their stance, while the feet are brought close to a midline beneath the body—which is an excellent design for rapid running. In these respects if the femur of *Coelophysis* is compared to the same bone in primitive reptiles, and even in most of the mammal-like reptiles, the head of the femur in these nondinosaurian reptiles is not sharply offset relative to the shaft of the bone, resulting in a rather sprawling pose with the feet spread far apart. Near the head of the femur of *Coelophysis* is a prominent ridge, the lesser trochanter, for the attachment of a strong muscle having its origin on the ilium; farther down and on the inside of the shaft is another ridge, the fourth trochanter, to which was attached a very strong muscle, the aforementioned caudofemoralis, running forward from the base of the tail—a muscle that helped to give a powerful thrust to the hind limb. The lower end of the femur terminates in two side-by-side rounded surfaces known as condyles, against which the tibia and fibula were able to swing back and forth, as the hind limb was alternately doubled up or stretched out almost straight during locomotion.

The tibia and fibula, the "drumstick" of your Thanksgiving turkey, are also hollow, very straight, and perhaps slightly longer than the femur. The two bones, which are closely appressed to each other, diminish in dimension from the top of the bone to well down their shaft. But at the bottom the two bones flare from side to side, to afford a broad lateral articulation for the upper bones of the hind foot (see figure 40). The junction between the lower ends of the tibia and fibula and the upper ends of the ankle in *Coelophysis* is characterized, as is the case in all the theropod dinosaurs as well as birds, by a midtarsal joint. In other words, the surface of articulation between the bones of the lower leg and the foot comes in the *middle* of the ankle, not at its upper edge as might be expected. This has been accomplished by the two upper bones of the ankle, the astragalus and the calcaneum, being firmly and immovably joined to each other and integrated into the tibia and fibula, to form the tibio-tarsus, with the lower surfaces of these conjoined bones rounded to form a pulley. This development allowed the foot to rotate freely and extensively back and forth, just as the joint between the femur and the lower leg bones allowed for rotation in the upper part of the limb.

Below the midtarsal joint in *Coelophysis* may be three small, flattened lower ankle bones, or tarsals. Or there may be only one, the outer bone that articulates with the upper end of the fourth metatarsal (i.e., of the fourth digit) while the two other tarsal bones have become fused into the upper ends of the third and second metatarsals, these two bones in turn often fused to each other at their upper ends. But the foot of *Coelophysis* varies considerably.

Five metatarsals form the upper parts of the toes in *Coelophysis*, but two of these are essentially rudimentary. The first metatarsal consists of only the lower end of the bone, to which is connected a small phalanx or finger bone, this in turn being joined at its lower end by a little dangling claw. The fifth metatarsal is a mere bony splint that was assuredly hidden beneath the skin of the foot. Therefore the functional foot of *Coelophysis* consists of three long metatarsals, the lower ends of which are attached to the three supple toes, terminating in sharp claws (as seen in figure 41). The foot is

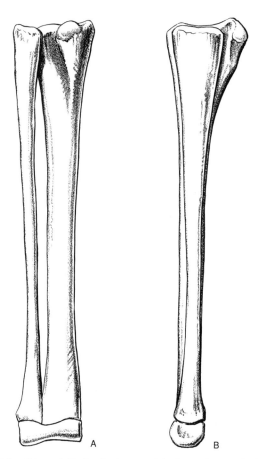

FIGURE 40   The tibia and fibula, the bones of the lower leg, in *Coelophysis bauri*, are long and straight, and, as in birds, the calcaneum and astragalus of the ankle are fused to form a single, pulleylike joint, while at the same time these two bones are closely appressed or even fused to the lower ends of the tibia and fibula, to become an integral part of those bones. These singular adaptations were part of an integrated mechanism that provided a large arc through which the hind limb was swung, thereby ensuring a long and speedy stride, as well as a smooth, cylindrical, transverse roller bearing, allowing for extreme back-and-forth flexibility of the foot. A: front view; B: right lateral view. (× 1/2)

indeed so birdlike that when dinosaur footprints were first discovered in the Triassic and Jurassic rocks of the Connecticut Valley in the mid-nineteenth century and studied by Professor Edward Hitchcock, the president of Amherst College, he thought he was looking at a record of the ancient wanderings of large, ground-living birds. It was not until after his

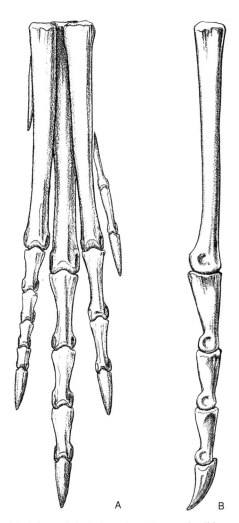

FIGURE 41 The hind foot of *Coelophysis bauri* is very birdlike in its structure. Although the foot had five toes, only three were functional. The first toe was reduced to a hanging appendage, not useful for locomotion, and the fifth toe was a mere splint (the remnant of the metatarsal), which was probably concealed beneath the skin. The foot was balanced, with the second and fourth digits of equal length (even though there were three phalanges in the second toe and only five in the fourth) flanking the large third or middle toe, which had four phalanges. The functional metatarsals were compressed against each other at their upper ends, thereby giving strength to the foot. The hind foot was as long as its tibia-fibula. A: front view of foot; B: side view of third toe. (× 3/4)

death that these tracks were recognized as having been made by early dinosaurs.

The combined length of the tibia-tarsus and the hind foot is double the
length of the femur in *Coelophysis*. Here we see an adaptation for swift
running—a swinging of the femur back and forth through an arc of about
90 degrees would have swung the foot through a similar but greatly magnified arc. Consequently, *Coelophysis* was able to run with very long strides,
as indicated by tracks that it or closely related theropod dinosaurs might
have made. *Coelophysis* was almost without doubt a fast-running dinosaur.

As has been mentioned, the forelimbs of *Coelophysis* are much smaller
than the hind limbs and almost certainly were of little use for locomotion.
On occasion *Coelophysis* may have come down on "all fours" as do kanga-
roos today, but the small forelimbs were used mostly as accessories to the
jaws in feeding. The forelimb, from the shoulder articulation to the tips of
the fingers, is about half as long as the hind limb, from pelvis to the tips of
the toes.

The shoulder blade of *Coelophysis*, known as the scapula-coracoid, was
of course attached to the body by muscles, as is the case for almost all land-
living backboned animals. This element consists of two bones, the upper,
bladelike scapula, enlarged at its upper and lower ends, and the lower
short coracoid, expanded fore and aft to about the same width as the lower
end of the scapula (see figure 42). The scapula and coracoid are firmly attached to each other by a long, immovable joint or suture (the scapula being
expanded along this joint to match the expansion of the coracoid) and at
the back, where these two bones come together, is a socket, shared by
both, for the rotation of the upper arm bone, the humerus. The humerus is
a small bone, somewhat shorter than the scapula-coracoid, and the two
lower arm bones, the radius and ulna, are even shorter than the humerus.

The hand of *Coelophysis* is composed of three functional fingers, each
consisting of a long metacarpal, with long, supple finger bones, terminating in a large claw. The metacarpals connect at their upper ends with a flexible wrist, composed of five bones, two broad upper elements join with the
radius and ulna respectively, and three lower bones, two of which are
broad and correspond to the upper bones of the wrist, the third being a
mere nubbin on the outer side of the wrist. This last bone articulates with
the metacarpal of the fourth finger, which is slender and short, and carries
at its lower end just one phalanx or finger bone. It is obvious that the fourth
finger in *Coelophysis* was rudimentary, perhaps visible as a short stub, per-

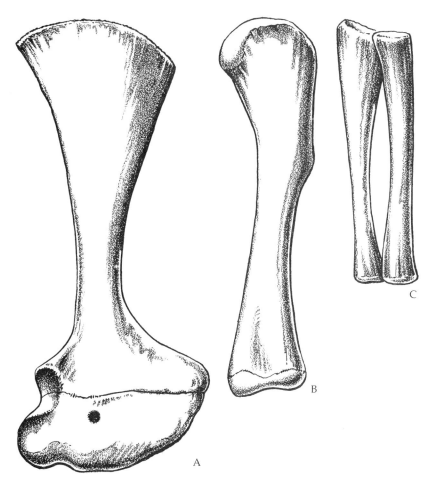

FIGURE 42   A: The scapula-coracoid, the two bones that form the "shoulder blade" of *Coelophysis bauri*, expand at each end, thereby affording an ample platform for the muscles that activated the arm. Note the cuplike depression (on the bottom left) for articulation with the head of the upper arm bone, the humerus.

B: The humerus of *Coelophysis bauri* is markedly smaller than the femur, the upper bone of the leg, as might be expected in this bipedal reptile. The long crest on this bone, the deltopectoral crest, forms an extended attachment for muscles from the shoulder and chest areas. Dorsal view.

C: The radius and ulna of *Coelophysis bauri*, the lower bones of the arm, are relatively short—shorter than the humerus, with which they articulate at their upper ends, and the hand, articulating their lower ends. Anterior view. (all × 3/4)

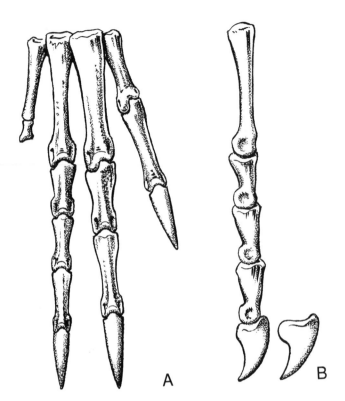

FIGURE 43   The hand of *Coelophysis bauri*, although rather large, is obviously not adapted for locomotion. Useful for grasping prey, it has three functional fingers, metacarpals, and phalanges, the terminal phalanges adapted as claws. The fourth finger is rudimentary, with only one phalanx, articulating with the metacarpal bone. A: front view, showing the typical reptilian formula of two phalanges in the first digit, three in the second, and four in the third; B: side view of third digit and claw of second digit. (× 1)

haps even buried within the skin of the hand. There is no trace of a fifth finger; it was completely lost during the course of evolution. The first of the three functional fingers of *Coelophysis* is much shorter than the other two, which are of equal length. The claws on all three fingers are large. This three-fingered hand is longer than the radius and ulna, and is about equal in length to the humerus—an indication of how strong and well designed the hand was for grasping and holding objects.

This detailed description of the *Coelophysis* skeleton is intended to provide a reasonably intimate view of this small dinosaur, one of the first of its kind, as it is known from the hard evidence of the fossils—the evidence on which almost all other knowledge about it is based. Fortunately, the evidence of the bones tells us a lot about *Coelophysis*, not only as to its adaptations for a particular mode of life, as will be discussed below, but also as to its particular position within the complex skein of dinosaur evolution. That subject will be considered in chapter 9—the position of *Coelophysis* relative to the classification of dinosaurs. If this appears less than exciting, one should remember that only through an understanding of the interrelations of animals and plants do we achieve a true understanding of organisms. A consideration of the roots and the relatives of *Coelophysis* provides the perspective necessary to see in this little dinosaur something greater than the delicate skeletons excavated at Ghost Ranch; fascinating though they may be as esthetic objects, they exist in their fossilized state as prime examples of biological engineering and as testaments to success and survival in an ancient world.

EIGHT

THE LIFE OF AN EARLY DINOSAUR

Chapter 7 provides a reasonably detailed description of *Coelophysis* as deduced from the hard evidence of the fossil remains unearthed at Ghost Ranch. These petrified bones are the foundation on which to base a broad, and in some respects speculative, portrayal of *Coelophysis* as a living, active animal. Paleontologists must use this method if the bones released from their rocky sepulchres are to have any *real* meaning as the relics of once-living animals. And in attempting to clothe the skeleton of *Coelophysis* with muscles and skin—and supply it with the internal organs essential to the life it once led—a certain amount of theorizing is necessary. Such speculation is valid so long as it is used with proper restraint, the theorist being cognizant of the limits of information to be derived from the bones and aware of what may be used in speculations from one's knowledge of living animals.

Goodness knows, speculation has been endless about the lives of dinosaurs—some of it good, some of it bad, some of it so far beyond the realm of reality as to soar into the cloud-cuckoo land of fantasy. It is hoped that the notions put forth in this chapter are reasonable and realistic.

From the web of arguments put forth by many authors to support their ideas as to the capabilities of dinosaurs to have led the lives invisaged for them, five important propositions emerge based on facts—as opposed to inferences. These factual bases are:

1. The size of individual dinosaurs and dinosaur species. Size may very well have been crucial in the development of dinosaurian body temperatures (as will be discussed).
2. The posture and gait of dinosaurs, as shown by the structure of the skeleton and the evidence of tracks and trackways. Such evidence reveals in no uncertain terms the levels of activity among dinosaurs.
3. The nature of the skull and teeth. Developments of the skull and dentition provide solid clues as to the type and amount of food the dinosaurs required for living from day to day.
4. The internal structure of the bones. This evidence, particularly as investigated by Armand J. de Ricqlès, gives sophisticated insight into growth rates in dinosaurs, and possible physiological developments in various genera.
5. The size of the brain as revealed by endocranial casts. Endocranial casts do not provide the exact size of the brain, but they do give us approximations on which to base conclusions concerning the development of the brain and its role in the evolution of the animal.

The inferences that have been put forward in the long and continuing debate regarding the lives of dinosaurs in general (and of *Coelophysis* in particular) must be regarded as supplementary to the five basic facts listed. These inferences include speculations concerning the supposed structure of the heart, the spatial relation of the heart to the brain, the nature of the food that kept various dinosaurs alive and provided them with the necessary energy to follow the life-styles for which they were adapted, the population ratios between carnivorous and herbivorous dinosaurs in any particular setting, and the environmental temperatures that dinosaurs may have experienced throughout the world.

When *Coelophysis* is viewed as a living animal, one impression stands out: the little dinosaur from Ghost Ranch must have been very active and capable of rapid movements. It was obviously a small predator, quick enough to pursue its small prey, and quick enough to avoid the attentions of the large predators with which it shared the late Triassic landscape. The well engineered skeleton attests to this, as do the tracks and trackways attributed with good reason to this dinosaur.

Let us consider the skeleton and the footprints. Walter Coombs, a paleontologist who has given considerable attention to the dynamics of dinosaurs, has shown that dinosaurian cursorial adaptations—that is, the ability to run fast and make quick movements—involved: an optimum body weight of perhaps 50 kilograms (about 110 pounds), long lower limbs having hingelike joints; relatively short upper limbs; the two bones of the lower limb joined into what amounts to a single bone; a long, slender foot having median symmetry (meaning that the line of the axis of the foot passed through the middle toe); and a digitigrade stance whereby the heel was carried well above the ground. All in all, *Coelophysis* fits the specifications set forth by Coombs as the ideals for a fast-running animal (Coombs 1978:399).

Indeed, the structure of the hind limbs of *Coelophysis,* as already described, is a textbook example of adaptation for fast bipedal running. The combined length of the lower hind-limb bones (which are so closely appressed as to function as a single unit), plus the extended length of the foot, is about double that of the femur (around which were concentrated the powerful muscles for propelling *Coelophysis* at great speed). Consequently, when the lower end of the femur was swung through an arc of about 45 degrees, the foot accordingly moved in a similar arc, but the distance covered was magnified by a factor of three. In brief, *Coelophysis* could run fast because it had a long stride, undoubtedly rapidly repeated. Furthermore, there is reason to think that during very rapid running *Coelophysis* probably had both feet off the ground during a portion of each stride.

Such an anatomical development of lower limbs has resulted in an efficient mechanism for swift running among numerous land-living vertebrates time and again over millions of years of evolution. One sees it today in horses and other fast-running hoofed mammals (though, of course, in quadrupedal mammals the forelimbs are equally adapted for rapid locomotion) and in such bipedal runners as ostriches and other large ground birds. In fact, *Coelophysis's* rapid running conformation is closely paralleled in the running birds—not a surprise to one who accepts the ancestry of the birds as having probably derived from the theropod dinosaurs.

However, we need not depend on the obvious cursorial conformation of the hind limbs in *Coelophysis* or the close anatomical similarities to ostriches and emus in order to visualize speed as a definitive attribute of this little Triassic dinosaur. There is the evidence of the trackways.

The abundant footprints made by dinosaurs walking and running across ancient mudflats and preserved for eternity as impressions in the rocks provide us with *direct* evidence as to the gait and speed of these extinct reptiles. We saw earlier that, in the nineteenth century, Professor Edward Hitchcock of Amherst College described dinosaurian footprints found in the Upper Triassic and Lower Jurassic rocks of the Connecticut Valley as having been made by large, ground-living birds of ancient age. After his death the footprints and trackways were recognized as those of very early dinosaurs, some of the track-makers being similar to *Coelophysis* or *Coelophysis* itself.

For many years after Hitchcock's pioneer work the study of dinosaur footprints was a sort of ho-hum branch of paleontology; numerous paleontologists described dinosaur footprints, tried to classify them, and that was that. But in recent years has come the dawning realization that footprints are extraordinarily valuable records of animal behavior. The footprints— and especially the association of footprints that make up trackways— show us exactly what particular dinosaurs were doing at a certain instant hundreds of millions of years ago. The immediacy of footprints and trackways are sometimes emphasized by the presence of impressions made by raindrops falling at the same time the dinosaurs were making their own impressions in the mud—a record of the dinosaurs traveling through a rainstorm a very long time ago! Such impressions convey, more than anything else, a feeling for dinosaurs as active, vibrant animals. Professor R. McNeill Alexander of the University of Leeds aptly remarked, "Fossil bones may remind us of a rotting carcass, but footprints are evidence of a living, moving animal" (Alexander 1989:27).

A dramatic instance of this is a large association of dinosaur footprints to be seen in the Cretaceous Winton Formation in Queensland, Australia (studied and described by Tony Thulborn of the University of Queensland and Mary Wade of the Queensland Museum). Here, in a rather circumscribed rock area known as the Lark Quarry, are some *three thousand* prints of small dinosaurs, some theropods, others ornithopods, that were obviously on a mud bank bordering a lake. Across one part of this surface are footprints made by a very large, carnivorous dinosaur. Evidently this big predator had appeared suddenly because the small prints show a literal explosion—a stampede born of terror—of hundreds of little dinosaurs, all running in one direction to escape a dreaded foe. And the intriguing thing about this dinosaurian escape a hundred million years ago is that the small dinosaurs, blocked from their preferred route of escape because of the waters of the lake (these were land-living reptiles) had, perforce, to doubleback past their giant foe, running in the direction from which he had come. These events are clearly depicted in the solid record of the rocks. There is, we think, little speculation involved in the recreation of a happening that took place—in a few seconds—in the distant geologic past (Thulborn and Wade 1979).

As revealing as the evidence of the footprints may be as a record of a short dinosaurian drama that took place many millions of years ago, even more can be learned from those impressions made in the Mesozoic mud of what is now Australia. How fast was the gigantic dinosaur going when he (or she) ventured onto the shore where the little dinosaurs had congregated? And how fast did the terrified small dinosaurs move in their attempts to escape? There are answers to these questions (to the first, *not very;* the second, *very*), thanks in large part to the studies of the aforementioned Professor Alexander.

As a result of his extensive work on dinosaur trackways and dinosaur skeletons (as well as numerous analyses of the dynamics of modern animals on the move—walking, trotting, and running), Alexander was able to establish some mathematical solutions to problems involving possible rates of locomotion in dinosaurs. Of particular importance is the length of *stride,* which is the distance from one footprint to the next made by the *same* foot. The *pace* is the distance between the left and the next right footprint. Alexander established that a relationship between the lengths of stride and the lengths of the limbs determines the approximate speed of locomotion, as revealed by a particular trackway. Furthermore, as a result of many comparisons between foot lengths and leg lengths in dinosaur skeletons, he determined that the leg, as measured from the hip joint to the ground especially in the bipedal dinosaurs, is about four times as long as the foot. Thus by measuring the size of footprints, from them estimating the length of the legs, and by measuring the lengths of strides, all in a single trackway, he could arrive at the approximate speed at which the dinosaur was traveling. Most dinosaurs would seem to have walked most of the time, but when suddenly stimulated these ancient reptiles, especially the small theropod dinosaurs, would break from a walk to a fast run.

In the desert of northern Arizona is a rock surface, discovered years ago by Roland T. Bird, covered with lowermost Jurassic dinosaur tracks and trackways, some of which are of the proper size and configuration to have been made by dinosaurs very similar in size to *Coelophysis.* This treasure trove of footprints recently has been carefully studied by Grace Irby at the Museum of Northern Arizona, and among the almost confusing melange of prints she has distinguished several trackways made by a *Coelophysis*-type dinosaur (Irby 1993a:Plate 1). All these particular trackways show the prints of the right and left feet in virtually a straight line—in contrast to trackways made by larger bipedal dinosaurs, in which the right and left footprints are somewhat offset from each other. It was probably a matter of weight. One *Coelophysis*-like trackway is noteworthy because of the length of stride, indicating a dinosaur that was running at about top speed. Moreover, it seems likely that during a part of each stride both feet were off the ground. Since in this trackway the stride is some three times as long as the limb, and since the estimated length of the limb is one meter, it would seem that the dinosaur was running at the rate of about three and a half meters per second, or something over eight miles an hour (Irby and Morales 1993).

Thulborn, in a comprehensive book on dinosaur tracks, has estimated a maximum speed for *Coelophysis* between twenty-three and thirty-one kilometers per hour, or fifteen to twenty miles per hour (Thulborn 1990). Alexander cites dinosaur trackways in Texas as indicating a speed of twelve meters per second or twenty-seven miles per hour. According to Alexander, "12 meters per second is fast. Good human athletes sprint at up to 10 meters per second" (Alexander 1989:41). Obviously there were some fast runners among the theropod dinosaurs, especially the smaller ones; of these *Coelophysis* was probably one of the swiftest.

It should be added that the analyses of many thousands of footprints and trackways of theropod dinosaurs, especially of small theropods including *Coelophysis*, quite clearly show that they did *not* hop, kangaroo fashion.

Still another point may be made from the analyses of small theropod dinosaur tracks, which may well apply to *Coelophysis:* scrapes within the toe prints of some tracks indicate that as the foot left the ground it moved forward and *laterally,* indicating that the leg was swung out away from the body during the initial phase of the stride, perhaps as an adaptation for "clearing" the pelvic region. But the footprints indicate that the leg was swung back in during the final phase of the stride, so that the foot was planted right on a midline beneath the body when it touched the ground.

Since the analyses of trackways made by small theropod dinosaurs, including *Coelophysis*, clearly indicate that such dinosaurs were indeed very active, what therefore might have been the level of their body metabolism? This brings us to a long-debated question—were the dinosaurs, or at least some of them, "cold-blooded," or *ectothermic*, with the body temperature dependent on the temperature of the environment, or were they "warm-blooded," or *endothermic*, with the body temperature dependent on a high and controlled rate of internal heat production? Ectothermy is typical of modern reptiles, such as alligators and lizards; endothermy is typical of modern birds and mammals.

In contrast to the rather definite information to be obtained from dinosaur trackways, we here enter a realm of speculation, which has been exploited by numerous paleontologists and biologists. Since we will never be able to test body temperatures in the dinosaurs directly, it has been the practice to evoke various criteria or inferred criteria in an effort to reach a solution to this vexing problem. Dinosaur people thus have an opportunity to indulge in a great deal of theorizing, some well-founded, some of questionable value.

Several years ago the American Association for the Advancement of Science sponsored a symposium on dinosaurian physiology, from which emerged a book, intriguingly called *A Cold Look at the Warm-Blooded Dinosaurs* (Thomas and Olson 1980). Eighteen authors contributed chapters to this book. As might be expected, opinions differed, from the uncompromising attitude of Robert Bakker, who categorically stated, "We need endothermic dinosaurs; evolutionary theory demands them; the empirical data confirm that they existed" (p. 352), to the measured words of James Hopson, who said, "I conclude that dinosaurs, with the possible exception of the coelurosaurs, were intermediate in their metabolic level between living reptiles on the one hand and living endotherms on the other" (pp. 309–10).

Generally speaking, most students who have delved deeply into this problem have concluded that the dinosaurs were very special reptiles, whose living habits we view through an imperfect glass. It has often been suggested that the dinosaurs were perhaps intermediate between what we think of as "cold-blooded" and "warm-blooded." (The aforementioned terms are anything but absolute; today, among the animals we know are numerous gradations between ectothermy and endothermy.) Furthermore, many people who have explored body temperatures among the dinosaurs believe that no simple statement is applicable to all ancient reptiles. So perhaps the large dinosaurs were essentially ectothermic, while the small coelurosaurs were largely endothermic.

John Ostrom, who has pioneered the study of possible dinosaurian endothermy, concludes his extended and carefully reasoned chapter in the *Cold Look* volume by saying: "Personally, I believe that some dinosaurs— especially the theropods, to which all lines of evidence seem to apply, were

probably endothermic. . . . The vast majority, however, I suspect were ectothermic 'homeotherms,' as first suggested by Colbert, Cowles and Bogert" (Ostrom 1980:54).

This last statement calls for some explanation. First of all, what is an "ectothermic homeotherm"? We have already encountered ectothermy,
meaning a pattern of temperature regulation in which the body temperature depends on the temperature of the environment; and endothermy,
meaning a pattern of temperature regulation in which the body temperature depends on a high and controlled rate of internal heat production. Ho-
meothermy is a pattern of temperature regulation in which variation in the
core body temperature is maintained within a small limit despite variations
in the environmental temperature. So an ectothermic homeotherm is basically an ectothermic animal that nevertheless maintains a rather constant
body temperature.

Many years ago, Raymond B. Cowles, a herpetologist at the University
of California at Los Angeles, and I became involved in an argument about
the extinction of dinosaurs, particularly about temperature tolerances—
the possible body temperatures of dinosaurs and the temperatures of their
environments. Our debate was carried on through letters back and forth,
and in the course of things my very close friend and colleague Charles M.
Bogert, herpetologist at the American Museum of Natural History, got
dragged into the fray. In the end the three of us decided to get together at
the Archbold Field Station, a research facility sponsored by the museum in
Florida, to look at some alligators. So we went there during August, with
plans for some experiments involving alligators.

We somehow assembled a dozen or so alligators, ranging in size from a
very young juvenile, perhaps eighteen inches in length, to an adult male
more than seven feet long. Some alligators even larger than our big fellow
would have been nice to have had, although I don't know exactly how we
might have handled them. We found the big 'gator exciting enough for the
three of us, particularly as he was not very cooperative. Nor did any of the
others look upon our efforts with favor. But the big fellow was especially
hostile; when we went to his enclosure after dark to check on him, shining
a flashlight to reveal a pair of very red, baleful eyes, he would hiss loudly
and charge us with all his might.

We subjected our reptiles to a series of experiments, on the land and in
the water, during the course of which we took their temperatures at frequent intervals. We even built some wooden frames so that we could pose

them as if they were theropod dinosaurs, standing on their hind legs, with their bodies at various angles to the ground.

In brief, we discovered what might have been expected, that the reactions of these alligators to the heat of the sun or to varying water temperatures closely correlated with their body sizes. The little alligators heated up rapidly, and when removed to the shade they cooled off rapidly. Those of intermediate size showed slower responses, heating and cooling at more moderate rates. And our big fellow was the most stable of all, his temperature rising slowly when he was in the sun and likewise falling at a slow rate when he was removed to the shade.

With these empirical findings in hand, we made some extrapolations involving dinosaurs of various sizes. It seemed to us that if it required five minutes for the temperature of an alligator of thirteen kilograms, or thirty pounds, to rise one degree centigrade, then a very long time period, a matter of many hours, must have been needed for the body temperature of a thirty-ton dinosaur, two thousand times the weight of the alligator, to have risen or subsided a degree. The net result it seemed to us was that the bigger dinosaurs, at least, would have maintained almost constant body temperatures—going up perhaps a degree or so during the heat of the day, and going down in like manner during the cooler night. Consequently, such a dinosaur, being an ectothermic homeotherm, would have enjoyed many of the advantages of a "warm-blooded" animal, with the added advantage of maintaining the optimum basic metabolism almost constantly with relatively little food intake (Colbert, Cowles, and Bogert 1946:372). Endotherms including humans lead very expensive lives, having to eat frequently in order to maintain physical health. (The largest modern land-living endotherm, the African elephant, in the wild has to spend about twenty to twenty-two hours of each day feeding.)

Would *Coelophysis* have fared well as an ectothermic homeotherm, or considering its high level of activity as indicated by trackways, would this coelurosaurian dinosaur necessarily have been a true endotherm?

To explore one aspect of this latter possibility, we turn to the interesting and truly exciting research on the microscopic structure of dinosaur bone, conducted over the years by Armand de Ricqlès of the University of Paris. And here we become involved with the fourth of the above-listed facts, bone histology, as a basis for making some inferences about dinosaurian body temperatures. It is a thorny problem, as was realized by de Ricqlès when he stated that "a review of this literature [about the microscopic, his-

tological structure of dinosaur bone] indicates that there is general agree-
ment about *facts;* the available data are reasonably concordant and well established. The functional interpretation of these data is quite another
matter" (de Ricqlès 1980:103).

What are the histological facts? The first histological fact is that *Coelophysis,* as is the case with other dinosaurs, possessed dense Haversian
bone, similar to the bone tissue in mammals (see figure 44). This was recognized several decades ago by D. H. Enlow and S. O. Brown, who pointed
out that: "The bone tissues of . . . dinosaurs . . . are distinctive among all
recent and fossil reptiles. In structure, the bone . . . is similar to, if not
identical with, the bone tissue of many living mammals, including man"
(Enlow and Brown 1957:200–203).

This resemblance led various students of dinosaurs to the conclusion
that dinosaurs had an endothermic physiology. Indeed such was the view
of Dr. de Ricqlès when he first began his monumental research on the mi-

FIGURE 44   Microphotograph of Haversian canals as seen in a dinosaur bone. These
secondary vascular channels, developed in the remodeling of bone tissue, are characteristic of the bones of dinosaurs, crocodilians, tortoises, birds, and mammals. It is now
thought that the Haversian canals, once considered an indication of endothermy, or
warm-bloodedness, may be related to size, rates of growth, and strength of bone.

crostructure of dinosaur bones. But the more this subject was investigated, the more it became apparent to de Ricqlès, and also to Dr. Robin Reid of the Queen's University, Belfast, who also was deeply immersed in this problem, that things were not so simple as at first they seemed.

Thus Haversian bone, when seen in cross-section under the microscope, is highly vascularized, with numerous closely packed channels for blood vessels, each surrounded by bony rings. This structure was thought to be the antithesis of reptilian bone, which is poorly vascularized. But continuing research revealed that highly vascular bone occurs in many living ectothermic reptiles, while small mammals and birds, which are remarkably endothermic, may have poorly vascularized bone.

It became evident that there are two types of highly vascular bone: "primary bone" first formed within a dense arrangement of blood vessels, which bring in bone materials such as calcium phosphate, and "secondary bone," which replaces the primary bone with the bony Haversian canals. This secondary bone is designed to withstand stress—an important feature for dinosaurs and other large land-living vertebrates.

Both de Ricqlès and Reid have now shown that dinosaurs possess various types of bony tissue, such types correlated with the functions of the bones during the lives of individual dinosaurs. Highly vascularized primary bone would seem to indicate rapid growth; thus it may be dominant in the leg bones of young dinosaurs. Later such bone was replaced by secondary bone, to support the great weight of the mature individual.

But to complicate matters, Reid has found evidence of seasonal growth in some dinosaurs, indicating that these dinosaurs may have been more active at some times of the year than at other times. Such growth patterns would seem to show a mode of life wherein activity was governed by seasonal changes (Norman 1991:118–19).

A recently published paper describes the presence of *growth plates* near the ends of long bones in juvenile dinosaurs. These structures, present in modern birds, are discs of cartilage that generate bone elongation during the early life of the bird. The bone elongation is very rapid and demands high metabolism and endothermy. Perhaps, therefore, we see in this histological detail within the long bones of young dinosaurs the indication of an avian type of growth, which might have been of crucial significance in the early life of a large or giant reptile (Barreto, Albrecht, Bjorling, Horner, and Wilsman 1993).

Then to complicate the picture even further, Dr. de Ricqlès found that some dinosaurs seem to have grown very rapidly when they were young, but after reaching adulthood the metabolic rate slowed down to an ecto-thermic reptilian level. The foregoing remarks make clear that the relation-ships between various bone tissues in the dinosaurs and the matter of basic metabolism, body temperatures, and probably physiology and habits in these ancient reptiles present the student with complicated facts that can lead to complicated interpretations.

In this connection, a microphotograph of a cross-section of a long bone of *Coelophysis* from Ghost Ranch taken by de Ricqlès is reproduced in figure 45. His explanation of the microphotograph follows in full. Perhaps some of his remarks may be a bit technical, but this firsthand information from an outstanding authority on the internal structure of bone in fossil verte-brates is worthwhile.

> The photo shows the structure of cortical, compact bone tissue forming the whole shaft cross-section of a long bone [of *Coelophysis*]. The magnifi-cation is fairly low. The bone tissue is quite homogeneous, entirely of

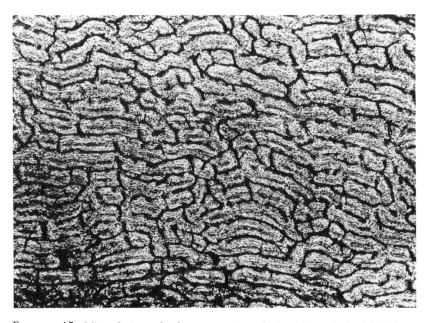

FIGURE 45   Microphotograph of a cross section of a long-bone shaft of *Coelophysis bauri*, showing "primary periosteal plexiform bone tissue." Courtesy of Armand de Ricqlès.

periosteal origin, with *no* reconstruction by secondary osteons (Haversian Systems). The tissue is entirely of the so-called plexiform bone tissue pattern, a three-dimensional meshwork of primary (not reconstructed) osteons organized around longitudinal, circular, and radial vascular canals trapped within a "background" of woven periosteal bone matrix (the bone matrix forming the primary osteons themselves is lamellar, so this bone tissue is an example of the wider category of "fibro-lamellar" bone tissues). In fact, this photo is a good example of a slight modulation of the plexiform tissue pattern because most vascular canals have a somewhat oblique course, hence the pattern here could be most precisely described as somewhat intermediate between "plexiform" and "reticular" bone tissues.

Whatever these minutiae, this bone tissue pattern is commonly observed in very fast growing animals. In this case it may be that the bone came from a somewhat immature individual, since no hints of secondary reconstruction are seen. There are no "growth rings" of any sort, either.   (de Ricqlès 1993, personal communication)

Compare this picture to figure 44, which is a microphotograph of a cross-section from a toe bone of a large, adult dinosaur of Cretaceous age. Here one sees characteristic secondary Haversian bone, highly vascular and well designed to withstand stress.

To conclude these remarks having to do with bone tissue and the possible physiology in dinosaurs, it is probably safe to say that the large and gigantic dinosaurs were probably ectothermic homeotherms, living in a tropical world in which temperature fluctuations from day to day and from year to year were minimal. As for the small dinosaurs, their body mass may have been insufficient to maintain constant body temperature. So we return to the notion that these dinosaurs may have been at least partly endothermic, as suggested by Ostrom. And one wonders if this might also have been true for the hatchlings and juveniles of large dinosaurs. The matter is far from settled, despite what may be said otherwise.

Another fact listed at the beginning of this discussion of *Coelophysis* as a very active dinosaur is the matter of brain size, as determined from the capacity of the brain cavity within the skull. James Hopson, who has studied this question, has determined that the relative size of the brain and the overall activity of the animal controlled by that brain are clearly correlated. As we have seen Hopson concluded that, *except for the coelurosaurs*, the behavior of dinosaurs as inferred from skeletal structure and trackways

This late Triassic thecodont evolved as an inoffensive plant-eating reptile, inhabiting the borders of streams and uplands, where it was subject to attacks by *Rutiodon* and *Postosuchus*. In a world of such aggressive carnivores, *Desmatosuchus* evolved a heavy defense of bony armor plates encased in heavy, leathery skin. Large spikes on the neck and shoulders protected these vulnerable parts of the body.

Postosuchus was a very large carnivorous thecodont reptile living in North America during late Triassic time. This predator dominated the uplands of Chinle landscapes. It was the ecological forerunner, but not the ancestor, of the giant carnivorous dinosaurs of Jurassic and Cretaceous age.

Placerias, a dicynodont reptile belonging to the order known as therapsids, or mammal-like reptiles, was one of the last of its kind. It was a strict herbivore, protected in part by its large size, comparable to that of an ox. Probably a dweller, for the most part, in upland environments, *Placerias* may have fed largely on roots and tubers that it uprooted with its strong tusks.

The streams and lakes of the late Triassic were ruled by phytosaurs such as
Rutiodon, some of which reached gigantic proportions. *Rutiodon* and
Postosuchus may have competed for food. *Rutiodon*, a thecodont reptile, was
a predecessor (but not an ancestor) of the crocodilians, which survive today.
The close resemblance between *Rutiodon* and crocodiles is an example
of evolutionary parallelism.

comes within the range of living ectothermic reptiles: "The evidence of relative brain size, combined with the bone histological evidence of Ricqlès (1974), suggests that most dinosaurs were intermediate in their metabolic rates between living reptiles and mammals. Only the coelurosaurs [and this includes *Coelophysis*] may possibly have been as metabolically active as living endotherms" (Hopson 1980:289).

It should be recalled here that *Coelophysis* and the other coelurosaurs (and most theropod dinosaurs, for that matter) had relatively large brains, when compared to all other dinosaurs.

So when all the factual evidence is carefully analyzed, and when proper inferences are made based on this evidence, one arrives once again at the conclusion made earlier on the basis of skeletal anatomy and footprints: that *Coelophysis* was a very active dinosaur, and as such it might very well have been an endothermic dinosaur, too. But for that we have no incontrovertible proof, nor will we ever have such proof, unless in the future someone invents a time machine that can carry him back to the late Triassic world.

If *Coelophysis* was either an ectothermic homeotherm or a true endotherm, how was this dinosaur protected against the vagaries of the climates in which it lived? Modern endotherms—birds and most mammals—have insulating coverings of feathers or hair. (Some modern tropical land-living endotherms of large size—elephants, hippopotamuses, and rhinoceroses,—manage with hairless skins, although during the last ice age the woolly mammoths and the woolly rhinoceroses were abundantly haired for protection against the cold. Moreover, although mankind has been a largely hairless endotherm during the past several hundred thousand years, he has had the intelligence and the means of protecting himself against the elements.)

Some paleontologists have gone so far as to restore *Coelophysis* with an outer covering of feathers. Not the slightest bit of evidence supports doing this. Those dinosaurs that have been fossilized with the skin or bits of skin preserved reveal a leathery covering that may be compared to the skin of crocodiles, alligators, or lizards. The world in which *Coelophysis* lived was probably a tropical world, so this dinosaur was able to do very well with a leathery outer covering.

Assuming that *Coelophysis* had a leathery skin, as was almost certainly the case, what did it look like? Was this dinosaur of a dark color, like crocodilians, or was *Coelophysis* a brightly colored reptile, as are many modern lizards? Again, we will never know. The artist restoring *Coelophysis* has fairly free reign for the imagination, although it seems safe to assume that this dinosaur probably was not lavender colored with pink polka dots. Dr. James Farlow has suggested that perhaps some dinosaurs may have been highly colored during the reproductive season, owing to hormonal influences, after which the color patterns may have faded.

The nature of the skull and dentition has been cited above as one of the five factual bases on which we can reconstruct the life pattern of *Coelophysis*. Certainly the teeth as described in chapter 7 leave little doubt as to the food that *Coelophysis* ate. This dinosaur was a thorough predator that fed on other animals. And what were the other animals? Anything that *Coelophysis* could catch and manage. Since *Coelophysis* was a comparatively small dinosaur it probably preyed on small game—little reptiles and amphibians, perhaps freshwater fish or even insects.

Recall that chapter 4 included a brief description of the bones of juvenile *Coelophysis*, found within the body cavities of two of the adult specimens from Ghost Ranch, namely American Museum of Natural History numbers 7223 and 7224. These little skeletons within the big skeletons are almost certainly the evidence of cannibalism; they are far too large and well-formed to have been embryos. Cannibalism in *Coelophysis* is not surprising; it is common among modern reptiles like crocodiles and alligators.

Thus Hugh Cott, who made an extended study of the Nile crocodile in Uganda and Zimbabwe, found that cannibalism was common in this reptile.

> Crocodiles are much addicted to cannibalism and this is doubtless one of the factors which accounts for their segregation in "age groups" on the basking grounds and elsewhere. . . . In Uganda, Hippel (1946) found crocodile remains in thirty-seven of the 587 crocodiles examined. . . .
>
> Of the seventeen occurrences of crocodile prey now recorded, only two of the predators measured less than 3 meters, and no fewer than eight were very large, ranging from 4.1 to 4.9 meters. Cannibalism thus appears to be a habit acquired with age. (Cott 1961:296)

As if in confirmation of Cott's observations, two of the larger skeletons among the Ghost Ranch dinosaurs contain the remains of young individuals within the body cavities.

Cott's mention of age groups points up another observation that he made in his study of the Nile crocodile: that young crocodiles, those less than a meter in length, are remarkably few in the aggregations of crocodiles to be seen along the rivers of Africa. Hunters and travelers have noted this for years. It probably is an indication that juvenile crocodiles avoid their adult peers.

Ironically, however, after having dug a nest and laid her eggs, the female crocodilian is very protective of the hatching babies. In fact, she vigorously guards the nest against intruders, a behavior pattern seen in the alligator as well. Furthermore, she assists the young as they emerge from the eggs and carries them in her mouth to the edge of the water, where they will be safe among reeds and other water plants. Then for the next three or four years the young crocodilians live a secretive life, feeding on insects and other small prey. It is only after they have become large enough to take care of themselves that they join the crocodilian populations of their home range. Even then, as noted by Cott, they stay with creatures of their own size, thereby lessening the chances of being attacked and eaten by large adults.

Walter Auffenberg, who studied the giant Komodo dragon lizard in its native habitat, found similar behavior patterns among these reptiles.

> Intraspecific predation is quite common. Pfeffer (1959) cited a native report that a female dug into an ora [Komodo lizard] nest just as the eggs were hatching, and that she attempted to eat the young and had to be driven away. They also kill and eat one another at later life stages. . . . Most intraspecific aggression occurs when small feeding aggregations are formed. Much of the antagonism is directed toward the smaller members of the group; when unable to escape they are sometimes killed and eaten.   (Auffenberg 1981:152)

In the light of these observations made of modern predatory reptiles of large size, it is perhaps significant that no truly small individuals of *Coelophysis* have as yet been discovered in the blocks removed from the Ghost Ranch quarry. One of the smallest specimens so far recovered is a juvenile skull, American Museum of Natural History number 7242, about one-third as long as an adult skull. This represents a small individual, but certainly one far removed from the hatchling stages. So one may wonder whether, as in the case of modern crocodilians, baby *Coelophysis*, for the sake of safety, retreated into a secluded environment for several years before joining their elders. Why not?

An interesting aspect of the Ghost Ranch dinosaur quarry is the size of the aggregation of dinosaur skeletons, representing thousands of animals.

Carnivorous vertebrates do not generally congregate in enormous numbers; this is a behavior pattern typical of herbivores, as seen, for example, in the truly huge local nesting population of the herbivorous hadrosaurian dinosaur *Maiasaura*, unearthed in Montana by Jack Horner and his colleagues. Carnivores commonly travel and hunt in small groups, or individually. Or do they?

William Bartram, the famous pioneer American naturalist who traveled in Florida during the latter part of the eighteenth century, has some interesting and exciting tales to tell about the habits and the abundance of alligators in that semitropical state two centuries ago. Remember, this was at a time before alligators had been diminished in numbers and size by continual pressure from human hunters.

> Should I say, that the river (in this place) from shore to shore, and perhaps near half a mile above and below me, appeared to be one solid bank of fish, of various kinds, pushing through this narrow pass of St. Juan's into the little lake, on their return down the river, and that the alligators were in such incredible numbers, and so close together from shore to shore, that it would have been easy to have walked across on their heads, had the animals been harmless?   (Bartram 1791 (reprint):118)

The incredible numbers of alligators seen by Bartram were attracted to one spot by a huge run of fish at the time. Ghost Ranch shows no indication of a prey species that would have attracted a comparably large gathering of carnivorous dinosaurs. One must remember, however, that crocodiles and alligators today gather on the banks of rivers in great numbers to bask in the sun. Could behavior like this account for the concentration of *Coelophysis* at Ghost Ranch? Of course, the burial of so many *Coelophysis* skeletons in one place is probably the result of stream action on carcasses, not the congregation of living dinosaurs.

There is every reason to think that *Coelophysis*, like its closest modern relatives, crocodilians and birds, and like all other dinosaurs for which we have evidence, was an egg-laying reptile. Dinosaur eggs are now known from many localities throughout the world, and in some cases the eggs have been associated with the dinosaurs that laid them. The dinosaur eggs found are similar to the eggs of birds; they are characterized by what were once calcareous shells. And in some cases, such as the discovery of dinosaur eggs and nests of *Maiasaura*, in Montana, embryonic skeletons have been found within the eggs (Horner 1982, 1984).

The structure of the pelvis in *Coelophysis* indicates that the eggs of this dinosaur must have been rather small, for the size of the opening between the pubic and ischial bones in the adult skeleton would have restricted the passage of eggs more than three or four centimeters, or an inch and a half, in diameter across their short axes. Therefore the eggs of *Coelophysis* might be compared in size with those of domestic chickens, although, as is the case of some dinosaur eggs, they may have been proportionately more elongated than are the eggs of modern birds. The eggs of *Coelophysis*, if these conclusions as to size are moderately accurate, were thus quite small compared with the egg-layer—which is consistent with the proportions of eggs of dinosaurs where the association of eggs and skeletons is known, and with the eggs of many modern reptiles. It is evident that dinosaurs, probably including *Coelophysis,* began their active lives as *very* small replicas of their parents.

Why were the nests and eggs of *Coelophysis* not found at Ghost Ranch, as the nests and eggs of *Maiasaura* were found in Montana? Probably because the environment in which the Ghost Ranch dinosaurs were entombed was not the environment in which the females made their nests and deposited their eggs. Perhaps some day *Coelophysis* eggs will be discovered.

Chapter 7, devoted to a description of the bony anatomy of *Coelophysis*, pointed out that the orbits, the openings for the eyes of this dinosaur, are very large, indicating that the eyes themselves were large, indicating in turn very perceptive sight. In this respect, *Coelophysis* would seem to have been very birdlike (or perhaps one should say that birds are very dinosaur-like, since, as has been mentioned, the evidence points to theropod dinosaurs, such as *Coelophysis,* as the putative ancestors of the birds). The resemblances between the eyes of *Coelophysis* and birds are further emphasized in that both the dinosaur and birds have sclerotic plates within the orbit—small, overlapping bony plates, it may be recalled, that articulate, each with its neighbor, to form a bony ring (in birds) within the sclera of the eye. The facts concerning the eyes in *Coelophysis* are those of large size and the presence of sclerotic plates. From these facts it is inferred that *Coelophysis* probably had very acute vision.

Modern birds have remarkably acute vision. Tests have shown that a kestrel—a small hawk—has vision so sharp that if it could read it would be able to distinguish newsprint at one hundred yards. Such marvelous vision is necessary for a bird circling in the air and searching the ground visually for the small rodents on which it feeds. The same might have been true for *Coelophysis,* even though it did not fly; visual acuity may have been a part of its adaptations for hunting small game. Certainly, acute sight was most useful for an animal that moved about as fast as *Coelophysis* did.

One may speculate as to whether *Coelophysis* could see color. If so, it looked out over a green world; late Triassic time was still within the age of gymnosperms, for the angiosperms or flowering plants, which lend so much color to our modern world, had not as yet come into being. Angiosperms arose with the advent of Cretaceous history; the last of the dinosaurs lived in a botanical world that was modern in its aspects.

The other senses of *Coelophysis* probably also were highly developed. We know from the form of the stapes, the single bone that occupies the middle ear in dinosaurs—and in birds—that this dinosaur must have had a fine sense of hearing. In the theropod dinosaurs, including *Coelophysis,* as in the modern birds, the stapes is a long slender bone, attached at its outer end to the eardrum, and fitting by means of a disclike footplate into an opening, the foramen ovale, in the brain-case. Thus sound vibrations were transmitted to the inner ear.

Since *Coelophysis* obviously had a keen sense of hearing, as do birds, it stands to reason that this dinosaur (as well as all dinosaurs) probably had a voice. Here we enter the realm of true inference, because there are no known preserved dinosaur hard parts, such as the syrinx in birds, adapted to the purpose of making sound. However the crocodilians, the closest reptilian relatives of the dinosaurs, are very noisy animals, and we can assume with some justification that *Coelophysis* and its relatives were able to call back and forth with a repertoire of signals that were essential to their social activities.

These final remarks, and the previous chapter describing the anatomy of *Coelophysis,* make abundantly evident that many comparisons have been made between *Coelophysis* and its relatives and birds. We have seen that in the structure of the hind limbs *Coelophysis* and other theropod dinosaurs are amazingly similar to birds. The similarities extend throughout the skull and other parts, as we have seen, and into various anatomical details. And for these reasons many paleontologists and zoologists believe that in the theropod dinosaurs we see the ultimate ancestors of the birds. If these dinosaurs are not actually bird ancestors, at least the two groups— dinosaurs and birds—probably have a common ancestry among the thecodont reptiles.

All this has led some paleontologists and zoologists to go off the deep end and classify birds as dinosaurs. This shows a certain imbalance in reasoning. Dinosaurs are dinosaurs and birds are birds, and designating birds as dinosaurs (as has been done) is no more justifiable than is designating mammal-like reptiles as mammals (as has also been done). To do so shows a certain lack of perspective. Of course, birds are similar to theropod dinosaurs, but during their evolution into birds they have undergone changes beyond anything seen in dinosaurs—such as the ability to fly. It is as if I should call myself a Frenchman, because I have some French ancestors dating back two centuries.

I close this chapter by quoting once again Armand de Ricqlès, who has carried out such epochal research on the structure of dinosaur bone, and who has given much thought to the implications of his work. "It makes no more sense to call a brontosaur a 'bird' than it does to delight in the song of a tiny 'dinosaur' on its nest in a nearby tree!" (de Ricqlès 1980:139).

———————————————————— ▬▬ ————————————————————

NINE

ROOTS AND RELATIVES

In chapter 7, *Coelophysis* was introduced as a saurischian dinosaur. Such a brief introduction was considered sufficient, because the Ghost Ranch dinosaur was being described there as "the elegant ancestor," and, as such, attention centered on the details of its skeleton—the refinements of bony structure that characterize this very early saurischian dinosaur as a truly elegant animal, even though it stands near the base of the dinosaurian tree. But having surveyed the details of anatomy that define *Coelophysis*, we now examine this dinosaur in a broader context—to explore its roots and to consider its relatives, in order to obtain a proper perspective of our dinosaurian subject; in short, to view it against the depth of time and the breadth of zoological relationships.

The classes of backboned animals include the reptiles, which have persisted from the Carboniferous period to the present. This long-lived class of vertebrates may be defined, and subdivided, in table 5.

Of course numerous other characters define the four subclasses, but the presence or absence of openings behind the eye (the temporal openings) and the relation of these openings (when present) to certain bones of the skull, offer convenient, basic criteria for distinguishing these major subdivisions of the class.

The subclass that concerns us here is the Diapsida, within which may be recognized several subdivisions, among them two superorders designated as the lepidosaurs and the archosaurs. The lepidosaurs consist of some fa-

TABLE 5
Definitions and Subdivisions of the Class Reptilia

Class	Definition
Class Reptilia	Tetrapods[a] that lack the specializations of birds and mammals and reproduce by the amniote egg.[b]
Subclass Anapsida	Reptiles in which there are no openings in the skull behind the eye, or orbit.
Subclass Diapsida	Reptiles in which the skull behind the orbit is penetrated on each side by two openings, separated by the postorbital-squamosal bones.
Subclass Euryapsida	Reptiles in which the skull behind the orbit is penetrated by a single opening located above the postorbital-squamosal bones.
Subclass Synapsida	Reptiles in which the skull behind the orbit is penetrated by a single opening located below the postorbital-squamosal bones.

[a] The tetrapods are backboned animals primarily adapted for life on land; in other words, nonfish.
[b] The amniote egg is basically the shelled egg, containing two sacs, the liquid-filled amnion within which the embryo develops, and the allantois that receives waste produced by the embryo during its development inside the egg.

miliar reptiles living today, notably the lizards and snakes and the tuatara of New Zealand, while the archosaurs are the crocodiles and various extinct diapsids (see table 6).

The basic classification of the archosaurs presented here is a conservative arrangement that has been widely accepted for many years. It is, for example, the classification used by Carroll in his comprehensive textbook *Vertebrate Paleontology and Evolution* (1988) and is here adopted as the most useful concept of archosaurian orders for the purposes of this book.

In recent years some students of the Archosauria have ceased to regard the Thecodontia as a valid order of reptiles. These authors, while not abandoning entirely the use of the word *thecodont,* use it as vernacular, not as a formal taxonomic term. And in the place of Thecodontia the several lesser divisions that previously had comprised the order are given independent status.

This is all very fine for those who specialize in the study of archosaurs, but for others it complicates the picture. Therefore the reptilian order Thecodontia is unabashedly recognized here to denote those archosaurs of Triassic age that established the reptilian evolutionary adaptations so dominant during Mesozoic times.

TABLE 6

Definition and subdivisions of the Superorder Archosauria

Order	Definition
Superorder Archosauria	Advanced diapsids, trending toward adaptations for efficient locomotion
Order Thecodontia	The basic archosaurs, of Triassic age
Order Crocodylia	Crocodiles and their relatives, Triassic to recent
Order Pterosauria	The flying reptiles, Triassic-Cretaceous
Order Saurischia Order Ornithischia }	The dinosaurs, Triassic-Cretaceous

As for the two orders of dinosaurs, they may be divided into suborders, as is shown in table 7. One suborder, that of the theropods, within the Saurischia, is further subdivided into its constituent families. It is here given detailed attention, because it is the suborder to which *Coelophysis* belongs. The staurikosaurians and theropods were all carnivores. The sauropodomorphs and ornithischians were all herbivores.

To introduce this survey of roots and relatives one might journey far back into the Paleozoic era, to the Upper Carboniferous, or Pennsylvanian, some 300 million years in the past, if a search for the roots of *Coelophysis* were to be carried to their utmost beginnings. This is not really necessary, for it would carry us back to the advent of *all* reptiles, which is beyond the scope of our inquiry. Our interest is rather in the more immediate roots of *Coelophysis*, which are in the transition between Permian and Triassic history, about 250 million years ago—to the years when the archosaurian reptiles were establishing themselves across the continents of those distant days as the forerunners of an evolutionary dynasty that was to dominate the world for considerably more than 100 million years.

During that transition, marked by widespread extinctions among many established reptilian lines, the hitherto rather inconspicuous diapsids experienced a sudden and dramatic development, namely, the almost instantaneous appearance of the thecodont reptiles, the earliest of the Archosauria. The archosaurs (*archos,* chief or principal *sauros;* lizard, or, by extension, reptile) were the diapsids destined to dominate Mesozoic history, arising as the thecodonts, and developing from them the two groups of dinosaurs, the crocodilians and the pterosaurs, or flying reptiles. Also as a part of this great flowering of the archosaurs arose the birds.

The earliest recorded thecodont reptile, *Archosaurus,* is insufficiently known from the Upper Permian beds of Russia, but except for this adumbration of thecodont evolution, the thecodont reptiles are strictly confined to the Triassic period. Two thecodonts are close to the ancestry of the theropod saurischian dinosaurs, one from the Lower Triassic beds of South Africa, the other from the Middle Triassic sediments of Argentina.

Of these, the African genus *Euparkeria* shows many approximations to the earliest theropod dinosaurs, particularly in the structure of the skull. The South American genus *Lagosuchus* is especially close to the theropods in its skeletal structure, but, unfortunately, the skull is imperfectly known. Both thecodont reptiles deserve more than a passing glance as we follow the evolutionary progress of the diapsid reptiles from their beginnings, as derived from primitive anapsid reptiles exemplified by a genus named *Hylonomus*, through the first diapsids of which *Petrolacosaurus* is a logical pregenitor, and into the early thecodonts that concern us here. There is good reason to suppose some thecodonts were close to the ancestry of the theropod dinosaurs, and therefore not far removed from the progenitors of *Coelophysis* itself.

Euparkeria, the skeleton of which is about a meter long, is to be found in the *Cynognathus* zone of the Upper Beaufort Series of South Africa, a strati-

TABLE 7
The Dinosaurs

Classification	Geologic Ages	Characteristics
Order Saurischia		
Suborder Staurikosauria	M-U Tr.	Ancestral saurischians
Suborder Theropoda	Tr.-Cret.	Carnivorous dinosaurs
Family Podokesauridae	U Tr.-L Jur.	Early theropods (*Coelophysis*)
Family Coeluridae	U Jur.-L Cret.	Small theropods
Family Ornithomimidae	U Tr.-U Cret.	Ostrich-like theropods
Family Dromaeosauridae	Cret.	Sickle-clawed theropods
Family Saurornithoididae	U Cret.	Large-brained theropods
Family Oviraptoridae	U Cret.	Egg-eating theropods
Family Megalosauridae	M Jur.-U Cret.	Large to giant theropods
Family Tyrannosauridae	U Cret.	Gigantic theropods
Suborder Sauropodomorpha	U Tr.-U Cret.	Giant herbivores
Infraorder Plateosauria	U Tr.-L Jur.	Early giants
Infraorder Sauropoda	L Jur.-U Cret.	The greatest giants
Order Ornithischia		
Suborder Ornithopoda	L Jur.-U Cret.	Duck-billed ornithischians
Suborder Pachycephalosauria	Cret.	Dome-headed ornithischians
Suborder Stegosauria	L Jur.-U Cret.	Plated ornithischians
Suborder Ankylosauria	U Jur.-U Cret.	Armored ornithischians
Suborder Ceratopsia	Cret.	Horned ornithischians

graphic level that is designated as the Burgersdorp Formation in the more recent literature devoted to the geology of the famous Karroo beds. It is not at the very base of the Triassic sequence in South Africa (a position occupied by the *Lystrosaurus* zone, or Katberg Formation) but rather is at a level already preceded by sediments that represent a significant segment of very early Triassic history. Even so, *Euparkeria* is a thecodont sufficiently primitive to have been near the beginning of several archosaurian evolutionary lines.

(Dealing with a problem of ancestry such as this calls for raising a certain warning. More often than not, one is looking at ancestral *approximations* rather than the very ancestors themselves. Certain anatomical details in *Euparkeria*—the structure of the ankle, for example—bar it from a direct ancestry of the first theropod dinosaurs. Yet a wealth of other details is so clearly antecedent to what we see in early theropod dinosaurs that *Euparkeria* may logically be taken as a model for the kind of archosaurian reptile from which the ancestral theropods derived.)

Take the skull, for instance. The skull of *Euparkeria* is almost a textbook example of what the precursor to the skull of an early theropod dinosaur must have been like. Indeed, Rosalie Ewer, who published a monographic study of *Euparkeria* in 1965, had this to say.

"When he first described *Euparkeria* Broom was quite clear that he was dealing with a progressive but relatively unspecialized member of a group that probably included the ancestors of all the major lineages of the later archosaurs. He stressed the dinosaurian characters of the skull of *Euparkeria* and noted that 'there is nothing in the post-cranial skeleton that is not just what we should expect to find in the dinosaur ancestor'" (Ewer 1965:430).

The skull of *Euparkeria* is deep and narrow, and very "open," like that of *Coelophysis*. Not only is the orbit large, as are also the temporal openings on each side of the skull behind the eye, but on the front of the skull is a very large opening between the eye and the nostril—a constant theropod feature. Also there is an opening in the side of the lower jaw. As in *Coelophysis*, a ring of sclerotic plates is within the opening for the eye. Furthermore, the daggerlike teeth both in the skull and in the lower jaw of *Euparkeria* are compressed from side to side, to form sharp blades, while along the front and back keel-like edges of these teeth are fine serrations—the beginnings of the strong sawtoothlike serrations so prominent in *Coelophysis* and other theropod dinosaurs. The teeth around the margin of the skull, and the teeth in the lower jaw of *Euparkeria*, are set in sockets, as they are in dinosaurs. Indeed, the name *thecodont* means socketed teeth, a character typical of these Triassic archosaurs.

However, *Euparkeria* is still primitive in that it has numerous fine teeth on the bones of the palate, a basic reptilian character that is lost in the dinosaurs.

As for the skeleton behind the skull, *Euparkeria* has fairly long hind limbs, much larger than the forelimbs. The difference is not so great, however, as to have made *Euparkeria* a strictly bipedal animal; it probably rose on its hind limbs when it needed to run fast, but it also could walk on all four feet—something that *Coelophysis*, so highly specialized for bipedal locomotion, probably could not do. In other words, *Euparkeria* was a facultative biped, having the option of walking on its hind legs, not an obligatory biped, having no choice in this matter, as was *Coelophysis*. In this respect the femur of *Euparkeria* is not so specialized as that in *Coelophysis*; the *Euparkeria* femur does not have a distinct, rounded head, set off at an angle from the shaft of the bone, as does the Ghost Ranch dinosaur. Therefore, *Euparkeria* probably did not move the hind leg in so strictly a fore-and-aft fashion as did *Coelophysis*, which means that the thecodont was perhaps a slower and more awkward runner than was the dinosaur.

The pelvis of *Euparkeria*, the crucial attachment between the vertebral column and the hind limbs, is clearly on the way to becoming a saurischian dinosaur type pelvis, but in this more primitive archosaur it consists of a platelike combination of bones, lacking the more open construction so typical of *Coelophysis* and other theropod dinosaurs.

It may be remembered from chapter 7 that *Coelophysis* had a midtarsal joint in the ankle; in other words in this dinosaur, as in other theropods and in birds, the two upper bones of the ankle, the astragalus and the calcaneum, are closely appressed or even fused to the lower bones of the leg, the tibia and fibula respectively, so that movement of the foot occurs between the two rounded, pulleylike ankle bones and the long bones or metatarsals of the foot, with which some of the lesser ankle bones may be associated or even fused. This arrangement in *Coelophysis* made, as we have seen, for very free but strictly fore-and-aft controlled action of the foot. In *Euparkeria* the structure of the ankle is more primitive in that the astragalus is functionally a part of the tibia while the calcaneum is part of the ankle. Consequently, the joint comes between those two ankle bones, all in keeping with a hind leg that was not so strongly restricted to fore-and-aft movement.

The forelimbs of *Euparkeria* are much smaller than the hind limbs, but the disparity is not so great as in the theropod dinosaurs. Furthermore, three bones of the primitive reptilian shoulder girdle, the two clavicles (the collarbones of the human skeleton) and the median interclavicle are still present, bones that are lost in the theropod dinosaurs.

Otherwise, the skeleton of *Euparkeria* is what one might expect in an unspecialized archosaurian reptile. Between the skull and the pelvis are twenty-two vertebrae, seven of which may be considered as constituting the neck. The two sacral vertebrae are characteristic of generally primitive reptiles, and at least thirty-seven vertebrae comprise the long tail. The tail obviously was in part to balance the body in front of the pelvis, so even if *Euparkeria* was not an obligatory biped it could walk on two limbs. The pelvic-hind limb articulation was a dominant feature in this early thecodont's skeleton.

Lagosuchus, an extraordinarily small thecodont reptile, shows numerous characters that would seem to put it on a direct line toward the theropod dinosaurs, particularly *Coelophysis.* In essence, this little thecodont from the Middle Triassic Chañares Formation of Argentina occupies an evolutionary position about midway between the Lower Triassic *Euparkeria* and the Upper Triassic *Coelophysis.* Furthermore, it is significant that the skeleton of a reptile so small as *Lagosuchus* has many theropod dinosaur characters—which illustrates that size must be carefully judged and allotted to its proper place in determining the relationships of any animal, fossil or recent. Indeed, size may not under particular circumstances be of evolutionary significance, a fact that applies most appropriately to the present discussion.

Lagosuchus is a rather small reptile, the articulated skeleton being about thirty-nine centimeters or approximately one foot long. Yet this small creature exhibits various skeletal characters that are almost directly antecedent to those seen in *Coelophysis.* Thus the skull, so far as can be interpreted from presently known incomplete fragments, would seem to be relatively small and shallow in comparison to its length. The anterior vertebrae within the vertebral column, which may be designated as cervical or neck vertebrae, are elongated, although not to the relative degree seen in *Coelophysis.* Yet one can see here a trend toward the long neck so characteristic of *Coelophysis* and those other small podokesaurs and coelurids, generally known as coelurosaurians. The skeleton pivots at the articulation between the hind limb and the pelvis, with the tail somewhat longer than the length of the body from pelvis to the tip of the nose. The pelvis more closely approaches the saurischian type of pelvis than does this structure in *Euparkeria*, since the pubis and the ischium, broad, platelike bones in *Euparkeria*, have in *Lagosuchus* become rather slender in their basal portions, like in some of the early theropods.

The femur, or upper bone of the hind limb, is shorter than the tibia and fibula, a characteristic seen time and again in vertebrates adapted to swift running, and in contrast to *Euparkeria*, whose femur and tibia are essentially equal in length. But of especial significance is the fact that in *Lagosuchus* the ankle is of the mesotarsal type, just as in *Coelophysis* and other theropod dinosaurs, and birds as well, with the astragalus and calcaneum, the two upper ankle bones, functioning as parts of the tibia and fibula respectively. This important character puts *Lagosuchus* directly on a line leading to *Coelophysis*. The hind foot is long and slender, and functionally three-toed, with the first and fifth toes so comparatively short that they could not participate in locomotion. *Lagosuchus* must have made tiny, birdlike tracks in the mud. The forelimb is slender, significantly shorter than the hind limb, but not so short (as it is in *Coelophysis*) as to prevent this thecodont from running on all fours. In short *Lagosuchus* was a facultative, not an obligatory biped (Bonaparte 1975).

So much for the roots of *Coelophysis*, roots that at their farthest extension include the first basic reptiles, and from them on through subsequently younger geologic ages involve the ancestral diapsid reptiles and after them the thecodont reptiles—some of which were the immediate ancestors of the theropod dinosaurs. What are the first known theropod dinosaurs, and when and where did they live?

If this question can be answered by any known forms, it is probably *Staurikosaurus*, a dinosaur of advanced middle Triassic age from the Santa Maria Formation of Brazil, or *Herrerasaurus* and *Eoraptor*, from the Ischigualasto Formation of Argentina—which are perhaps slightly younger than the Brazilian sediments. Since I named and described *Staurikosaurus* quite a few years ago I am, of course, pleased that many paleontologists regard it as at or near the beginnings of dinosaurian history (Colbert 1970a:39). As for the name, *staurikos* means cross, a designation I chose because the skeleton on which the description was based was found in southern Brazil, where the constellation of the southern cross traverses the night sky, far below the equator.

Staurikosaurus, unfortunately, is based on an incomplete skeleton, but in paleontology one does the best one can with whatever is at hand. Perhaps some day a complete skeleton will be found to complete the picture we have of this supposedly oldest dinosaur. The skull is not known, but the lower jaw is present, and its length—approximately equal to that of the femur or upper hind limb bone—makes clear that the skull was relatively large. The teeth in the lower jaw are sharp. The vertebral column, the pelvis, and the hind limbs (without the feet) are known, but the forelimbs are missing, as are the ribs. Enough is present, however, to show that *Staurikosaurus* was almost certainly an obligatory biped—an active predator, about two meters, or six feet, long. Thus it is comparable in size to *Coelophysis.*

Herrerasaurus was first described about thirty years ago on the basis of rather fragmentary remains. It has long been thought to be of particular importance because of its age—Upper Triassic, a bit younger than *Staurikosaurus* and a bit older than *Coelophysis.* Recently, Paul Sereno of the University of Chicago and his paleontological colleague Fernando Novas of the Argentine Museum in Buenos Aires discovered a complete skeleton with skull of this early dinosaur, in the previously mentioned Ischigualasto Formation of northwestern Argentina—the same formation and general area where the first fragmentary remains were collected. Moreover, Sereno and his colleagues discovered and have described the skull of another theropod dinosaur in the Ischigualasto Formation. This skull, whose owner they have named *Eoraptor,* is obviously the most primitive known theropod skull; as such *Eorapter* represents the base from which the theropod dinosaurs evolved. So now we have available the well-documented remains of two early dinosaurs very close to the base of the dinosaurian evolutionary tree (and therefore more satisfactory as models of dinosaur beginnings than the still incomplete, even though possibly older, *Staurikosaurus*). What can these ancient dinosaurs tell us? (Sereno, Forster, Rogers, and Monetta 1993).

Herrerasaurus was a carnivorous dinosaur, an obligatory biped, with a large, narrow, deep skull, a moderately long neck, a long tail to balance the body, very strong hind limbs with the upper leg bones, the femora, joining a primitive type of saurischian pelvis, and relatively small forelimbs but not so reduced as the forelimbs of *Coelophysis.* Like *Staurikosaurus,* this was an active predator, a rapid runner on long hind limbs, with a large skull and lower jaw, thus providing a large "bite," capable of handling relatively large prey victims.

A word should be added as to the "primitive" saurischian pelvis noted above. This pelvis is remarkably similar to that of *Staurikosaurus,* and the pelvis of both these early dinosaurs, *Staurikosaurus* and *Herrerasaurus,* may quite logically be derived from the pelvis of *Lagosuchus.* In both dinosaurs and the thecodont, the upper bone of the pelvis, the ilium, is comparatively short and deep, the kind of pelvis that in 1964 I had the temerity to designate as of the brachyiliac, or "short ilium" type. In this pelvis the pubis and ischium are elongated and slender as compared to those bones in the pelvis of *Euparkeria,* yet even so they retain some of the broad, platelike features of the earliest thecodont pelvis. In contrast, the pelvis of *Coelophysis* is distinguished by a very long and comparatively low ilium. This kind of pelvis I designated as of the dolichoiliac, or "long ilium" type (Colbert 1964b:9, 18).

Therefore on the basis of pelvic structure, as well as the nature of the skull, the vertebral column, and the limbs, it would seem that although *Staurikosaurus* and *Herrerasaurus* are at present the oldest known theropod dinosaurs, they are not on a direct line between the thecodont *Lagosuchus* and the geologically younger *Coelophysis.* The relationships of the thecodonts and the theropod dinosaurs here discussed are shown in chart 1.

The genus *Coelophysis* was one of a very few late Triassic dinosaurs, perhaps a dozen genera or so, living on continents that were home to nondinosaurian reptiles. It might be said that in late Triassic time *Coelophysis* and its relatives had barely gained their several footholds in the regions where they lived; they were the scattered precursors of what were to be the vast hordes of dinosaurs that dominated the lands of Jurassic and Cretaceous history. They were dinosaurs living in a largely nondinosaurian world; the largest part of dinosaur evolution still lay ahead.

CHART 1
Relationships of Thecodonts and Theropod Dinosaurs

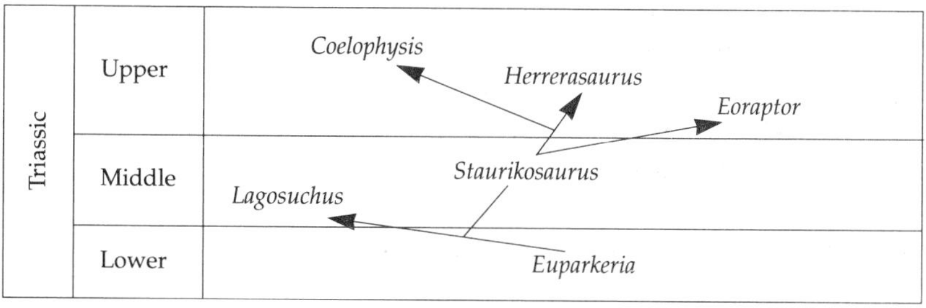

The Upper Triassic dinosaurs were mostly theropods, mostly belonging to the family that has been designated as the Podokesauridae—from the genus *Podokesaurus* found in the Triassic of the Connecticut Valley. Let us review briefly the story of *Podokesaurus,* a story with a sad ending. In 1911 the skeleton of a very small dinosaur came to the attention of Mignon Talbot, professor of geology at Mount Holyoke College, Massachusetts. Miss Talbot described her discovery of this dinosaur in the following words.

> In a bowlder of Triassic sandstone which the glacier carried two or three miles, possibly, and deposited not far from the site of Mount Holyoke College, the writer recently found an excellently preserved skeleton of a small dinosaur. . . . The bowlder was split along the plane in which the fossil lies and part of the bones are in one half and part in the other. These bones are hollow and the whole framework is very light and delicate.   (Talbot quoted by Lull 1953:13)

Although the skeleton suffered somewhat from the accident that had split the boulder into two pieces, it was nevertheless a reasonably good specimen, and was described and illustrated by Miss Talbot. She named it *Podokesaurus holyokensis.* Then in 1916 it was completely destroyed by a fire that gutted Williston Hall, the building containing the college's geological museum. Fortunately a cast of the specimen had been made at the Peabody Museum of Yale University, to be preserved for posterity. But a cast is not as good as the original specimen, especially if a study is to be made.

Back in the 1950s my good friend and colleague Don Baird, then of Princeton University, discovered in the collections of the Boston Society of Natural History a block of Triassic sandstone containing the *natural* casts of an associated pubis, tibia, and some ribs, all belonging to a small dinosaur. This block was found among the stones used in the construction of a nineteenth-century New England fort, Fort Adams, and was probably of the same kind of stone used for the society's museum. In fact, it was a "brownstone" block, of the type used so extensively in building the brownstone structures of Manhattan. It probably came from the Portland brownstone quarries, near Middletown, Connecticut. The block containing the fossil casts was presented to the society in 1864 by Professor William B. Rogers, and that same year a plaster replica of it was exhibited at the British Association for the Advencement of Science meeting in Bath, by Henry Rogers, a brother of William Rogers.

The preservation of these bone casts is unusual enough to merit an explanation here. In 1958 Don and I wrote,

Adhering to the surface of the block are traces of a soft red shale which evidently represents the alluvial plain on which the bones had come to rest, half embedded in silt. This silt became indurated enough to retain the imprints of the bones after the bones themselves had been swept away by the early freshets of the rainy season. Overflowing streams soon mantled the flood plain with arkosic sand from the fault-scarp uplands to the east, and this sand filled the bone impressions just as it did the footprints of dinosaurs and pseudosuchians on the plain.

(Colbert and Baird 1958:2)

Don and I studied the natural casts and described them in the article from which the above quotation is taken. We determined that the bone casts are from a small dinosaur, and we designated them as *Coelophysis* sp., thereby indicating that although the fossils probably represent *Coelophysis*, they are insufficient to warrant giving a species name. Measurements indicate that if these bone casts are of *Coelophysis* they represent an individual slightly larger than the then-known largest Ghost Ranch specimens. (It should be added that recently the preparation of a Ghost Ranch block has revealed the skeleton of a very large *Coelophysis*. Therefore the bone casts cannot be excluded from *Coelophysis* because of their size.)

In 1964 I made a comparative study of *Podokesaurus holyokensis*, as based upon the cast of the original skeleton, and of *Coelophysis bauri* based on Ghost Ranch specimens, and concluded that *Podokesaurus* is probably the same as *Coelophysis*. Although *Podokesaurus* is small compared to most *Coelophysis* specimens, measurements show that certain bones of the Connecticut Valley specimen, notably the femur and the tibia, when plotted on a graph showing femur length as related to tibia length, lie along the same straight regression line as do the corresponding bones from various specimens found at Ghost Ranch. So I concluded that the Triassic of North America may have two valid species of *Coelophysis: Coelophysis bauri* from New Mexico and *Coelophysis holyokensis* from Connecticut. This conclusion has been questioned by some paleontologists, and perhaps it is not justified. But whether correct or not, during late Triassic time small dinosaurs of the *Coelophysis* persuasion probably lived across the breadth of North America (Colbert 1964a).

Aside from *Podokesaurus*, the closest *Coelophysis* relative is a dinosaur discovered three decades ago, and half a world away, in what was then Rhodesia (now Zimbabwe) Africa. This dinosaur *Syntarsus rhodesiensis*, as it was named by its describer, Michael Raath, was found on the bank of a small stream about twenty miles northwest of the city of Bulawayo, entombed within a sandstone bed that is known as the Forest Sandstone—a horizon that may be equated with the Upper Karroo sediments of South Africa (Raath 1969). At the time of its discovery it was generally placed within the Upper Triassic sequence of southern Africa, but with the passing of years and the increased sophistication of knowledge of African geology, many authorities now consider the Forest Sandstone containing *Syntarsus* as of lowermost Jurassic affinities. Also, with the passing of years, additional materials of *Syntarsus* have been discovered at localities other than the original one near Bulawayo. In 1968 a well-preserved femur was found some four hundred fifty kilometers to the northeast of the original site, along the Maura River, in the central Zambezi River Valley. Of greater significance was the discovery in 1972 of a productive site on the Chitake River in the Zambezi Valley and some eighty kilometers to the west of the Maura River locality. This locality has yielded in a concentrated area the remains of more than thirty individuals of *Syntarsus*—an occurrence that may be compared to the Ghost Ranch deposit of *Coelophysis* skeletons. Raath has suggested that the concentration of skeletons in the Forest Sandstone of the Zambezi River Valley may indicate that some sort of a catastrophic event was responsible for the entombment of these particular dinosaurs.

Syntarsus, now known from a considerable sample of skeletons, is so remarkably close to *Coelophysis* in all aspects of its anatomy that some paleontologists have considered the genus from Africa to be synonymous with the North American form. Yet the differences, some subtle and some of considerable magnitude, make it reasonable to think that the African and North American dinosaurs are generically distinct. Let us stand the skeletons up, side by side.

Of course one cannot help being impressed by the similarity in size and appearance of the *Coelophysis* and *Syntarsus* skeletons. The *Coelophysis* skeleton (one of two extraordinary skeletons found side by side in the Ghost Ranch quarry, the specimen designated as American Museum of Natural History number 7223, is here chosen for the purpose of comparison with *Syntarsus*) is 254 centimeters, more than eight feet long, extended from the tip of the skull to the tip of the tail. The *Syntarsus* skeleton, as put together by Dr. Raath, is a little more than 200 centimeters long, or almost seven feet. The difference is not important, for the Ghost Ranch specimen is one of the larger individuals from the quarry; many other skeletons are comparable in size or even smaller than the skeleton of *Syntarsus,* as restored by Raath.

The meaningful differences between *Coelophysis* and *Syntarsus* are small and generally qualitative, and although they are not sufficiently great to mask the overall similarities between the two genera, they are numerous enough to indicate a schism that had occurred perhaps several million years in past Triassic history, as these two dinosaurs arose and developed from a common ancestor. To go into the details, point by point, that separate *Coelophysis* from *Syntarsus* would certainly be tedious and boring but a brief recounting of some of the characters that separate the two forms may give some idea of the gaps between them.

For example, *Coelophysis* has a few more teeth in the upper and lower jaws than does *Syntarsus;* twenty-six to thirty upper teeth on each side of the skull in *Coelophysis,* compared with twenty-three to twenty-four in *Syntarsus.* In the lower jaw the first-named genus has twenty-seven teeth on each side, while the second has twenty-five. As seen in side view, the large opening in the skull in front of the eye—the antorbital fenestra—is noticeably larger in *Syntarsus* than it is in *Coelophysis.* The skulls of the two genera show several other differences, especially in the relationships of the bones of the palate and of the occiput, but these will not be recounted here, important though they may be to the paleontological taxonomist involved up to his or her ears in such matters.

As for the skeleton behind the skull—the postcranial skeleton in anatomical jargon—it would appear that *Coelophysis*'s neck is relatively longer than is that of *Syntarsus,* on the order of more than twice the length of the skull, while in *Syntarsus* the neck is less than double the skull length. In the back, the flattened transverse processes of the *Coelophysis* vertebrae extend out laterally on each side, while in *Syntarsus* these features are swept back so that when seen from above, they appear shaped like the wings of a delta-wing aircraft. The difference between the two in the size of the forelimb, and especially the hand is quite noticeable. The hand of *Coelophysis* is comparatively large, its extended length being half again the length of the forearm. In *Syntarsus* the hand is considerably shorter than the forearm. Moreover, the three fingers of the *Coelophysis* hand are robust and terminate in large, curved claws. Evidently this was a strong, grasping hand, well suited to catching and holding prey, and in contrast to the small, apparently weaker hand of *Syntarsus.*

In *Coelophysis* the bones composing the pelvis were evidently discrete throughout life; in *Syntarsus* the pelvis in the adult animal is strongly ossified, so the component bones, the ilium, pubis, and ischium, form a single structure. The bones of the hind foot are usually distinct in *Coelophysis,* while in *Syntarsus* these bones commonly show considerable ossification, or binding together of certain bones in the foot, especially in adult animals. The two upper bones of the ankle, the calcaneum and astragalus, may be quite separate from each other in *Coelophysis* or they may be fused to form a single unified bone, a sort of pulley by means of which the hind foot rotates up and down, or back and forth, on the lower limb bones. Ossification of the two bones is a characteristic feature in *Syntarsus*.

Perhaps even this abbreviated list illustrates that the differences between *Coelophysis* and *Syntarsus* were numerous but small, and constant enough to show that the two dinosaurs were distinct animals. They almost had to be, since *Syntarsus* is geologically slightly younger than *Coelophysis*.

In 1989 Timothy Rowe of the University of Texas described a new species of *Syntarsus* from the Lower Jurassic Kayenta Formation, in northeastern Arizona. The Kayenta Formation is probably correlative in age with the Forest Sandstone of Africa. Dr. Rowe named this new species, based on a partial skull and skeleton, and fragments from sixteen additional individuals, *Syntarsus kayentakatae* (Rowe 1989). Two facts in particular should be mentioned concerning this new *Syntarsus*. First and most obviously, the geographic range of *Syntarsus* has been markedly extended, from a relatively restricted area in southern Africa to a distribution extending halfway around the world. (As we shall see later, the North American and African *Syntarsus* sites were probably not so far apart when these dinosaurs inhabited the early Jurassic world as they are today.) The second fact has to do with the skull of *Syntarsus kayentakatae*. On each side of the skull, on the skull roof just in front of the eye, a small, thin, but distinct crest formed of the lacrymal bone runs fore and aft above the antorbital foramen, the big opening in the skull in front of the eye. (Some skulls of *Coelophysis* show a subtle hint of such a crest, where the top of the skull makes a very sharp angle at its junction with the side of the skull in this location.) The two crests in the Arizona *Syntarsus* look very much as if they were the forerunners of the two large crests on the skull of *Dilophosaurus*, a theropod dinosaur, also from the Kayenta Formation.

In much of the literature about dinosaurs, one reads that the theropod dinosaurs, the only predatory dinosaurs, are divided into two great moieties, the "Coelurosauria" and the "Carnosauria." The former group comprises the "little" theropods, of which *Coelophysis* is a prime example. These are the theropod dinosaurs with skeletons commonly less than ten feet long, and often much less, with assumed body weights of at most a few hundred pounds, and often much less, slender bones, elongated hind limbs adapted for rapid running, small forelimbs, a rather long neck, and a relatively small, rather delicate skull. The latter group includes the "big" theropods, some of which are giants, such as the well-known *Tyrannosaurus*. These are the theropod dinosaurs with skeletons that may be as much as forty feet long, with assumed body weights frequently of several tons, stout bones as would have been necessary for the support of such large bodies, large, heavy hind limbs, again correlated with the necessity for gigantic bipeds to move with some degree of efficiency, often with ridiculously small forelimbs, and with huge, heavy skulls, supported by short, powerful necks.

This presumed dichotomy presents all too simple a picture, as we have come to realize with the passage of time and the consequent discovery of ever more theropods in the ever widening circle of fossil localities. Many theropods seem to share characteristics of both coelurosaurs and carnosaurs; the line between the two postulated groups is indeed fuzzy. Perhaps it is best to forget about coelurosaurs and carnosaurs, except in the most generalized of discussions, and to adopt a more fragmented and probably a more realistic classification of theropod dinosaurs.

Dilophosaurus, already briefly mentioned, is one of those theropods that seems to split the difference between small coelurosaurs and large carnosaurs. In fact, in various recent books and papers this dinosaur finds itself either towering over its supposed coelurosaurian relatives or dwarfed by its carnosaurian cousins. It is here suggested that *Dilophosaurus* is one of the podokesaurs (which places it among the coelurosaurs even though it is very much larger than the other theropods that have been assigned to the family of Podokesauridae).

Dilophosaurus was discovered by Dr. Sam Welles of the University of California at Berkeley, within the lower part of the Kayenta Formation in northern Arizona. Thus it is very close in its stratigraphic position as well as in its geographic locality to *Syntarsus*, also from the Kayenta Formation and also from northern Arizona. This occurrence, both in time and place has some interesting implications.

The *Dilophosaurus* skeleton is about six meters, or twenty feet, long—perhaps twice as long as the largest *Coelophysis*. In spite of its size it is lightly built, more like an enlargement of a *Coelophysis* skeleton than like the robust skeleton that so typifies the large carnosaur dinosaurs. Moreover the neck is elongated, and the skull, although somewhat enlarged, relatively speaking, over the skulls seen in *Coelophysis* and *Syntarsus*, is not the huge, deep skull that is so characteristic of the giant theropods of Jurassic and Cretaceous age. However, the skull *looks* big, because on each side of the skull roof there arises a large, longitudinal bony crest formed of the lacrymal and nasal bones. Consequently, two crests decorate the top of the skull of *Dilophosaurus*, side by side, and extend from the nares, the openings for the nostrils, at the front of the skull, to a point behind the eye. Furthermore, they are so high as effectively to double the apparent depth of the skull. Seen from the side, the upper contour of each crest is rounded, so that it appears on top of the skull like half a platter set on edge. The two crests diverge outwardly from their bases along the skull roof (Welles 1984).

Syntarsus kayentakatae from Arizona has a very small crest on each side, formed by a part of the lacrymal bone, while a slight indication of things to come may be seen on some skulls of *Coelophysis*, where this bone meets the skull roof, in front of the eye. It is therefore reasonable to think that we see in these late Triassic–early Jurassic podokesaurs a local example of evolutionary development in one skull character, taking place during the transition from Triassic to Jurassic time (see chart 2).

The transition from the small crests on the skull of *Syntarsus kayentakatae* to the very large crests that so dominate the skull of *Dilophosaurus* (if this proposed line of descent is properly interpreted) must have taken place during a short period of time, geologically speaking, since both forms are

CHART 2
Skull Development in Podokesaurs

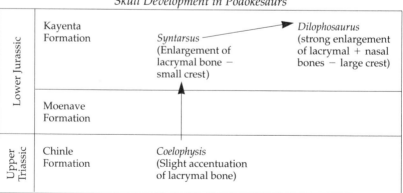

Lower Jurassic	Kayenta Formation	*Syntarsus* (Enlargement of lacrymal bone – small crest)	*Dilophosaurus* (strong enlargement of lacrymal + nasal bones – large crest)
	Moenave Formation		
Upper Triassic	Chinle Formation	*Coelophysis* (Slight accentuation of lacrymal bone)	

found in the lower part of the Kayenta Formation. But it is not surprising; the fossil record displays so many examples of bursts of evolutionary development that Niles Eldredge and Stephen Jay Gould coined a term, "punctuated equilibrium," to explain the usual process of evolutionary development as they saw it—long periods of stasis or evolutionary stagnation, punctuated by bursts of rapid evolution. Whether evolution is dominantly a matter of fits and starts interrupting long periods of quiescence or occurs by gradual steps is a matter that can be debated. I do not propose to get into the argument here (Eldredge and Gould 1972).

Dilophosaurus is probably the first and one of the few, theropod dinosaurs to have large outgrowths on the skull. A few later theropods have horns on the skull, but for the most part the skull roof in these dinosaurs is relatively smooth, which is what might be expected. Carnivorous reptiles and mammals do not ordinarily have horns, antlers, or crests on the skull, unlike the herbivores—the plant-eating ornithischians among the dinosaurs and the so-called ungulates, or hoofed mammals, in the modern world. It is hard to envision a tiger with horns; such growths on the skull would probably be disadvantageous to a predator, an animal that must concentrate its functions for survival in the powerful jaws and sharp teeth.

Therefore, what is the meaning of two large crests on the skull of *Dilophosaurus,* a most predatory dinosaur? Some students have maintained that the crests were nothing more than display devices, anatomical features that perhaps made the dinosaur look bigger to other dinosaurs than it really was, therefore enabling it to establish dominance. The modern frilled lizard of Australia, for example, can erect a frill, or collar of skin, that encircles the neck, thereby making itself look like a large and terrifying object when it faces an adversary. This is known as agonistic behavior. But the crests on the skull of *Dilophosaurus* were permanent structures that could not be changed to suit the occasion. Perhaps they served as do the antlers in modern male deer, which if antagonistic face each other, and often the one with the larger antlers prevails; he faces down his opponent without having to resort to combat. Is it possible that the crests of *Dilophosaurus* may have been limited to males? There is not sufficient material to determine this.

As opposed to the hypothesis of display, is it possible that the cranial crests of *Dilophosaurus* were temperature regulating devices, which because of the considerable area of skin that covered them were able to absorb heat from the sun, or conversely to radiate heat if the animal were in the shade? But why should such radiators be confined, so far as we know, to just one genus among the theropod dinosaurs? Here we have a problem that remains totally within the realm of speculation—and there we must leave it.

All this has taken us away from *Coelophysis*, but it illustrates lines of evolutionary development that may have been followed by some close relatives, or perhaps even the descendants of the Ghost Ranch dinosaur.

In 1990 a massive, comprehensive book edited by David Weishampel, Peter Dodson, and Halszka Osmólska was published, entitled *The Dinosauria*, in which numerous dinosaurian authorities contributed chapters pertaining to their particular fields of expertise. In one chapter, called "Ceratosauria," Tim Rowe and Jacques Gauthier of the California Academy of Sciences argue that *Coelophysis*, *Syntarsus*, *Dilophosaurus*, and four other theropods, including *Ceratosaurus* from the Upper Jurassic Morrison Formation of North America, should be placed together within a group that they designated as the Ceratosauria (Rowe and Gauthier 1990). *Ceratosaurus* was first described by O. C. Marsh in 1884, who placed it in a family of its own—the Ceratosauridae. Other paleontologists through the years either followed Marsh, or have considered this genus as not requiring a separate familial allocation and have grouped it with the giant theropod *Allosaurus*.

It seems to me that *Ceratosaurus* probably deserves to be given a family of its own. So *Coelophysis* is here regarded not as a ceratosaur but as a podokesaur, as it has been through the years, a member of a group of early theropod dinosaurs retaining many primitive theropod characters that were established as these dinosaurs became differentiated from their Triassic thecodont ancestors.

An almost universal trend in the various evolutionary lines of the dinosaurs was growth to large and even gigantic size through the years. Yet this was not always the case. Thus we find certain later Mesozoic theropod dinosaurs that, having evolved from origins not far removed from *Coelophysis*, continued the "coelurosaurian" pattern of small size. These little theropods probably lived protected lives sheltered by friendly vegetation and preyed on very small animals such as little lizards, snakes, insects, or even some of the early primitive mammals, many of which were no larger than shrews or very small rodents.

One striking example is *Compsognathus*, known from two skeletons found in the Upper Jurassic rocks of Europe, one from the famous Solnhofen Limestone of Germany, the locality and horizon that has yielded the seven skeletons of the first bird, *Archaeopteryx*. The Solnhofen *Compsognathus* reveals a tiny theropod less than a meter, or three feet, long, including a very long tail, with a probable body weight, as estimated by Dr. John Ostrom, of about three kilograms, or six and a half pounds (Ostrom 1978). This smallest of the theropods is in essence a reduced version of *Coelophysis*, with relatively longer hind limbs. The hand of *Compsognathus* is so specialized that it has only two small fingers. It probably originated from a base in common with that of *Coelophysis*, or perhaps it was an offshoot from the podokesaurid evolutionary tree, not far removed from *Coelophysis*. That *Compsognathus* was an effective predator is proved by the presence of a small lizard skeleton within the body cavity of the Solnhofen specimen.

Another coelurosaurian dinosaur, not very far removed from *Coelophysis*, is *Ornitholestes* from the Upper Jurassic Morrison Formation of Wyoming, the region and the geologic level that has yielded so many skeletons of giant dinosaurs: brontosaurs and the gigantic theropods, including *Ceratosaur::s*, that may have preyed upon them. *Ornitholestes*, a small and modified version of the *Coelophysis* pattern (see figure 46), is a theropod about two meters, or six feet, long, whose skull is shorter and deeper, and forelimbs larger compared to *Coelophysis*. The relatively large arms and hands of *Ornitholestes* indicate that it may have used them for catching prey. (Professor Osborn, who described this dinosaur, named it with the rather far-fetched supposition that it may have preyed on the ancestral bird *Archaeopteryx*. *Ornitholestes* means "bird-robber" [Osborn 1917:735–38].)

Certain late Cretaceous theropods designated as ornithomimosaurs carry the *Coelophysis* structural pattern, with modifications, into the latest years of dinosaurian history. *Struthiomimus*, often called the "ostrich dinosaur" because it is about the size of an ostrich (but with a long tail, of course), is in some ways like an enlarged version of *Coelophysis*, more than four meters, or about fourteen feet, long. This dinosaur has long, strong hind limbs, clearly adapted for fast running, and its forelimbs are fairly large, with long, three-fingered hands, well engineered for grasping and manipulating food. The long and supple neck supports a relatively small and fragile skull, without teeth (Osborn 1917:738–61). In fact, the skull of the *Struthiomimus* and its closely related genera are remarkably birdlike. It seems evident that, having lost its teeth, the jaws of *Struthiomimus* were covered with a horny beak, as in modern birds. In short, *Struthiomimus* was

FIGURE 46   *Ornitholestes hermanni,* from the Upper Jurassic beds of Wyoming. Restoration by Charles Knight. Here one sees a small theropod dinosaur, very similar to *Coelophysis* in size and adaptations, but some seventy-five million years younger than the Ghost Ranch dinosaur.

a theropod dinosaur that anticipated by many millions of years (but is not ancestral to) the modern ostrichs in general adaptations, and probably in habits. *Struthiomimus* is but one of several genera of these ornithomimosaurs that are widely represented in the Upper Cretaceous beds of western North American and northeastern Asia.

An amazing discovery has recently been announced by Sankar Chatterjee, who has described from the Upper Dockum Formation of Texas— stratigraphically equivalent to the Upper Chinle from which *Coelophysis* has been collected—a toothless theropod dinosaur that seems to be a form ancestral to the ornithomimids of late Cretaceous age. Though smaller than the Cretaceous ornithomimids, this new dinosaur, which Chatterjee has named *Shuvosaurus inexpectatus* (most definitely an unexpected theropod), bears an uncannily close resemblance to the well-known Cretaceous "ostrich dinosaurs." Of course, it might be an early theropod that followed an evolutionary path parallel to that of the late Cretaceous ornithomimosaurs, or it might be that the toothless, birdlike ornithomimosaurs had a long evolutionary history, going back almost to the beginnings of dinosaurian evolution. All of this demonstrates that those who collect and study fossils must be prepared for surprises, great and small.

A footnote: it should be said that in Mongolia a discovery was made years ago of a pair of forelimbs, or "arms," of an ornithomimid-like dinosaur, *Deinocheirus*, of unbelievably huge size, whose three-fingered hands terminated in great, curved claws of such large dimensions as to make the claws of a grizzly bear seem puny. This dinosaur could have picked up an animal the size of a grown man with ease. What was it? To date only the arms and hands are known. But from them we know that in late Cretaceous time a gigantic ornithomimosaur, a giant almost beyond imagination, roamed the landscapes of Central Asia.

The role call of theropods heretofore set forth—the various podokesaurs including *Dilophosaurus*, the ostrichlike ornithomimosaurs, and such persistently small coelurosaurs as *Compsognathus* and *Ornitholestes*—has introduced us to the close and reasonably close relatives of *Coelophysis*. These are the theropod dinosaurs that have largely retained the structural pattern of the skeleton, albeit with modifications, that is so abundantly exemplified by *Coelophysis* from Ghost Ranch. What now can be said about the numerous other theropod dinosaurs?

They may be characterized as those theropods that departed from the *Coelophysis* pattern in one way or another. Some departures were along the lines of highly modified anatomical characters, adaptations for specialized modes of life. Others were along the line followed by so many dinosaurs, the line leading to giantism. Even though some consideration of these divergent lines of theropod evolution will lead us away from the protagonist of this story—*Coelophysis*—it may be helpful to discuss them briefly in order to appreciate the degree to which the various theropods adapted to widely differing modes of life during Jurassic and Cretaceous times.

One of the most remarkable of the theropod dinosaurs is *Deinonychus*, excavated from the Lower Cretaceous Cloverly Formation in Montana by John Ostrom of Yale Peabody Museum, and described by him in detail (Ostrom 1969). *Deinonychus* is not a large theropod but it is not exactly small, either, its total length being between three and three and a half meters, or about ten feet. The skeleton, although mostly of conventional theropod form, is distinguished by an overlay of remarkable specializations that make this dinosaur one of the most unusual predatory dinosaurs. Yet the adaptations that make *Deinonychus* seem so weird a creature at first sight are the logical results of evolutionary specializations for a very definite kind of life. What are the features of the *Deinonychus* skeleton that so distinguish this predator?

First, even though the skeleton is not very large, the skull is relatively large, similar in shape and proportions to those of the large gigantic carnosaurian dinosaurs of late Jurassic and Cretaceous times. It is robust and deep, quite different from the long, low skull so characteristic of podokesaurids like *Coelophysis*. Because of this enlargement of the skull, the jaws have a large bite, of prime importance to the aggressive predator that *Deinonychus* is believed to have been. The enlargement of the skull was accompanied by a shortening of the neck, by shortening each neck vertebra and in particular skewing the articulations between the individual vertebrae so that its neck was carried in a more upright position than was that of small-skulled theropods like *Coelophysis*.

This is not particularly unusual; large skulls and short necks are seen in many big theropods. It is in the skeleton behind the skull that one sees the distinctive characters of this highly specialized theropod.

Thus the forelimbs of *Deinonychus* are comparatively large—larger in relation to the body than in any other theropod dinosaur—and the hands are enormous for a dinosaur of this size, with the three fingers terminating in large, sickle-shaped claws. But perhaps the most astonishing feature of *Deinonychus* is the structure of the foot. There are the usual five toes, two of them reduced in size, as is common in theropod dinosaurs. The fifth toe is diminished to a mere splint—the remnant of a metatarsal being all that remains. The first toe is so short that it probably never touched the ground. Even so, it had a large claw. Three toes are functional, again as is common in theropod dinosaurs, but of these only two, the third and fourth, are so constructed as to have been useful during locomotion. These two toes are essentially equal in length (toe number three, the middle toe of the foot, being no longer than toe number four) for it is evident that they were the "running" toes of this dinosaur. In other words, *Deinonychus* was a didactyl, or two-toed, runner, which was most unusual in the dinosaur world. The second toe of the foot is remarkable because of its enormous claw, which was held in an elevated position, ready for instant use as a weapon. In other words, this second toe was no longer a part of the locomotor apparatus; it was strictly a weapon.

Another feature in the skeleton of *Deinonychus*, almost as amazing and unexpected as the huge slashing claw of the second toe, is the strange tail, the posterior two-thirds of which is stiffened by long bony rods above and below the vertebrae; this part of the tail must have functioned like a long staff, almost but not quite unbending. The rods that stiffen this part of the tail are offshoots from the prezygapophyses—the bony knobs that carry the supplementary articulations between vertebrae—on the upper side of the tail and from the chevron bones, which in reptiles are located between the vertebrae on the lower side of the tail. Each individual rod laps over about eight vertebrae, so that as this occurs to successive vertebrae, the long rods form stiff bundles on the upper and lower parts of the tail throughout the back part of its length. (It may be recalled that in *Coelophysis* elongated bony rods developed from the cervical ribs in the neck, but these obviously were flexible.)

The front part of the tail, in which the vertebrae are of normal structure, must have been rather flexible, but from about the tenth tail vertebra to the tip of the tail this part of the appendage acted very much as a single unit that could be swung from side to side. It has been suggested that the stiff tail in *Deinonychus* acted as a balancing device, enabling this dinosaur to maintain its posture while running on its two-toed feet, or leaping during an attack, and to change direction quickly while running at top speed.

Dr. Ostrom has visualized *Deinonychus* as a fearful predator—a very tough customer among a host of aggressive predators. Perhaps, he thinks, *Deinonychus* hunted in packs; several individuals might attack a large, inoffensive, plant-eating dinosaur, like wolves attacking a moose in the snows of Canada, or like hyenas attacking a wildebeest on the African veldt. It is suggested that *Deinonychus* might have held its victim in the iron grasp of its large clawed hands, while slashing and tearing the unfortunate object of its hunt with the huge claws of the second toes in the hind feet. It seems a reasonable interpretation of this highly evolved predator.

Even though *Deinonychus* seems far removed from other theropod dinosaurs because of its extreme specializations, an analysis of all its anatomical characters indicates that it probably derived from a coelurosaurian ancestor, not so very distant from *Coelophysis* and its Triassic–early Jurassic relatives. *Deinonychus* belongs to a moderate-size group of theropods largely of late Cretaceous age, known as dromaeosaurs. Many of the dromaeosaurs show the specialization of the second toe that has a large claw similar to that of *Deinonychus*. But of particular significance in the evolution of the dromaeosaurs was the enlargement of the brain; as can be seen from the structure of the skull, the brain in the dromaeosaurs was comparable in relative size to that in many birds and in primitive living mammals. These theropods may be generally regarded as the "wolves" of the Mesozoic—dinosaurs that not only were specialized for very aggressive hunting but also were more intelligent than most of their dinosaur contemporaries.

Various other small theropods descended from beginnings not far removed from *Coelophysis*. One interesting small theropod from the Cretaceous sediments of Mongolia is *Oviraptor*. This dinosaur, more or less the size of *Coelophysis*, exhibits the usual primitive theropod structural pattern except for the skull, which is short and toothless, and appears to have a small horn on the nose. The lower jaw is very deep and also toothless. It seems probable that this dinosaur had horny coverings on its jaws, forming a sort of beak, and it may have fed on the eggs of other Cretaceous dinosaurs. Recently David Smith has advanced convincing arguments that *Oviraptor* was in fact unique—an herbivorous theropod (Smith 1992).

Almost all the theropod dinosaurs that have been described up to this point have been small or moderate in size, which is not surprising because obvious ecological niches existed for small and medium-size theropods inhabiting the forests and plains of Jurassic and Cretaceous times—theropods that retained, frequently with remarkable modifications, the primitive pattern exemplified in many respects by *Coelophysis*. But the giant predators also were there and through the years have received a tyrannosaur's undue share of attention because of their fearsome size. These large and gigantic theropods, the often styled carnosaurs, make a fitting ending to this survey of the theropods.

One of the first two dinosaurs to be described was a large theropod, *Megalosaurus*, named in 1824, as mentioned by the Reverend William Buckland, almost two decades before the concept of Dinosauria was established by Richard Owen in 1842. *Megalosaurus*, which was more fully described by von Meyer in 1832, became during the middle years of the nineteenth century such a standard in Europe for giant predatory theropods that dinosaurs of this general type were often referred to as megalosaurs.

But with the passage of time, more large theropods were discovered, especially in western North America. The discoveries of giants included the finding of *Allosaurus* in the Upper Jurassic Morrison beds of Colorado and Wyoming and of *Tyrannosaurus* (today perhaps the best-known of the giant theropods) in the late Cretaceous Hell Creek beds of Montana. During the past several decades many gigantic theropods have come to light from around the world.

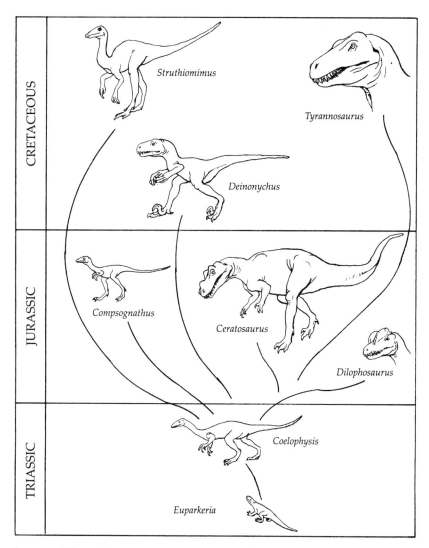

FIGURE 47 Evolution of the theropod dinosaurs. To approximate relative scale. Drawing by Margaret Colbert.

One might say that the giant theropods of late Jurassic and Cretaceous times, call them what you will, are cut from a single pattern—but, as must always be said when describing dinosaurs, a pattern with modifications. The giants were, literally, giants, with skeletons of ten or fifteen meters, or thirty to forty feet, and more in length. When alive these giant predators weighed several tons, perhaps as much as eight tons in the case of *Tyran-nosaurus*. And being of such size they show the modifications necessary in an animal of great weight.

The skull in the giant predators—as exemplified by the greatest of the giants, *Tyrannosaurus*—is huge, thus providing these carnivores with long jaws capable of opening to facilitate huge bites. Such jaws, armed with dag-gerlike teeth, were necessary in carnivores that preyed on other giants— the vegetarian sauropods, or brontosaurs, and the various herbivorous or-nithischian dinosaurs. Of course, a skull like the one in *Tyrannosaurus* can-not be supported by a long neck of the kind common in the small theropods, and so in this giant and its relatives the neck is short and very strong. Likewise the vertebral column is robust, while the sacrum, the at-tachment between the vertebrae and the pelvis, is exceedingly strong, it had to be. The hind limbs are heavy, as necessary to support such great weight, while the three-toed hind foot is remarkably compact, with the metatarsal bones being squeezed together to form in effect a solid, unified structure. Giant theropods like this have left their footprints in stone, which show us that the big bipeds walked majestically across the land-scape. They probably lacked the fleetness of foot that characterized the smaller, lighter theropods, but nonetheless the giant carnivores must have been capable of moving at considerable speed. Finally, the forelimbs in the giant theropods are relatively small, sometimes ridiculously small, an indi-cation that the predatory functions of these big reptiles were concentrated in the powerful jaws. The tiny hands of *Tyrannosaurus*, for example, consist of but two fingers, the first and second digits of the original five-fingered hand typical of primitive reptiles (Osborn 1917:761–71).

It has been suggested that because of their puny arms, these giant theropods were scavengers rather than predators. Perhaps, but it seems more likely that they were both predators *and* scavengers. Consider the lion today in Africa. This great cat is a fearsome predator, but it does not hesitate to scavenge now and then. Most predators aim to obtain their food with the minimum expenditure of energy and risk. Costly predation, in terms of energy output and injury, is self-defeating.

It was a long journey in time from the Upper Triassic, and *Coelophysis*, to the Upper Cretaceous, and *Tyrannosaurus*. But through this journey the theropods, despite the diversity of their evolutionary lines, maintained the basic structural pattern of bipedal predators: strong jaws usually supplied with sharp teeth, the body pivoted where the hind limbs join the pelvis, the long tail counterbalancing the body, and the forelimbs commonly rather small. It was a pattern for predation—valid in *Coelophysis,* one of the first theropods to follow this pattern, and valid in all the modified relatives and descendants of *Coelophysis,* from the consistently small coelurosaurs, to the ostrichlike struthiomimosaurs, to the viciously aggressive dromaeosaurs, particularly as exemplified by *Deinonychus,* finally to the gigantic tyrannosaurs and their carnosaur cousins of late Jurassic and Cretaceous times. Yet in spite of the diversity seen in the theropod dinosaurs it is possible to look beyond these varied predators to the beginning of it all, represented in essence by the little dinosaurs of Ghost Ranch.

———————————— ▬ ————————————

TEN

CONTEMPORARIES AND COMPETITORS

The animals living with *Coelophysis* in the tropical landscape that once spread across today's American Southwest were numerous and varied, and most of them were anything but dinosaurian. *Coelophysis*, although a fully developed theropod dinosaur, by virtue of its status as an evolutionary pioneer—indeed, one of the first of its kind—was destined to play a lonesome phylogenetic role among the vertebrates that lived during Chinle times. The days when dinosaurs were to dominate the continents were still millions of years in the future; consequently, the rulers of the Chinle scene were reptiles other than dinosaurs, some of them much larger and in many cases more aggressive than the small, one might say fledgling, dinosaurs of the late Triassic.

One may speak of the amphibians and reptiles that lived during the late Triassic time in the American Southwest as the Chinle fauna, but actually two different faunas are found in the Chinle Formation: a rather rich assemblage in the lower part of the formation and a somewhat more restricted fauna in the upper part. We have seen that *Coelophysis* occurs at such a high level in the Petrified Forest beds at Ghost Ranch that some workers would place it within a distinct stratigraphic zone, the siltstone member above the Petrified Forest Member, as it is called by some; the separate Owl Rock Member as it has been designated by others. In the Petrified Forest of Arizona the Lower and Upper units of the Petrified Forest Member of the Chinle Formation are separated from each other by the very distinct Sonsela Sandstone, but in other areas, as at Ghost Ranch, there is no such convenient separator.

The distinction between the low and high faunas in the Chinle Formation is not so much a difference in the nature of the included fossils—although this is a factor—as it is a matter of the presence or absence of various genera and species of amphibians and reptiles. A few specific differences occur among genera at both levels, and these may be attributable to evolutionary advances during the course of Chinle history. The major differences between the lower and upper faunas may be summarized as follows.

The lower fauna shows an abundance of fish, compared to the upper fauna. The difference may be a result of the accidents of discovery, or it may reflect a real difference in environments—between swampy lowlands at the lower level and drier, more upland landscapes that prevailed near the end of Chinle time and consequently were recorded in the upper level fauna. This same environmental difference may be responsible for the perceived occurrences of amphibians, notably the gigantic, heavy-skulled labyrinthodont, *Metoposaurus*—a genus that is abundant at lower levels, but rare in upper Chinle sediments. By contrast, various genera and species of phytosaurs, all of which were water-loving reptiles comparable to the crocodilians of our modern world, are abundant not just in the lower levels of the Chinle Formation, along with *Metoposaurus,* but also with *Coelophysis* at Ghost Ranch and at very high levels in the Chinle Formation at other localities.

The absence at high Chinle levels of the little lizardlike procolophonid, probably of the genus *Hypsognathus,* of the large lizardlike reptile *Trilophosaurus,* and of the small long-necked swimmer *Tanytrachelos*—all well represented at lower levels, or in equivalents of the lower levels, such as in the Dockum beds of Texas—may very well be due to the accidents of discovery or perhaps even the extinction of these forms during the passage of Chinle time. On the other hand, the large mammal-like dicynodont *Placerias*—a very large reptile of oxlike proportions—is notably absent, perhaps because it was extinct by the time *Coelophysis* roamed the land. (It is probable that soon after this book is published, somebody will find nice *Placerias* bones at the very top of the Chinle Formation, nicely intermingled with the bones of *Coelophysis.* Such are the risks of making positive statements when dealing with paleontological possibilities.)

With the foregoing remarks in mind, we may now turn to a consideration of the contemporaries of *Coelophysis*. This chapter analyzes how *Coelophysis* might have lived among the animals of Chinle time and its ecological relationships with vertebrate contemporaries with which the little dinosaur might have come into contact; as a benign neighbor, as a predatory competitor for food or for living space, or as a wary fugitive ever alert to avoid annihilation from some of the larger nondinosaurian predators that dominated the Chinle forests and waterways. This assessment will consider the vertebrate fossils from both the lower and upper levels of the Chinle sedimentary sequence. *Coelophysis* obviously experienced confrontations with the upper-level vertebrates, but discussion will also cover those fossils found in lower Chinle deposits, on the assumption that some of them might have existed in late Chinle times, as we know others did. The vertebrates under consideration are the Chinle fish, amphibians, and reptiles, while brief attention will be given to the possibility that primitive Chinle mammals might have been present in the world where *Coelophysis* lived.

FISH

Abundant fish roamed the freshwater streams and lakes of Chinle time, especially the waterways that were so widely distributed early in the period. Since the remains of fish, usually rather fragmentary, have been found at the Ghost Ranch quarry, one may ask the obvious question: was *Coelophysis* a fish-eater as well as a predator of various land-living animals? Perhaps. It seems reasonable to think that a reptile probably as quick and alert as was *Coelophysis* might very well have probed the shallows of rivers and ponds for whatever fish could be caught there. And perhaps it scavenged dead fish along drought-diminished shores.

The opportunities were plentiful, for in Chinle time the waterways were inhabited by a considerable array of primitive bony fish—known as chondrosteans (related in a general way to the modern paddlefins and sturgeons) and those known as holosteans (related, also in a general way, to the modern bowfins). There were also some small freshwater sharks, as well as two interesting fish belonging to groups that were more or less along the lines leading to the earliest land-living vertebrates—ancestral amphibians. These were *Ceratodus*, a lungfish closely related to its modern counterpart, the Australian lungfish (*Neoceratodus*), and *Chinlea*, related to the modern coelacanth fish *Latimeria*.

As for the bony fish, represented by such chondrostean genera as *Turseodus, Cionichthys, Lasalichthys, Synorichthys,* and *Tanaocrossus* and by the

holostean genera *Semionotus* and *Hemicalypterus*, we see an array of generally small fish, three to eight inches (six to twenty centimeters) long,
mostly of primitive, fusiform shape, and covered by rather heavy, rhom-
boid scales. *Hemicalypterus* is a deep-bodied fish, very peculiar in that the
front of the body is covered with the heavy scales so characteristic of
these fish, while the back part seems to lack such scales. Perhaps the outer covering of heavy scales in all these fish may have protected them from
predators; conversely, perhaps *Coelophysis* was capable of handling these
little fish.

Lungfish tooth plates, well adapted for crushing small mollusks, are not
uncommon in the Chinle Formation—an indication that these versatile
fish may have been fairly abundant in Triassic freshwater environments.
As has been mentioned, *Ceratodus* from the Chinle Formation is anatomi-
cally close to its modern relative, *Neoceratodus*, which lives today in the rivers of Australia. The Australian lungfish, about three feet or a meter long,
surfaces to gulp air when the waters in which it lives become so foul as to be
depleted of oxygen. The same must have been true in Triassic time, and
such behavior, which made *Ceratodus* vulnerable when it came up for air,
may have made it tempting to a hungry *Coelophysis* wandering along the
edge of a pond or even wading in the shallow water.

Along with *Ceratodus*—which with its relatives and descendants were
evolving toward living out of the water but never quite made it—is *Chinlea*,
a crossopterygian fish, a member of a large category of so-called lobefin
fishes with lungs, some of which did make the transition to land, to become the ancestors of the first amphibians. But *Chinlea* belongs to that sub-
division of the crossopterygians known as coelacanths, which evolved toward continued life in the water, especially in oceanic waters. These
particular crossopterygian fish were long supposed to have become extinct
with the end of the Cretaceous history, until the discovery a little more than
a half century ago of *Latimeria*, a coelacanth living in the ocean off the east
coast of Africa. The discovery of *Latimeria*, a large fish as much as six feet (2
meters) long, was one of the most exciting events of modern evolutionary
zoology.

In Triassic time the freshwater coelacanths, as exemplified by *Chinlea*,
were comparatively small, ranging from six to twenty inches (fifteen to sixty centimeters) long. This lobefinned fish was probably an aggressive
predator, preying on other small fish in the Chinle rivers and lakes (Schaeffer 1967).

AMPHIBIANS

One of the most prevalent inhabitants of Chinle streams and ponds, judging by the abundance of its fossil remains (equaled only by the abundance of phytosaur bones and teeth), was the gigantic amphibian *Metoposaurus*, commonly found in the lower Chinle sediments and in reduced numbers in the upper sediments. (See figure 48.) (One should not be confused by the linguistic stem *saurus* in this generic name; the animal is a true amphibian in spite of the original designation, conferred in the early days of paleontological studies, when the exact natures of some fossils were not fully understood.) *Metoposaurus* is a labyrinthodont amphibian, so designated because of the structure of its tooth enamel, which, instead of being a simple layer covering the tooth, is complexly infolded to form (when seen in cross-section) sinuous curves of remarkable intricacy. This big amphibian is about six to eight feet (2 to 2.5 meters) long with a huge, flat, and heavy skull, a strange shoulder girdle the lower bones of which (clavicles and interclavicle) are likewise large, flat, and heavy, weak vertebrae, a rather

FIGURE 48   A section of the Petrified Forest National Park mural, showing late Triassic Chinle life. At the bottom of the picture, in the water, is a long-snouted phytosaur that has just caught a large lungfish. In front of it is the large labyrinthodont amphibian *Metoposaurus*. Coming to the river shore, immediately above the phytosaur, is the armored, horned thecodont *Desmatosuchus* and, to the right, the dicynodont *Placerias*. Descending a slope behind *Placerias* is the armored thecodont *Typothorax*. Dinosaurs also appear in the far distance.

small pelvis attached to the spinal column by a single vertebra, and small, weak limbs. This grotesque (to us) vertebrate was evidently an almost full-time inhabitant of the water, where it rested on the bottom of shallow streams and ponds, waiting for unwary fish to come within reach of its widely gaping jaws. In fact, it has been suggested that perhaps a part of the *Metoposaurus* tongue was specialized as a sort of colorful fish-lure, to entice fish into the mouth of the big amphibian; of course, this must remain speculation (Colbert and Imbrie 1956).

Coelophysis and *Metoposaurus* probably had little close contact, even though the dinosaur may frequently have traversed the mud flats contiguous to the habitat of the big amphibian, leaving trackways of such crossings. Perhaps it is significant that at the Ghost Ranch quarry, where the fossils consist overwhelmingly of *Coelophysis* remains, there are some other reptilian fossils, and even some fish, yet *Metoposaurus* is notably absent, as is usually the case in upper Chinle strata. *Coelophysis* and *Metoposaurus* seemingly did not frequent the same ecological environments, even though they may have been contemporaries.

REPTILES

During pre-Triassic Permian history, the largest and most dominant reptiles were synapsids, or mammal-like reptiles. Many of these were aggressive predators, others were large herbivores. All of them were quadrupedal animals, in which the adaptations for walking and running across the land were refinements, after a fashion, of the primitive reptilian methods of locomotion. These reptiles were competent but perhaps not altogether efficient walkers, with legs that were not notably elongated, so that steps were short, and with the elbows everted so that the forelimbs, at least, did not move forward and backward in a straight vertical plane, but in a rotary fashion. The hind limbs may have been more efficiently utilized, but these therapsids probably were not particularly fast at covering ground.

Then came the transition into Triassic time—and enter the thecodonts, with a radical new plan for locomotion and feeding that has been described above. To recapitulate, the limbs are frequently elongated, and from the beginning a trend developed toward bipedal locomotion, for running on the hind limbs, which are notably larger than the fore limbs. Such a change in the structure of the reptiles increased their speed, often quite dramatically, and freed the forelimbs for other uses—particularly as adjuncts for feeding—for grasping their prey. Furthermore, the evolutionary trends in the skull and jaws frequently toward increased size and decreased weight introduced new and more efficient means of predatory feeding. Such were the innovations that appeared with the initiation of Triassic history—innovations that pointed directly toward the theropod dinosaurs. Indeed, *Euparkeria*, which appeared in southern Africa with the onset of the Triassic, has a very theropod-like skull. Then as Triassic history unfolded some of the thecodonts veered away from the ancestral carnivore pattern, to develop as large herbivores, heavily armored against attacks from their predatory cousins.

To look a little more closely at the thecodonts, these first of the archosaurian reptiles are particularly distinguished, as has been mentioned, by a marked difference in size between the fore and hind limbs, so that even though the thecodonts were for the most part quadrupedal reptiles, they had mostly established a bipedal manner of locomotion. Otherwise, as outlined in chapter 9, the carnivorous thecodonts may be particularly defined by a narrow, deep skull, with the two openings on each side behind the eye characteristic of diapsids and by a large antorbital opening in front of the eye. Sharp teeth are set in sockets, and although this is the basis of the name for the order (*thece*, a receptacle; *odont*, tooth) the condition is not unique to the thecodont reptiles. Among the herbivorous thecodonts the skull is much reduced in size. All the thecodonts have a strong vertebral column, connected to the pelvis by two vertebrae. The pelvis is characterized by a closed acetabulum, forming a socket where sits the head of the femur, this socket being at the junction of the three bones of the pelvis. The head of the femur is not turned inwardly to any appreciable degree, which is a primitive condition, and all the digits are present in the hands and feet, although some digits on the outer sides of hand and foot may be small.

Three types of large thecodonts were dominant in Chinle and equivalent time: *Postosuchus*, a land-living predator; *Rutiodon* and related genera, crocodile-like inhabitants of streams and ponds; and *Desmatosuchus*, *Typothorax*, and *Calyptosuchus*, three heavily armored herbivorous reptiles.

Postosuchus (the name comes from the town of Post, Texas, near which the original materials of this reptile were discovered in the Dockum Formation, the Texas equivalent of the Chinle) was without doubt a kingpin among the land-dwelling Chinle reptiles. It is a large archosaurian reptile, some twelve to fifteen feet (four to five meters) long. The skull is large for an animal of its size, about two feet or seventy centimeters long, and is deep and strongly constructed. Indeed, the skull is remarkably similar in many respects to that of *Tyrannosaurus*, a fact that, in combination with other features, led the describer of this thecodont, Sankar Chatterjee of Texas Tech University, to postulate that *Postosuchus* was on the evolutionary line leading to the huge tyrant dinosaur of late Cretaceous time. His conclusion has been disputed by other paleontologists, who think that the structure of the hind limb and the hip and ankle joints indicate another evolutionary direction. Whichever is the case, in late Triassic time *Postosuchus* was an ecological counterpart of the much larger tyrannosaurs that so dominated the late Cretaceous scene (Chatterjee 1985).

Even though *Postosuchus* was a fearsome predator, it probably did not pose a very serious threat to *Coelophysis* if the two ever met, because it very likely could not match the speed of the small dinosaur. Chatterjee, in his original description of this large, predatory thecodont, illustrates it as a fully bipedal reptile; however, it may not have been an obligatory biped, for the forelimbs are large enough that it might have occasionally assumed a quadrupedal pose. Certainly, the closest relatives of *Postosuchus*, known as the rauisuchid thecodonts—as exemplified by *Rauisuchus* itself from South America and *Ticinisuchus* from Switzerland—evidently were dominantly quadrupedal reptiles. But as an optional biped, *Postosuchus* probably pursued its victims by running on its long, strong hind limbs—a strategy for hunting that was undoubtedly effective except perhaps when it attempted to catch *Coelophysis* or other similar archosaurs. By analogy with modern times, it would have been like a lion trying to catch a jackal.

The other large predators of the Chinle environment were phytosaurs like *Rutiodon* which lived in streams and ponds and along their shores (see figure 49). Actually, there were several genera of Chinle phytosaurs, but the nomenclature of these reptiles has become so enmeshed in Byzantine technicalities that for our purpose the simplest procedure is to use the name of the dominant Chinle phytosaur as representative of this type of reptile.

The phytosaurs are typical of Upper Triassic sediments across the northern hemisphere, and their remains are among the most common Chinle fossils. It is indeed ironic that the prototype of these highly carnivorous reptiles should have been named *Phytosaurus* by the German paleontologist Georg Friedrich Jaeger in 1828, on the supposition that it fed upon plants (*Phyto*, plant; *sauros*, lizard or reptile). This shows that under the rules of zoological nomenclature, which had become established, if not codified, in Jaeger's day, a name cannot be rejected because it is inappropriate.

The close parallelism between phytosaurs and crocodilians is one of the

FIGURE 49   A Chinle scene showing a number of characteristic late Triassic tetra-pods, namely, *Metoposaurus*, the large amphibian, and the phytosaur *Rutiodon*, in the foreground. In the middle distance is *Hesperosuchus*, a small reptile related to crocodiles; at the back are two *Coelophysis* on the left and the thecodont *Desmatosuchus* on the right. This scene depicts the vegetation characteristic of Chinle times, dominated by the large conifer *Araucarioxylon*, ferns, and large horsetails, *Neocalamites*.

prime examples of parallelism in the fossil record. On casual examination a phytosaur like *Rutiodon* might easily be mistaken for a crocodile because it looks so very crocodilian by virtue of its long skull, whose jaws are set with numerous sharp teeth, and by virtue of its long, scaly body and short limbs. Only when seen more closely is it apparent that the phytosaur's nos-trils, instead of being at the tip of the snout as in crocodilians, are located just in front of the eyes, very commonly on a sort of volcano-shaped emi-nence, which raises them to or above the level of the skull roof. (There are other differences in the skull, notably in the structure of the palate, and in details of the skeleton, which clearly separate phytosaurs from crocodiles, but these are technicalities of interest mainly to paleontologists who dote on details [Colbert 1947]).

In short, the phytosaurs "invented" the crocodilian body form and mode of life, and then as they became extinct at the end of the Triassic period the crocodiles arose, to imitate the phytosaurs in a most uncanny fashion, and to live as supremely successful reptiles through millions of years from early Jurassic time to the present. Indeed, if it were not for modern firearms and the propensity of certain human beings to use these firearms, the crocodilians would still be abundant throughout the tropics of our modern world. Why the phytosaurs failed, when their imitators have been so successful, is one of the puzzles of paleontology.

In late Triassic time the phytosaurs must have dominated the Chinle waterways beyond all challenges. And as in the case of modern crocodilians, many of the phytosaurs were gigantic—twenty to thirty feet long, with enormous skulls to match. *Rutiodon,* like *Postosuchus,* was a fearsome predator, but one that could be readily avoided by alert and fast-moving upland dwellers, particularly by such reptiles as *Coelophysis.* It is probable that *Rutiodon* was a predator that lived for the most part on fish.

Desmatosuchus, Typothorax, and *Calyptosuchus* belong to a subgroup of thecodonts known as aetosaurs, all distinguished by their heavily armored bodies. These are often large thecodonts, ten to fifteen feet (three to five meters) or more in length, which probably inhabited uplands within the Chinle forests. Living as they did in an environment frequented by the likes of *Postosuchus* and *Rutiodon,* they could hardly have survived had it not been for the heavy, bony plates (in turn undoubtedly covered by very thick, leathery skin, as in modern crocodilians) that made them, if not invulnerable, at least very difficult for attacking predators to overcome. These were fully quadrupedal thecodonts; they had to be, considering the weight of armor that they carried, and they walked about on sturdy but relatively short legs. Their resistance to attack was of the static kind; it is difficult to imagine them trying to run away from a large, ravenous *Postosuchus.* The bony armor plates are transversely broad, especially in *Typothorax,* covering the back and extending down on the sides of the body. The neck in these thecodonts is short and is protected by armor plates that terminate in pointed spikes, extending laterally on each side of the neck. *Desmatosuchus* has very long spikes on each side of the neck, increasing in size from front to back, that terminate in a pair of long, curved spikes over the shoulders, in shape not unlike the horns of a long-horned bull. Small, pointed plates run along each side of the body and along the tail. *Typothorax* shows a somewhat similar arrangement, but without the excessively long spikes over the shoulders that characterize *Desmatosuchus.* A predator would have to be adventurous indeed to attempt to confront such large, spiky reptiles. It is not unreasonable to think that these big aetosaurs, when attacked, would crouch down on the ground or in the mud, thus presenting to the attacker a low, broad surface of armor plate, difficult to get through and difficult to turn over. *Typothorax*, in particular, revealed to its enemy a broad, immovable dome that seemed to merge into the surroundings.

The skull in these aetosaurs is quite small relative to the size of the body, while the comparatively short jaws bear remarkably small teeth. The front of the skull, composed of the nasal and premaxillary bones, is extended forward as a narrow, toothless snout. It seems probable that it had a piglike nose and burrowed in the mud or soil for roots and tubers (Long and Houk 1988:50–51).

These plant-eating neighbors of *Coelophysis*, the only herbivorous thecodonts, were of little consequence to the dinosaur. They must have been too large and too well protected by their armor to have been objects of a *Coelophysis* attack, even if the little dinosaur had attempted to launch multiple, packlike assaults on the aetosaurs. Consequently they were probably largely ignored by *Coelophysis* as it searched for food in the Chinle forests.

A reptile that may have received some attention from *Coelophysis* was *Hesperosuchus*, known from upper Chinle sediments; a small, lightly built predator, it was about four feet (a little more than a meter) long and well adapted for rapid running. (See figure 49, above.) This reptile, originally described and named by the author, was formerly thought to be a thecodont, but now most paleontologists have come to regard it as a little crocodile-like reptile known as a sphenosuchian—an early forerunner of the typical crocodilians, which in Jurassic time took over the ecological roles of the phytosaurs (Colbert 1952).

Hesperosuchus agilis is the full name given to this reptile, a name that indicates the possible nature of its movements. The original description portrayed it as a bipedal reptile. However, the relative length of the forelimbs, about two-thirds that of the hind limbs, has led some paleontologists to picture *Hesperosuchus* as a quadrupedal runner. Perhaps it may have adopted both styles of locomotion; the lengths of both fore and hind limbs were such that whatever pose this reptile adopted, it must have been a fast traveler. It was small enough to be preyed on by adult *Coelophysis*, yet fast enough to escape, unless taken by surprise or subterfuge. Who knows?

Perhaps at times *Hesperosuchus* turned the tables and attacked *Coelophysis*. *Hesperosuchus* and *Coelophysis* probably competed for food as they were both primarily hunters of small game.

Coelophysis was probably not the only dinosaur in the Chinle fauna. Long and Houk have suggested that anchisaurs were present, although the evidence for this is tenuous. Yet there is no reason why these dinosaurs might not have lived in the Chinle forests. They are known from the Upper Triassic and Lower Jurassic sediments of eastern North America, as well as from other parts of the world. As always, much of what we do and do not know about Chinle vertebrates is subject to the accidents of preservation and the accidents of collecting.

The anchisaurs, as typified by *Anchisaurus* from the Connecticut Valley, are rather small prosauropod dinosaurs, that is, forerunners, if not ancestors, of the gigantic sauropod dinosaurs. The *Anchisaurus* skeleton is about eight feet (2.5 meters) long and shows many of the features that were to become typical of the gigantic middle and late Mesozoic sauropods. Thus the neck and the tail are long, the forelimbs are heavy and almost as long as the hind limbs (strongly suggesting a dominantly quadrupedal pose), while the skull is relatively small and the jaws have spatulate or leaf-shaped teeth, with serrations along their edges. There has been some disagreement over the diet of these prosauropods—whether they were scavengers, or omnivores eating anything that came their way, or pure herbivores (Lull 1953:98–107).

Perhaps the last suggestion offers the best interpretation of the diet of *Anchisaurus*. If valid this concept makes *Anchisaurus* and its close relatives among the earliest of the plant-eating dinosaurs, and the first of the herbivorous saurischian dinosaurs.

Anchisaurs, if present in the Chinle fauna, were certainly no threat to *Coelophysis*. Indeed it may have been the other way around, with *Coelophysis*, perhaps acting in packs, attacking and feeding on the harmless anchisaurs. *Coelophysis*, in spite of its small size, which determined its usual role as a hunter of small prey, was probably at times an aggressive, fast-moving slasher with tooth and claw, not infrequently preying on reptiles that surpassed it in size.

There seems to be good evidence that, whether or not herbivorous anchisaurs were members of the Chinle aggregation, some other dinosaurian herbivores, known as fabrosaurs, were present to feed on the vegetation of those distant days. The fabrosaurs are ornithischian dinosaurs; in fact they may be regarded as the ancestral representatives of this order, which is composed entirely of plant-eating dinosaurs.

Fabrosaurs have not yet been described in detail from Chinle sediments, but fragments have been found, and recently Hunt has described some small teeth of ornithischian type from the Bull Canyon Formation of New Mexico—an equivalent of the Chinle Formation. He created a new genus and species for these teeth, *Revueltosaurus callenderi* (Hunt 1989). But as Padian (1990) has shown, although these teeth are no doubt related to ornithischians, their classification at a lower taxonomic level is hardly justified. It should be noted that similar teeth have been found in the Chinle beds at the Petrified Forest.

In the overlying Kayenta Formation of Arizona an armored ornithischian dinosaur, *Scutellosaurus,* perhaps a forerunner of the stegosaurians of Jurassic age, is known from a nearly complete skeleton (Colbert 1981). Since such a dinosaur lived in Kayenta time, it is reasonable to think that its more primitive fabrosaurian cousins may have lived alongside *Coelophysis* in the Chinle forests.

The fabrosaurs, known from *Fabrosaurus* itself from the Lower Jurassic of South Africa and from *Technosaurus* from the Upper Triassic Dockum Formation of Texas, are small dinosaurs, smaller even than *Coelophysis.* They are characterized by the ornithischian type of pelvis. Furthermore, the fabrosaur skull is small, and the teeth are flattened and leaf-shaped, with well-developed serrations along their edges. They are obviously teeth designed for cropping vegetation, not for eating meat. The front of the lower jaw in the fabrosaurs is devoid of teeth; in place of anterior teeth is a new bone, the *predentary,* shaped like a beak, that must have been useful for cutting vegetation. The development of this new predentary bone in the fabrosaurs and other ornithischians established a definitive character that persisted throughout ornithischian evolution to such an extent that these dinosaurs are often designated as "predentates." As for the ecological relationships between *Coelophysis* and any possible Chinle ornithischian dinosaurs, the little plant-eaters were probably fair game for the theropod predator of Ghost Ranch.

One other archosaurian reptile may have been present in the Chinle forests, namely, an early flying reptile, or pterosaur. *Eudimorphodon* has been described from Upper Triassic rocks in Italy; indications of pterosaur bones are reported from the Chinle beds of the Petrified Forest in Arizona, listed as *Eudimorphodon* sp. by Robert Long and Rose Houk (Long and Houk 1988:60–61). Pterosaurs of the *Eudimorphodon* type were small winged reptiles about the size of a robin. The skull in *Eudimorphodon* is elongated, and the jaws are armed with long teeth, well adapted for catching fish from the surface of the water. The long, narrow wings, supported by an elongation of the fourth finger, consisted of a leathery batlike membrane, as is known from other pterosaurs preserved in fine sediments. *Eudimorphodon* had a very long, bony tail and probably a triangular rudder at its end, if the evidence from related pterosaurs preserved in fine-grained shales, in which such a rudder is to be seen, can be accepted. *Coelophysis* probably did not have much interaction with flying pterosaurs, but it is conceivable that on rare occasions the dinosaur, so swift and agile, may have leapt up and snatched a low-flying pterosaur out of the air.

However, the Chinle pterosaur (whatever kind of flying reptile it may have been) was not the only vertebrate in this fauna to have been airborne: a little protolizard *glided* from tree to tree in the forests of that ancient time. A virtually complete skeleton (named *Icarosaurus* by the author) is known from the Upper Triassic black shales of the New Jersey Lockatong Formation, discovered some years ago just acròss the Hudson River from Manhattan. In fact, this little fossil may be geographically the closest fossil vertebrate to the American Museum of Natural History, being about three miles in a direct air line from that institution. Furthermore, some miscellaneous jaws and teeth fragments that may be attributed to *Icarosaurus* have been found in the Chinle Formation at the Petrified Forest, so there is every reason to think that this little reptile was well established in the Southwest during late Triassic time. The paucity of the fossil record of such a small and delicate reptile in this region may be attributed to the nature of the sediments that comprise the Chinle Formation—a succession of sandstone and siltstones, the quality of which usually precludes the preservation of fossils as fragile as *Icarosaurus* (Colbert 1970b).

Indeed, the fortunate preservation of a complete skeleton of *Icarosaurus* in the fine-grained Lockatong black shales of New Jersey is due to the fact that this specimen probably represents an individual that inadvertently fell into a Lockatong lake, sank to the bottom, and was rapidly covered with fine mud before the skeleton could disintegrate. It is a situation that parallels the preservation of the first bird, *Archaeopteryx*, in the extraordinarily fine-grained white Jurassic limestones of central Germany—the difference being that *Archaeopteryx* fell into a clear tropical lagoon, not into a muddy lake, as did *Icarosaurus*.

During Permian and Triassic times several lines of reptiles took to the air by gliding rather than flying. This was independently accomplished within at least two early diapsid groups by an elongation of the ribs to form supports for a gliding membrane on each side of the body. That it was and still is a successful tactic is demonstrated by the presence of *Draco*, a gliding lizard that today inhabits the forests of the Philippines and elsewhere in Asia. These little lizards, in which five ribs on each side form the "wing" supports, are able to glide as far as sixty meters (two hundred feet) from one tree to another, and, moreover, they are able to direct their flights most efficiently. When the lizard is scrambling around through the trees in search of insects its "wings" are folded up over the back. One secret of *Draco*'s success is the ability to spend a lifetime in the trees, without having to come down to the ground, where danger lurks from every side. And an important part of this pattern for success is the freedom to move from tree to tree high above the ground, even when trees are not close together, thereby giving *Draco* an extended area in which to live. The gliding reptiles of Permian and Triassic times probably lived in a manner similar to that of *Draco*.

Interestingly, *Icarosaurus* was more effectively adapted for gliding than is the modern *Draco*, for whereas the modern lizard has rather small "wings," rounded in silhouette when seen from above, *Icarosaurus* has widely spread "wings" supported on each side by ten elongated ribs, of which the first is very straight and thus furnishes a strong leading edge, an important aerodynamic advantage. In addition, the ribs that follow are arched, to provide to the wing an aerodynamically efficient camber—convex on the upper surface, concave below, as in the wing of a bird. *Icarosaurus*, about ten inches (twenty-five centimeters) long, is classified within an ancient group of lizards known as eolacertilians, far removed within the Order Squamata (comprising the lizards and snakes) from *Draco*, an agamid lizard. These independent and parallel developments of gliding reptiles provide striking illustrations of how a "desirable" adaptation can be developed time and again by similar but distantly related animals. We saw it in the case of the Triassic phytosaurs and the later crocodiles; we see it today, for example, in the hedgehogs (insectivores) of Eurasia and the porcupines (rodents) of North America.

It is interesting that some of the first lizards, so distinctly primitive compared to the later lizards as to be restricted by students of this segment of vertebrate evolution to a separate group (the Eolacertilia, or "dawn lizards") were nonetheless highly specialized with the adaptation for gliding, described above. Perhaps this is an indication that life on the ground was very dangerous for small vertebrates, particularly with such active, quick predators as *Coelophysis* lurking through the underbrush. It would seem that lizards did not proliferate until Jurassic time.

Yet lizardlike reptiles had an ecological niche in the Triassic years, a niche that was filled to some degree by small reptiles known as procolophonids. These were nonlizard "lizards" of ancient lineage and primitive anatomy, members of the basic reptilian group Anapsida (see chapter 9) characterized by a solid skull, pierced only by the openings for the nostrils and the eyes, with a single opening in the top of the head, the pineal opening, a sort of "third eye" seen in the labyrinthodont amphibians and their descendents, the early anapsid reptiles, and as well in lizards, *Sphenodon* (the tuatara of New Zealand) and synapsid reptiles.

Hypsognathus, a procolophonid known from complete skeletal fossils found in the Upper Triassic beds of Newark, New Jersey and from fragmentary materials, particularly a jaw fragment from the Petrified Forest, was a small lizardlike reptile, the skeleton of which is about a foot or thirty centimeters long. It was a sprawling reptile, with a broad body, short limbs, and short, wide feet. The skull is particularly interesting, because on each side are several long spikes or horns quite obviously developed as protective devices. These spikes would have made *Hypsognathus* a something less than delectable meal for a reptilian predator such as *Coelophysis;* indeed they may have made *Hypsognathus* nearly invulnerable to various predators of the time. In many respects, *Hypsognathus* parallels the horned lizard, or "horned toad" (which is not a toad) *Phrynosoma,* of the American Southwest today, except in one important feature. Whereas the modern horned lizard is an insect eater, *Hypsognathus* quite obviously fed on plants. The teeth in the front of the skull and jaws are pointed, as is common among reptiles, but those in the sides of the jaw are in the shape of transverse chisels, suited to chopping up vegetation (Colbert 1946).

Two reptiles mentioned at the beginning of this chapter, both herbivores, are prominent members of late Triassic faunas in North America, one being *Trilophosaurus,* again a lizardlike nonlizard, some six feet or two meters long, the other being *Placerias,* a mammal-like reptile, as has been said, about the size of a small ox and like nothing in the modern world. Even if these reptiles and *Coelophysis* had any interaction—which they probably did not, for they seemingly were not contemporaries—it is conceivable that the dinosaur was not at all loath to attack *Trilophosaurus,* an inoffensive, lumbering herbivore, while steering clear of *Placerias,* which was simply too large to be assaulted.

Trilophosaurus, a highly modified diapsid reptile, in which a single upper opening is behind the eye with an extraordinarily deep, solid bar beneath it, is a sprawling reptile with enormous feet. The front of the skull and lower jaw lack teeth and are in the form of a very strong beak that must have had a tough, horny covering, while the teeth in the sides of the jaws are transverse, chisel-like structures, an adaptation, as we have seen, independently developed in *Hypsognathus.* This reptile was well adapted for tearing at tough plants with its strong beak and chopping them into small pieces with the opposing chisels of the skull and the lower jaw. It is best known from the Dockum Formation, but its presence in the Chinle Formation is well attested (Gregory 1945).

Placerias is a holdover from an earlier age; as mentioned, it is one of the synapsids, or mammal-like reptiles, and it belongs to that branch of the synapsids known as the dicynodonts. These were very specialized mammal-like reptiles or therapsids, having large, capacious bodies (one probable indication of a herbivorous diet) with large, broad feet, with a short tail, and with a huge skull, the front of which is in the form of a large, pointed beak, as is the front of the lower jaw. The jaws lack teeth, except for a pair of tusks in the skull. Some dicynodonts were tuskless, which suggests sexual dimorphism. These jaws must have been sheathed with horny beaks (Camp and Welles 1956).

Placerias is one of the last and one of the largest of the dicynodonts. It is well known from a quarry near St. Johns, Arizona, where years ago paleontologists from the University of California at Berkeley collected literally thousands of its bones.

Although *Placerias* is a mammal-like therapsid, it is quite off to one side from the line of mammal-like reptiles known as cynodonts that were the direct ancestors of the mammals. Cynodonts are abundantly known from southern Africa and from South America, but their remains are sparse in North America. Supposed teeth of such therapsids have been found in the Chinle Formation, but these teeth are so equivocal that nothing very definite can be said about them at present.

MAMMALS

Some very early mammals, descended from therapsid cynodonts, may have lived in Chinle times. Farish Jenkins and A. W. Crompton of Harvard University and Will Downs of Northern Arizona University have described an early mammal that they named *Dinnetherium*, from the Kayenta Formation, just above the Chinle Formation in northern Arizona. This very

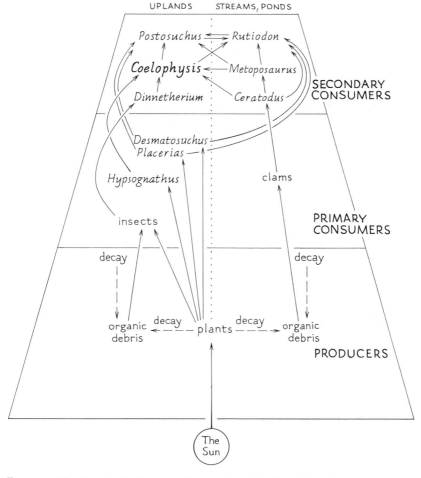

FIGURE 50 Hypothetical ecological pyramid and food web, involving some of the late Triassic Chinle plants and animals. The arrows show the flow of energy from the sun to plants (producers) and on to animals (primary and secondary consumers). The pyramidal form indicates the progressive decrease of available energy.

early mammal, known from teeth and from a lower jaw, about two centimeters long, represents an initial stage in the evolution of the mammals. No larger than a modern shrew, it must have lived a furtive life among the ubiquitous reptiles of those early Mesozoic days. If it or something like it was present in the Chinle fauna, it probably showed itself seldom by day; rather it was very likely a crepuscular animal, living underground and coming out at twilight or at night to feed on small insects. And very possibly it was occasionally seen by *Coelophysis*, which would quickly snap it up as a small tasty morsel, giving the diet of the dinosaur some variety (Jenkins, Crompton, and Downs 1983).

This assessment of the contemporaries and competitors of *Coelophysis* has concentrated on the animals that *Coelophysis*, an active predator, might have eaten, and the animals that in turn might have eaten *Coelophysis*, a small animal compared to some of its carnivorous thecodont neighbors. The world in which *Coelophysis* lived was anything but benign, as has been the world of nature through the ages, even now. There is the ever-present struggle to survive, a struggle that we experience in terms other than eating or being eaten, in ways different than those experienced by our stone age ancestors.

As we survey modern ecological systems, we see the relationships between the animal and plant worlds, between plants and plants, and between animals and animals as a complex mosaic of interactions whereby the primary feeders, the herbivores, eat plants that get their energy from the sun, while the secondary feeders, the carnivores, get their energy largely by preying on the primary feeders. In the accompanying diagram (figure 50) an attempt is made to depict the system as it existed in Chinle time, and especially to show the position of *Coelophysis* within that system.

ELEVEN

EQUATORIAL NEW MEXICO

The preceding chapter depicted the rich vertebrate life of New Mexico in late Triassic time, more than 200 million years ago. If our interpretation of the fossils is reasonably correct, the streams and rivers, the lakes and ponds, and the low often swampy lands between abounded with fish, giant amphibians, and reptiles, giving the scene an exotic cast quite at variance with the land of high deserts and cliffs that we know today. The same may be said for the plants that shared the land with the ancient animals belonging to the Chinle fauna. Everything about the fossils indicates that this was a tropical land.

Our new knowledge and interpretation of the geology of New Mexico, and of the world for that matter, shows that in the Triassic years the American Southwest was situated much farther south than is the case today; in fact New Mexico and the surrounding terrain was only about ten degrees north of the equator, compared to the present latitude of thirty-five degrees. In other words, the relationship of what is now Ghost Ranch, the home of *Coelophysis*, to the equator was comparable to that of the present Panama Canal, Nigeria, or Thailand. So it is not surprising that *Coelophysis* lived in a moist, humid environment where summer reigned throughout the year (Smiley 1985:10).

However, *Syntarsus* (described in chapter 9), the very close cousin of *Coelophysis*, lived in a region, namely southern Africa, that was on the other side of the equator and some forty-five degrees away from it. Thus *Syntar-*

sus lived farther south of the equator than is the location of its burial ground today, in Zimbabwe. Yet the fossils, plant and animal, seem to show that the habitat in which *Syntarsus* found its home was as tropical as was the homeland of *Coelophysis*. This all indicates that the Triassic world was different from today's—it was one world geographically and climatically, a tropical world (Calder 1972:23).

If this seems strange, consider that the world today is quite atypical compared to the world during much of geological time. And yet we are strongly influenced, perhaps unconsciously, by the nature of the world in which we live. Many of us have flown through varied climatic zones, and frequently into the polar regions, experiencing the changes from palm-lined shores to hardwood forest, to great belts of conifers and on to the tundra and the lands of perpetual snows. But during much of earth history there were no distinctly defined climatic zones, and certainly no polar ice-caps. It was a generally benign world, climatically speaking, and a unified world, geographically speaking, as we shall see.

The tropical aspects of Triassic New Mexico, a subject that has not yet been considered in detail, may be seen in the composition of the Chinle flora; a flora that was primitive, as the animals were primitive, and markedly less varied than the tropical-subtropical floras of today.

If we were able to use a time machine to journey back to the American Southwest of late Triassic years, we probably would be impressed by two botanical aspects of the landscape: first, great coniferous forests dominating rolling hills, flatlands and marshy borders of numerous rivers and lakes, and second, ferns everywhere beneath the trees. And if large conifers are not in one's mental image of a tropical land, remember that these are primitive trees known as gymnosperms, in which the seeds are naked. They prevailed when forests were primitive—not as primitive as 300 million years ago, when the truly primitive coal forests covered large continental regions, but much more primitive than at the end of Cretaceous time, when the flowering angiosperms, with enclosed seeds, including a remarkable variety of deciduous "hardwood" trees, had explosively evolved, to dominate tropical forests from then until the present. The ubiquitous coniferous trees of the Chinle forests were overwhelmingly of one kind, a tree designated by the generic name *Araucarioxylon*—comparable, but not ancestral to the modern *Araucaria* and its relatives, so widely distributed in Brazil and other southern hemisphere regions.

One interesting aspect of the Chinle forest was the very dominance of

Araucarioxylon, which resulted in the broad expanse of woodlands pre-
dominantly made up of a single species. In this respect, the forest that we
see preserved in the great fossil logs of the Petrified Forest of Arizona is in a
way similar to the modern ponderosa pine forest that covers so much of
northern Arizona, both being strictly limited in the variety of trees that
compose them. This contrasts with the tropical forests of today—in the
vast forest of the Amazon Basin, for example, because these modern tropical forests, composed as they are of deciduous or angiosperm trees, are
most particularly characterized by the remarkable variety of tree species
within their boundaries. Thus a square kilometer of Amazonian forest will
contain scores, even hundreds of species of trees forming the high wood-
land canopy within and beneath which the rich variety of lesser plant species and of animals flourish. This shows the different yet parallel ecologies
that have prevailed in two geologic ages, each separated from the other by
millions of years of organic evolution.

Not only were the *Araucarioxylon* forests of Chinle time widely established throughout the region that is now New Mexico and Arizona, but
these were remarkably dense forests. The trees—which commonly grew
to several feet or two meters and more in diameter and more than a hundred feet or thirty to forty meters high—were evidently closely arranged,
to form forests not unlike stands seen in modern redwood forests. The result of such dense growth was the inevitable struggle for light, causing the
trees to have tall, unencumbered trunks and large crowns of needles at the
very top. Consequently, the *Araucarioxylon* forests of the Triassic must have
been particularly similar to the modern redwood forests in that beneath
their high crowns were large areas of dim light, while on the ground were
lush carpets of ferns (Ash 1972).

Perhaps such an environment was not conducive to abundant populations of large reptiles; perhaps these ancient forests were special havens for
small reptiles that fed on insects, rather than for the large thecodonts that
dominated reptilian assemblages of the time. Since large reptiles were active animals, it seems reasonable to assume that the Triassic forests were
traversed by wandering thecodonts, as well as by the tusked *Placerias* and
by *Coelophysis,* too.

But the Chinle woodlands were not so completely dominated by the
huge conifers as to lack botanical variety. Other trees and other plants interrupted the dense stands of *Araucarioxylon* to lend some primitive differences to the Triassic scene. For example, occasionally interspersed among

the dominant pines, was a conifer named *Woodworthia,* a tree considerably smaller than *Araucarioxylon* and characterized by small, short branches extending along the trunk, giving the tree a prickly appearance. But *Woodworthia* seemingly was not very numerous in the Chinle forests.

Another tree, the relationships of which are not well understood, was *Schilderia.* This was a moderate-size tree in which the trunk, when seen in cross-section, displays a radiating pattern of growth—quite different from the rings that typify the trunks of the conifers. Large *Schilderia* trees had interesting fluted bases, not unlike the bases of bald cypress trees, indicating that such Triassic trees, like their modern analogues, grew in watery swamps. Generally speaking, the *Araucarioxylon* forests seem to have occupied dry lands that bordered the rivers and swamps of the Chinle landscape, so perhaps *Schilderia* trees grew in wetlands immediately adjacent to the forest borders.

The forest floor, and open spaces throughout the woodlands, were covered with cycads, or seed-bearing coniferous plants typified by a low bulbous trunk, not unlike a giant pineapple in shape, or often a columnar stem a few feet high. These plants are distinguished by a crown of leaves that look like gigantic fern fronds. Within this spreading crown of leaves are cones.

Also in the Chinle forests were tree ferns, plants that, like cycads, persist in our modern world. As the name implies, these are gigantic ferns that grow as tall as trees, with trunks that may be several meters high. Stands of tree ferns are found today in tropical and subtropical environments. In the Chinle forests they may have flourished along the edges of the woodlands, not far removed from watercourses.

As has been mentioned, many waterways, in the form of streams and rivers, ponds and lakes, traversed and bordered the Chinle forests, their edges frequently bounded by broad mudflats and sandbars, on which Chinle reptiles left the footprint records of their comings and goings. These ancient flatlands show not only the trackways of the backboned animals that lived in the Chinle streams and ponds but also those of the "upland" reptiles, such as *Coelophysis,* that came down to the water to drink, or even to prey on such aquatic creatures as they might be able to catch. And in these wet, muddy, swampy areas grew various plants that were particularly adapted to wet environments.

Schilderia, the tree with a fluted base, has already been mentioned. Particularly characteristic of these lowland areas, however, were the giant horsetails known from their abundant fossil remains.

Horsetails persist today as the genus *Equisetum* (why it is called "horse-tail" baffles me) and are common inhabitants of wet, marshy soil along the edges of streams. Today's horsetails are small plants, growing two or three feet tall, consisting of jointed, hollow stems, with whorls of branches and leaves protruding from each joint of the stem. At the top of each stem is a single cone. Horsetails similar in size to the modern *Equisetum* are seen in the Chinle environment; these belong to the genus *Equisetites*. But the truly impressive horsetails of Chinle time are the giant specimens, characterized by the genus *Neocalamites* that grew profusely in swamps and low places forming dense communities of these plants, each jointed stem having the dimensions of a small telephone pole. Thick bands of *Neocalamites* evi-dently bordered many Chinle streams, their strange, jointed stems ris-ing twenty or thirty feet—seven to ten meters—above the swamps in which they grew, in decided contrast to the tall trees that rose majestically behind them.

Beyond the wide stands of *Araucarioxylon* forests, away from the low riv-erine habitats in which grew the stark palisades of *Neocalamites* and in which the crocodile-like phytosaurs, the huge, clumsy amphibian *Metoposaurus*, and various fish made their homes, were the so-called up-lands of the Chinle landscape. These were low hills covered with low shrubs and other vegetation, decidedly different from the tall trees of the *Araucarioxylon* community. Most of what we know about these upland bo-tanical aggregations must be learned from microscopic fossils, from spores and pollen and varied fragmentary remains. As Ralph Chaney, a paleo-botanist who studied Chinle plant fossils, remarked in 1964: "Only rarely can insight be gained from plant macrofossils regarding the forests that lived in the uplands" (Chaney, in Gottesfeld 1972:69). And to continue the speculation as to the upland Chinle woodlands, Gottesfeld remarked that "a diverse upland gynmospermous community is hypothesized" (p. 69). Thus we can see in our mind's eye the upland hills rather openly covered by small, shrubby gymnosperms, including various conifers, as well as by ginkgos, with their distinctive, fan-shaped leaves.

It has been suggested that it was in these upland woodlands, which were in fact not very elevated above the dense conifer forests, that many large thecodont reptiles made their homes, as possibly did *Coelophysis*. This is a subject about which one cannot be very definite. It seems likely that many of the Chinle reptiles ranged freely through all three Chinle bo-tanical communities—the riverine and lacustrine lowlands, the tall conifer forests, and the open uplands.

One other aspect of the Chinle environment should be mentioned. There is ample evidence that to the southwest was a mountain range now known as the Mogollon Highlands, within which were active volcanoes; this range extended from west to east along the southern border of present-day Arizona and on into present-day New Mexico. Here was the source for the bentonitic deposits, the layers of fossil volcanic ash, that are so prevalent within the Chinle Formation (although not present in the siltstone member at Ghost Ranch, as Schwartz has shown). It seems apparent that during much of Chinle time ash falls were found throughout large areas of what is now the American Southwest, blown by winds from the Highlands toward the north and east. Such volcanic activity has been a part of earth history through the ages and continues unabated today. The ever-present ranges of volcanoes are prominent features of many tropical regions today—Java, for example—thereby giving us some idea of what environmental conditions were like in tropical Chinle times (Smiley 1985:11).

The foregoing picture has focused on the American Southwest, as it is supposed to have existed during late Triassic history. But the picture of the Southwest, with its tropical setting and its ancient amphibians and reptiles, may be evoked for almost all other parts of the Triassic world; for eastern North America, for South America, for northern Europe, for India, for other parts of Asia, for Africa, for Australia, and even for Antarctica. So the theme of this chapter—as for the whole Ghost Ranch story—is that in Triassic time—as indeed for all of Mesozoic history—the world was one world, a tropical world in which plants and animals were widely distributed across continents that were closely connected. Which is why, of course, *Coelophysis* is so closely related to its cousin *Syntarsus* in southern Africa, and in Arizona as well. Why should this have been the nature of the earth and its continents, millions of years ago? This is a question that opens up the subject of plate tectonics—a very big subject indeed—and that reminds us that paleontology, properly viewed, is but one aspect of earth history. Consequently, the little dinosaurs of Ghost Ranch involve much more than a local tale of life and death some 200 million years ago. The contemplation of these earliest dinosaurs brings us to a consideration of why they were so close to dinosaurs that lived on the other side of the world, and of why the continents should have been so intimately related in the days of *Coelophysis*. The key to the puzzle is our new-found knowledge of plate tectonics.

If I had been asked a half-century ago to explain the close relationship between *Coelophysis* and *Syntarsus*, my answer to this request would have been rather simple and uncomplicated: both these dinosaurs descended from a common ancestor, probably living in North America, and then *Syntarsus*, or rather its ancestors, "migrated" from this center of origin to southern Africa by way of a long route—up through western North America, across the Bering Strait region, down through Asia to the Middle East, and from there southwardly to the southern tip of Africa. The direction of movement would have been thus, rather than from Africa to North America, since *Syntarsus* is slightly younger than *Coelophysis*. But is not such a long, tortuous route rather improbable? Yes and no. The way is long, something on the order of fifteen thousand miles, but if the "migrating" dinosaurs had made the journey at the rate of a half mile per year, the trip would have been accomplished in about thirty thousand years—a segment of time that is essentially instantaneous when one is dealing with earth history at a remove of some 200 million years. (One must not think of such a journey having been a conscious movement in one direction, but rather the spread of the range of the species involved, such as we see today in the northward spread of such North American birds as cardinals and titmice. Just by extending their living space by a small distance each year these birds have moved into new ranges in a way that is noticeable even to the casual observer. So it might have been with the Upper Triassic dinosaurs.)

However, in those days before World War II, there was a concept known as Continental Drift, according to which all continents in the world had once been a part of a single supercontinent that in due course broke apart, its several fragments drifting to the positions of our modern continents. The idea was championed by a German meteorologist named Alfred Wegener just before, during, and after World War I. It was not popular among most members of the geological fraternity, particularly northern hemisphere geologists, because it seemed to be based on very tenuous evidence, which it was (Wegener 1966). It did find favor among some southern hemisphere geologists, especially Alex DuToit of South Africa, who was a great disciple of Wegener (DuToit 1937).

At the time I was working at the American Museum of Natural History, with colleagues including George Simpson—a firm believer in the permanence of continents, and an outspoken critic of Wegener. Furthermore, Simpson was a most formidable scientist, and I was rather overwhelmed by him.

But in the years after World War II, some geologists began detailed studies of the oceanic basins, using sonar techniques that had been developed during the war for detecting enemy submarines. One of them was Maurice Ewing of Columbia University, who, like me, was associated with the Geology Department. Under Ewing's direction two other Columbians, Bruce Heezen and Marie Tharp, set out on the formidable task of mapping the bottom of oceans all over the world. To make a long story short, they discovered that the oceanic basins not only are different from the continents but also are relatively young. Core samples from the sea floors show that the South Atlantic, for example, is no older than the Jurassic, and this seems to show that the crust of the earth is very dynamic, with continents shifting and oceanic basins being formed during such continental shifts.

Thus Wegener's idea of continental drift was refined as plate tectonics. According to this concept, the continents we know *were* at one time part of a single continent known as Pangaea, this in turn consisting of a northern half-Laurasia, composed of North America and Eurasia, lacking the Indian Peninsula, and a southern entity of Gondwanaland (more properly, Gondwana), consisting of Africa, South America, Peninsular India, Australia, and Antarctica (see figure 51). Within this pangaean supercontinent the northeast border of North America was fitted against the western border of Europe, the Mauritanian bulge of Africa fitted very nicely into the eastern coast of North America, the eastern convex border of South America nestled against the western concave border of Africa, while the northern part of South America was in contact with the southern edge of North America, Antarctica was joined to the southeastern edge of Africa, one side of Peninsular India fit against the northeastern edge of Africa, with Madagascar wedged between them, the other side of the Indian peninsula being joined to Antarctica. Finally the Wilkes Land edge of Antarctica fit very neatly into the Great Australian Bight. This was the situation during Permian time.

With the advent of Mesozoic history Pangaea began to break up, featured by rifts developing within the supercontinent along lines that would define the future separate continents. The embryonic continents pulled apart from one another, and new oceanic basins developed between the separating land masses. (Which is why the South Atlantic is no older than the Jurassic, the time when this ocean began to appear between South America and Africa, as the two continents drifted apart.)

The rifting of Pangaea and the movements of its several fragments across the globe were not a matter of the new continents plowing through

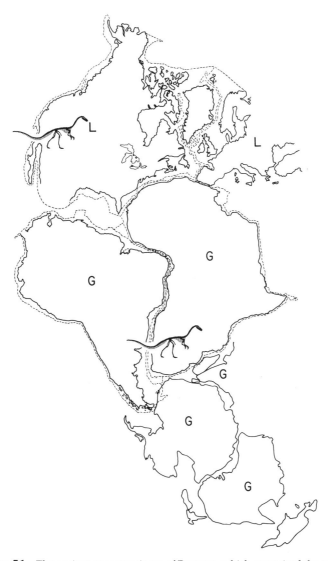

FIGURE 51   The ancient supercontinent of Pangaea, which comprised the two lesser
continents Laurasia (L), composed of present-day North America and Eurasia (except
India), and Gondwana (G), made up of present-day South America, Africa, peninsular
India, Antarctica, and Australia. This map shows the relationships of the various blocks
constituting Pangaea, just before the breakup of that supercontinent, which began during the transition from Triassic to Jurassic time. The map shows the approximate location
of the Chinle beds containing *Coelophysis* and the Forest Sandstone of Zimbabwe containing *Syntarsus*.

the crust of the earth as had been imagined by some geologists in those early days of the concept, but rather of the shifting of great crustal plates, on which the continents were contained like logs of wood in blocks of ice. An immense body of geophysical evidence has accumulated since the end of World War II to support this picture of crustal development through Mesozoic and Cenozoic time (Hallam 1974).

But what about the fossil evidence? A good fossil with accurate geologic and geographic documentation as to its position in time and space cannot be denied. Would the fossil evidence accord with the evidence of plate tectonics, or was the original earlier idea of fixed continents and long "migrations" of land-living animals sufficient to explain the distribution of fossil and recent vertebrates? In the opinion of numerous geologists, especially paleontologists, the answer to this question was to be found in Antarctica. Here in our modern world is the South Polar continent, isolated by thousands of miles of ocean from the other land masses of the earth. It is a continent that could not have been reached by land-living animals if the continents of past time were arranged as are the continents today. But if Antarctica was once part of Pangaea, then one might hope to find the fossils of land-living animals within Antarctic rocks, particularly the fossils of animals with African relationships. Quite by accident, or perhaps it would be more proper to say by serendipity, I became involved in the search for ancient land-living animals in Antarctica—Triassic amphibians and reptiles.

In 1968 a fragmentary fossil bone had been discovered in Triassic sediments in the Transantarctic Mountains, about four hundred miles from the South Pole. The fossil had been found by a party from the Institute of Polar Studies of Ohio State University, and by chance it was submitted to me for identification. The fossil might very well have been sent to any one of a dozen people around the country but I happened to be chosen to look at it. It proved to be a part of a lower jaw of a Triassic amphibian, and in due course it was described in a paper jointly written by Ralph Baillie, who had first seen the specimen in the field, Peter Barrett, a New Zealander who has since become one of the outstanding authorities on Antarctic geology, and me.

The specimen created a lot of interest among paleontologists, as well as among people at the National Science Foundation in Washington. They suggested that I go to Antarctica in search of more fossils, and that is how in late October 1969, I came to be at McMurdo Station, about eight hundred miles from the pole, together with Bill Breed of the Museum of Northern Arizona, Jim Jensen of Brigham Young University, and Jon Powell of the University of Arizona. We were part of a larger team, under the direction of David Elliot of the Institute of Polar Studies, a veteran of many Antarctic expeditions. (During the interval between my first contact with that single Antarctic fossil and my journey to the South Polar continent, I had retired after forty years at the American Museum of Natural History in New York City and had settled with my wife, Margaret, in Flagstaff, Arizona, where I became associated with the Museum of Northern Arizona.)

We established ourselves at a field camp about four hundred miles from McMurdo Station, near the Beardmore Glacier, the great glacier up which Scott and his companions painfully made their way to the pole, only to find that they had been preceded by Amundsen and his party. We immediately found fossils and continued to find them during the extent of the 1969–1970 austral summer. And our initial sally into the snow and ice of Antarctica was followed by several subsequent expeditions (in which I did not participate) whose members found more fossils. But in 1969–1970 we had the pleasure of discovering a fossil vertebrate fauna on a continent where no fossils of land-living vertebrate animals had ever been discovered before. Nobody will ever do that again.

What we found was the Lower Triassic reptile *Lystrosaurus,* so characteristic of the Lower Triassic beds in South Africa that these sediments have been known for many years as the *Lystrosaurus* zone. And the fossils that we found in Antarctica not only were *Lystrosaurus* but also belonged to the same species—*Lystrosaurus murrayi*—that characterizes the lowest Triassic sediments of the Karroo Series of South Africa. Furthermore, as a result of our expedition and of expeditions in following years, other constituents of the *Lystrosaurus* zone fauna have been found in Antarctica, such as a mammal-like reptile, *Thrinaxodon,* and a small primitive reptile, *Procolophon,* both of the same species in Africa and in Antarctica. Additional members of the *Lystrosaurus* fauna have since been found in Antarctica.

These fossils established a final corroboration for the close physical connection of Antarctica with Africa during Triassic time. In addition, as a result of field studies in India (in some of which I participated) the *Lystrosaurus* fauna is known from the Lower Triassic beds of that subcontinent. The *Lystrosaurus* fauna is identifiable down to species, found in locales now thousands of miles apart; when Gondwana is restored to its supposed original limits, it may be confined to an area comparable to the eastern part of the United States—an area quite compatible for the range of single species.

The *Lystrosaurus* fauna is of Lower Triassic age, millions of years before the Upper Triassic of Ghost Ranch. But since our original work in Antarctica, fossil reptiles have been found in later Triassic beds there, and in Lower Jurassic as well as in Cretaceous sediments. These discoveries have included the finds of some of the later dinosaurs, closely related to the Jurassic and Cretaceous dinosaurs of other continental regions. Consequently, during Mesozoic times Antarctica evidently was a part of Gondwana, in turn a part of Pangaea. During the Jurassic and Cretaceous periods Pangaea was beginning to split apart, yet even so the continental connections were so close that the land-living animals of those days could extend their distributions across parts of the world that today are far apart and separated from one another by broad oceans.

So we return to the question posed earlier—why are *Coelophysis* and *Syntarsus* so closely related? Because they lived on a single large continent, where active, land-living animals could become established, over distances much shorter than the distances that now separate their fossil remains. One may say that *Lystrosaurus* and *Thrinaxodon* and *Procolophon*, that *Coelophysis* and *Syntarsus*, lived and died in regions that subsequently became separated, to drift for thousands of miles to their present locations. The natural tombs of these various fossils were transported, like the remains of Viking warriors in their funeral ships, to resting places far removed from the places where they had lived.

The story of *Coelophysis* is more than a local story, restricted to Ghost Ranch; it pertains to the vast stretches of ancient continents.

———————————————— ▰▰▰ ————————————————

TWELVE

AN END AND A BEGINNING

The world in which *Coelophysis* lived—a tropical world dominated by great pine forests and inhabited by a broad variety of reptiles, as well as by the last of the labyrinthodont amphibians and the first of the mammals—was an evanescent world, that would soon (in geological terms) give way to a new and different world. And in this respect it followed the course of the worlds of preceding geologic ages as well as the worlds to come. If anything can be learned from the study of geology, it is that through the millenia, the earth has been an ever-changing planet, a planet very different from the earth of "everlasting hills" so dear to the heart of the poet. And in this changing world plants and animals always have been under constant pressure to change as the earth has changed. This is the driving force of organic evolution (Elliott 1986).

During the past two centuries, the years in which mankind has at last begun to learn something about the mobile planet that is his home, the word *extinction* has taken on a pejorative meaning in many minds, to be equated with *failure* in discussions of the history of life. It is thought that to have become extinct is to have failed—as we see, for example, in the common, frequent concept applied to dinosaurian evolution. The dinosaurs were failures, it is often said, because they are no longer with us. Nothing could be farther from the truth; the dinosaurs were supremely successful animals—among the most successful ever to have lived on earth. That they are now extinct is a part of their evolutionary history, as sooner or later it is

a part of the evolutionary history of all plants and animals. We think of ourselves as supremely successful beings, the rulers of the earth, but there is
every reason to think that we, too, will become extinct (perhaps sooner
than later) as did those earlier rulers of the earth.

Extinction is truly not a bad thing; rather, it is a creative process, the
counterpart of origin, a method of sweeping away the old in favor of the
new so that progressive evolution may bring about the "improvements"
among plants and animals that have made the organic world what it is today. Without extinction the world would long since have become a static
planet, inhabited by organisms of the most primitive kind. In short, without extinction little evolutionary advancement would have occurred during the long history of life. It has been the dualistic force of the origin and
extinction of species that has made the long history of life a vibrant, ever-
changing evolutionary drama. And important contributing factors to the
never-ending succession of animals and plants on earth, behind the varied
origins of new species and the concomitant extinctions of old species, have
been the movements of earth's tectonic plates, that, as we have seen, have
resulted in profound changes in the environments that have harbored living things around the globe. The movements of tectonic plates determined
that during Triassic time New Mexico should have been a tropical land,
probably no more than ten degrees of latitude north of the equator.

The transition from late Triassic to early Jurassic time was so gradual
that geologists who have spent their careers studying the geology of the
Southwest have had great difficulty in defining, from the evidence of the
rocks, just where the break between Triassic and Jurassic sediments should
be placed. This is as it should be, because the sedimentary record of earth
history ideally should be a continuous series of rocks, corresponding with
the continuum of time. More often than not, there are breaks in the record
of the rocks that enable the student of earth history to establish divisions
within what would otherwise be an undisturbed sequence of sediments.
But where the geological evidence seems to show a gradual passage from
one great division of earth history to another, as is the case for the Triassic-
Jurassic transition in the American Southwest, it is often necessary to look
at the fossils for clues of the change (Colbert 1986a).

When one analyzes the fossil tetrapods, notably the amphibians and
reptiles that are found in southwestern sediments, it becomes evident that
an extinction event of great consequence took place during the Triassic-
Jurassic transition. Yet a simple one-to-one relationship between the disap-

pearance of various Triassic amphibians and reptiles and the movement of tectonic plates is not easy to establish. For it would seem that with the opening of Jurassic history the geographic position of New Mexico was essentially what it had been during the final days of Triassic history—that is, about ten degrees north of the equator. (This may be contrasted with the situation during late Jurassic time, when the North American segment of Laurasia had shifted at least twenty degrees to the north, perhaps more.)

Where was the plate tectonic "driving force" during the Triassic-Jurassic transition that theoretically brought about earth changes, which in turn determined the directions of evolutionary changes among the animals that inhabited the early Mesozoic continents? The answer would seem to be that in early Jurassic time the tectonic plates had not yet moved enough to change the continental relationships from what they were in late Triassic time. However, the extensive shifts in the tectonic plates during Jurassic history determined that by the end of this geologic period the continents were populated by tetrapods quite advanced over those living at the beginning of Jurassic time. Dinosaurs of early Jurassic history were not far removed from those ancestral types of late Triassic time (note, for example, the extraordinarily close resemblances between *Syntarsus*—Jurassic—and *Coelophysis*—Triassic), but by the close of Jurassic history the continents in their changed positions were populated with dinosaurian giants.

Thus it seems probable that such differences as may be seen between late Triassic and early Jurassic tetrapod faunas were largely the result of extinctions that removed various characteristic Triassic amphibians and reptiles from the early Mesozoic scene. In fact, three waves of mass extinction occurred, involving the evolution of tetrapods during Mesozoic history. The first was at the end of Permian time, when thirty-two families of tetrapods disappeared, to inaugurate associations of basal Triassic amphibians and reptiles very different in composition from the tetrapod faunas that had characterized Permian history. The second was at the end of the Triassic period, when thirty-one tetrapod families became extinct. And the third was the well-known extinction at the end of Cretaceous history, when fifty-two tetrapod families disappeared from the face of the earth— this being the extinction event that brought to a close the reign of the dinosaurs. Although the first two of these three tetrapod mass extinctions were not so great as the Cretaceous extinction, they were in each case about two-thirds as large as the Cretaceous event; moreover, they bracketed Triassic history in such a way as to set apart the Triassic amphibians, reptiles, and mammals (such as they were) as distinctive in their own right (Colbert 1986b).

The tetrapods that lived during late Triassic, Chinle time may be divided into two groups, namely, what may be called the "oldtimers"—the amphibians and reptiles that survived the extinction marking the end of Permian history, thus making their way during Triassic times as relics of animals that had once been numerous and dominant, but whose numbers had been largely reduced by the end of Permian extinction—and the "newcomers"—the amphibians, reptiles, and even mammals that appeared as evolutionary innovations with the advent of Triassic history, destined to establish new ways of life designed to fit new environmental strictures in a changing world. Among the oldtimers within the Chinle assemblages were almost the last of the gigantic labyrinthodont amphibians, represented by *Metoposaurus;* the last of the procolophonid reptiles, *Hypsognathus,* a parallel to lizards before lizards had become well-established in the Mesozoic world; and the last of the mammal-like dicynodont reptiles, as exemplified by *Placerias,* the last member of a long evolutionary line. These oldtimers all became extinct with the closing of Triassic history.

The Triassic newcomers, which gave the faunas of Chinle age much of their distinction, were the "lizardlike" trilophosaurs, as represented by *Trilophosaurus; Tanytrachelos,* belonging to a minor Triassic reptilian group known as the Protorosauria; the kuehneosaurs, which may be categorized as gliding proto-lizards and represented in the late Triassic of North America by *Icarosaurus;* and above all the initial burgeoning of the archosaurs, represented in Chinle time by the first pterosaurs; the very first crocodilians; and above all, the varied thecodonts, such as the crocodile-like phytosaurs, and the various armored thecodont reptiles; and, of course, the first dinosaurs. Finally, the very first mammals, exceedingly small, primitive, "warm-blooded" tetrapods were in late Triassic time establishing new living styles, destined to become dominant in the far distant future. Most, but not all, of these newcomers were the founders of evolutionary lines destined to dominate not only Jurassic and Cretaceous history but, in the case of the mammals, post-Cretaceous history down to the present.

As a result of recent studies, particularly by Dr. Michael Benton of the University of Bristol, England, it seems very likely that two extinction events took place in late Triassic time; one of Carnian age, about 225 million years ago, and a second one of Norian age, some 15 million years later, approximately 210 million years ago. According to this scenario the first Triassic extinction involved most of the thecodonts and most of the mammal-like reptiles, as well as the rhynchosaurs (a Eurasian and southern hemisphere group that has not previously been introduced into the discussions, since it is largely irrelevant to the *Coelophysis* story). This opened the field to very late Triassic, or Norian, dinosaurs—the theropods, prosauropods, and ornithischians. It would appear that perhaps the second, or Norian, extinction was less extensive than the Carnian extinction. In relation to the Carnian extinction, Benton has said that "the dinosaurs, and other replacing groups, appear to have radiated only *after* the extinction event, thus suggesting an opportunistic replacement rather than one involving long-term competition" (Benton 1986; 1989a:196; 1989b).

Benton's analysis is logical; his explanation that the extinction of the thecodonts, in particular, left open niches that were to be exploited by the descendants of *Coelophysis* and other dinosaurs contemporaneous with the Chinle dinosaur best fits the evidence of the fossils. The alternative explanation involves direct competition between dinosaurs and thecodonts, and it is indeed difficult to picture a theropod such as *Coelophysis* contending in a direct way with a large, aggressive thecodont such as *Postosuchus*. This sort of competition would have involved the elegant ancestor that is the subject of our attention face to face with a large predator several times its size, yet in some ways a clumsy reptile, in many respects hardly the equal of even the earliest theropod dinosaurs. Part of this problem has to do with comparative anatomy.

The thecodont reptiles, as discussed earlier, introduced a new sort of functional anatomy into the world of Triassic reptiles. As we have seen, some of these new reptiles were distinguished by their large, narrow, open skulls in which the very long jaws were provided with sharp, bladelike teeth, and by their elongated limbs, particularly the hind limbs, so constructed that the feet were brought in close to a midline beneath the body, and more often than not locomotion was bipedal. Such a design was integrated toward rapid running and the efficient killing of their prey (see figure 52). It contrasted with the previously perfected design for predation as developed during Permian times by many of the mammal-like reptiles and continued into the Triassic; this design involved compact skulls in which

FIGURE 52   *Coelophysis,* as depicted by Margaret Colbert in the mural now at the New Mexico Museum of Natural History.

the teeth in the sides of the jaws were frequently of complex shape and adapted to the chewing and crushing of food, while the limbs were not particularly elongated and the gait was thoroughly quadrupedal.

Although the mammal-like reptiles were very much on the wane even before the advent of Triassic time, some of them were disappearing not because of extinction in the usual sense of the word but because they were evolving into mammals and thus developing a distinctive mode of life, quite at variance with other new living styles that appeared during Triassic history—like that of the thecodont reptiles, the initial archosaurs. The emphasis in the archosaurian reptiles was on efficient, rapid locomotion, which reached its culmination among the theropod dinosaurs, and generally on an increase in size. In the first mammals, directly derived from certain advanced mammal-like reptiles, the trend was toward very small size, "warm-bloodedness," expansion of the brain, and intimate maternal care of the young.

Yet the question remains—why did the thecodont reptiles disappear so completely before effective dinosaurian dominance became established?

For that matter, why did the aquatic phytosaurs die out, to be so closely imitated by the crocodilians? One might say that even the earliest theropods, *Coelophysis* being a prime example, were so much more efficiently adapted for a life of active predation that they were almost bound to prevail. Based on examination of anatomical structures, the dinosaurs were the more efficient running and killing machines, to state the case in mechanical terms.

To repeat Benton's argument, the dinosaurs became what they were by reason of an opportunistic replacement—*after* the thecodonts had become extinct. Which leaves a large question still unanswered: if there was no real competition between the first dinosaurs and the last of the thecodonts, why did the thecodonts become extinct? They were doing very well as the Triassic period drew to its close; and ironically they were performing well roles that would be independently developed and exploited by the later dinosaurs. Thus certain small carnivorous thecodonts known as ornithosuchids were living in late Triassic time and enjoying successful evolutionary histories, even in the presence of parallel early dinosaurs as exemplified by *Coelophysis* (see figure 52). These small carnivores—thecodonts and theropods—must have had similar behavior patterns, similar in their generalities but notably different in details. The ornithosuchids failed, while the early theropods were the ancestors of successful dinosaurian lines of evolution.

Perhaps more striking examples may be found in the comparison of the very large carnivorous thecodonts, such as *Postosuchus*, and the gigantic theropods of Jurassic and Cretaceous times, such as *Allosaurus* and *Tyrannosaurus*. It might be said that the disappearance of *Postosuchus* and its relatives left open a large ecological niche that would not be occupied until after a lapse of many millions of years, when the big dinosaurian carnivores came to dominate the scenes in which they lived. And the same scenario applies to the herbivorous armored Triassic thecodonts, such as *Desmatosuchus* and *Typothorax*, which disappeared, leaving a gap that would be occupied after many millions of years by *Ankylosaurus* and its dinosaurian relatives.

One may wonder how the evolutionary picture might have developed if the thecodonts had not become extinct in the late Triassic. How might they have fared as true, contemporaneous competitors of the dinosaurs? However, there is little point in so speculating, because the end-of-Triassic extinctions that left open ecological niches for subsequent exploitation by the dinosaurs were as much a fact of life as were the consequent unopposed occupations of these niches by the dinosaurian analogues of their theco-dont predecessors.

So late Triassic history was a time of endings and of beginnings—of extinctions and of origins, acting in tandem as creative forces that set the course of middle and late Mesozoic dinosaurian evolution along the lines that have become known to us through a century of field and laboratory research. Such efforts by many paleontologists, working over a century and a half and around the world, have revealed this history of endings and of beginnings; of the ends of diverse lines of thecodont evolution because of extinctions during the transition from Triassic to Jurassic time; of the beginnings of even more diverse lines of dinosaurian evolution that extended through Jurassic and Cretaceous history—resulting in a rich evolutionary radiation of dinosaurs that far exceeded the range of adaptations that had been reached by the thecodonts. It is a familiar sequence, repeated time and again among evolving organisms: the sequence of death and renewal, of extinctions and of origins, of the two seemingly opposed but actually congruent forces that have determined the creative role of evolution in the history of life.

At Ghost Ranch, where the *Coelophysis* quarry revealed such an astonishing richness of dinosaur skeletons, more can be seen than a Triassic graveyard. For here we may view the last of the thecodonts, the end of one highly diverse evolutionary line in the history of reptiles and the beginning of another, as represented by *Coelophysis*, ancestral to many of the multitudinous and varied reptiles that we call dinosaurs, which were to rule the earth for 150 million years.

BIBLIOGRAPHY

Alexander, R. McNeill. 1989. *Dynamics of Dinosaurs and Other Extinct Giants.* New York: Columbia University Press.

Anonymous. 1947. *Life* (magazine) 23 (August 17, 1947): 49–52. (Restoration of *Coelophysis* by R. Freund, p. 52.)

Ash, Sidney R. 1967. "The Chinle (Upper Triassic) Megaflora of the Zuni Mountains, New Mexico." In *New Mexico Geol. Soc. Eighteenth Field Conference:* 125–31.

———. 1972. "Plant Megafossils of the Chinle Formation." *Mus. Northern Arizona, Bulletin Series* 47:23–43.

———. 1974. "Upper Triassic Plants of Cañon del Cobre, New Mexico." In C. T. Siemers, ed., *New Mexico Geol. Soc. Twenty-Fifth Field Conference, Ghost Ranch:* 179–84.

Auffenberg, Walter. 1981. *The Behavioral Ecology of the Komodo Monitor.* Gainesville: University of Florida Book.

Baker, A. A., C. H. Dane, and J. B. Reeside, Jr. 1947. "Revised Correlation of Jurassic Formations of Parts of Utah, Arizona, New Mexico, and Colorado." *Bull. Amer. Assoc. Petroleum Geologists* 31: 1664–77.

Bakker, Robert T. 1986. *The Dinosaur Heresies.* New York: Morrow.

Barreto, Claudia, Ralph M. Albrecht, Dale E. Bjorling, John R. Horner, and Norman J. Wilsman. 1993. "Evidence of the Growth Plate and the Growth of Long Bones in Juvenile Dinosaurs." *Science* 262:2020–23.

Bartram, William. [1791]. *Travels of William Bartram.* Mark Van Dorn, ed. New York: Dover (no date).

Bellairs, Angus. 1969. 2 vols. *The Life of Reptiles*. London: Weidenfeld and Nicolson.

Benton, Michael. 1983. "Dinosaur Success in the Triassic. A Noncompetitive Ecological Model." *Quart. Review Biol.* 58:29–55.

——. 1986. "The Late Triassic Tetrapod Extinction Events." In K. Padian, ed., *The Beginning of the Age of Dinosaurs: Faunal Changes Across the Triassic-Jurassic Boundary*, 303–20. Cambridge: Cambridge University Press.

——. 1989a. "End-Triassic." In D.E.G. Briggs and R. R. Crowther, eds., *Palaeobiology: A Synthesis*, 194–98. Oxford: Blackwell.

——. 1989b. "Mass Extinction Among Tetrapods and the Quality of the Fossil Record." *Phil. Trans. Roy. Soc. London* B 325:369–86.

——. 1991. "What Really Happened in the Late Triassic?" *Historical Biology* 5:263–78.

Bonaparte, J. F. 1975. "Nuevos materiales de *Lagosuchus talampayensis* Romer (Thecodontia-Pseudosuchia) y su significado en el origin de los Saurischia. Chanarense inferior, Triasico medio de Argentina." *Acta Geologica Lilloana* 13:5–90.

Breed, Carol S. and William J. Breed, eds. 1972. "Investigations in the Triassic Chinle Formation." *Mus. Northern Arizona, Bulletin Series* 47.

Broom, Robert. 1913. "On the South African Pseudosuchian *Euparkeria* and Allied Genera." *Proc. Zool. Soc. London*: 619–33.

Buckland, William. 1824. "Notice on the *Megalosaurus*, or Great Fossil Lizard of Stonesfield." *Trans. Geol. Soc. London* series 2, vol. 1: 390–96, pls. 40–44.

Calder, Nigel. 1972. *The Restless Earth: A Report on the New Geology*. New York: Viking.

Camp, C. L. and S. P. Welles. 1956. "Triassic Dicynodont Reptiles." *Memoirs Univ. California* 13:255–348, pls. 30–33.

Carroll, Robert L. 1988. *Vertebrate Paleontology and Evolution*. New York: Freeman.

Case, Ermin C. 1927a. "The Vertebral Column of *Coelophysis* Cope." *Contributions Mus. Geology, Univ. Michigan* 2:209–22, pl. 1.

——. 1927b. "Genus *Coelophysis* in the Upper Triassic Beds of Western Texas." *Bull. Geol. Soc. Amer.* 38:227.

Charig, Alan. 1979. *A New Look at the Dinosaurs*. New York: Mayflower.

——. 1981. "Cladistics: A Different Point of View." *Biologist* 28:19–20.

Chatterjee, Sankar. 1985. "*Postosuchus:* A New Thecodontian Reptile from the Triassic of Texas and the Origin of Tyrannosaurs." *Phil. Trans. Roy. Soc. London* B 309:395–460.

——. 1993. "*Shuvosaurus:* A New Theropod." *National Geographic Research and Exploration* 9:274–85.

Colbert, Edwin H. 1946. "*Hypsognathus:* A Triassic Reptile from New Jersey." *Bull. Amer. Mus. Nat. Hist.* 87:229–74.

——. 1947. "Studies of the Phytosaurs *Machaeroprosopus* and *Rutiodon.*" *Bull. Amer. Mus. Nat. Hist.* 88:53–96.

——. 1952. "A Pseudosuchian Reptile from Arizona." *Bull. Amer. Mus. Nat. Hist.* 99:561–92, pls. 48, 49.

——. 1964a. "The Triassic Dinosaur Genera *Podokesaurus* and *Coelophysis.*" *Amer. Mus. Novitates,* no. 2168:1–12.

——. 1964b. "Relationships of the Saurischian Dinosaurs." *Amer. Mus. Novitates,* no. 2181:1–24.

——. 1970a. "A Saurischian Dinosaur from the Triassic of Brazil." *Amer. Mus. Novitates,* no. 2405:1–39.

——. 1970b. "The Triassic Gliding Reptile *Icarosaurus.*" *Bull. Amer. Mus. Nat. Hist.* 143:85–142.

——. 1973. *Wandering Lands and Animals.* New York: Dutton.

——. 1974a. "*Lystrosaurus* from Antarctica." *Amer. Mus. Novitates* no. 2535:1–44.

——. 1974b. "The Triassic paleontology of Ghost Ranch." In C. T. Siemers, ed., *New Mexico Geol. Soc., Twenty-Fifth Field Conference:* 175–78.

——. 1981. "A Primitive Ornithischian Dinosaur from the Kayenta Formation of Arizona." *Mus. Northern Arizona, Bulletin Series* 53.

——. 1983. *Dinosaurs: An Illustrated History.* Maplewood, N.J.: A Dembner Book, Hammond.

——. 1985. "The Petrified Forest and Its Vertebrate Fauna in Triassic Pangaea." In Edwin H. Colbert and R. Roy Johnson, eds., *The Petrified Forest Through the Ages,* 33–43. *Mus. Northern Arizona, Bulletin Series* 54.

——. 1986a. "Historical Aspects of the Triassic-Jurassic Boundary Problem." In Kevin Padian, ed., *The Beginning of the Age of Dinosaurs,* 9–19. Cambridge: Cambridge University Press.

——. 1986b. "Mesozoic Tetrapod Extinctions: A Review." In David K. Elliott, ed., *Dynamics of Extinction,* 49–61. New York: Wiley.

——. 1989. "The Triassic Dinosaur *Coelophysis.*" *Mus. Northern Arizona, Bulletin Series* 57:1–160.

Colbert, Edwin H. and Donald Baird. 1958. "Coelurosaur Bone Casts from the Connecticut Valley Triassic." *Amer. Mus. Novitates* no. 1901:1–11.

Colbert, Edwin H. and John Imbrie. 1956. "Triassic Metoposaurid Amphibians." *Bull. Amer. Mus. Nat. Hist.* 110:399–452.

Colbert, Edwin H., Raymond B. Cowles, and Charles M. Bogert. 1946. "Temperature Tolerances in the American Alligator and Their Bearing on the Habits, Evolution, and Extinction of the Dinosaurs." *Bull. Amer. Mus. Nat. Hist.* 86:327–74, pls. 36–41.

Colbert, Edwin H., Alan J. Charig, Peter Dodson, David D. Gillette, John H.
Ostrom, and David Weishampel. 1992. Case 2840. "*Coelurus bauri* (Cope
1887) (currently *Coelophysis bauri*: Reptilia, Saurischia): Proposed Replacement of the Lectotype by a Neotype." *Bull. Zool. Nomenclature* 49:276–79.

Coombs, Walter P., Jr. 1978. "Theoretical Aspects of Cursorial Adaptations in
Dinosaurs." *Quart. Rev. Biol.* 53:393–418.

Cope, Edward Drinker. 1887a. "The Dinosaurian Genus *Coelurus*." *Amer. Naturalist* 21:367–69.

——. 1887b. "A Contribution to the History of the *Vertebrata* of the Trias of
North America." *Proc. Amer. Philos. Soc.* 24:209–28, pls. i, ii.

——. 1889. "On a New Genus of Triassic *Dinosauria*." *Amer. Naturalist* 23:626.

Cott, Hugh B. 1961. "Scientific Results of an Inquiry into the Ecology and Eco-
nomic Status of the Nile Crocodile (*Crocodilus niloticus*) in Uganda and
Northern Rhodesia." *Trans. Zool. Soc. London* 29:215–337.

Dickens, Charles. 1989. *Bleak House*. Oxford: Oxford University Press.

Dubiel, Russell F. 1989a. "Depositional Environments of the Upper Triassic
Chinle Formation in the Eastern San Juan Basin and Vicinity, New Mexico."
U.S. Geol. Surv. Bull. 1801–B–D: B1–B22.

——. 1989b. "Sedimentology and Revised Nomenclature of the Upper Triassic
Chinle Formation and the Lower Jurassic Wingate Sandstone." In *New Mexico Geol. Soc., 40th Field Conference Guidebook*.

DuToit, A. A. 1937. *Our Wandering Continents*. Edinburgh: Oliver and Boyd.

Eldredge, N. and S. J. Gould. 1972. "Punctuated Equilibria: An Alternative to
Phyletic Gradualism" In T.J.M. Schopf, ed., *Models in Paleobiology*, 82–115.
San Francisco: Freeman, Cooper.

Elliott, David K., ed. 1986. *Dynamics of Extinction*. New York: Wiley.

Enlow, Donald H., and Sidney O. Brown. 1956. "A Comparative Histological
Study of Fossil and Recent Bone Tissues, Part I." *Texas Jour. Sci.* 8:405–43.

——. 1957. "A Comparative Histological Study of Fossil and Recent Bone Tissues, Part II." *Texas Jour. Sci.* 9:186–214.

——. 1958. "A Comparative Histological Study of Fossil and Recent Bone Tissues, Part III." *Texas Jour. Sci.* 10:187–230.

Ewer, Rosalie F. 1965. "The Anatomy of the Thecodont Reptile *Euparkeria capen-
sis* Broom." *Phil. Trans. Roy. Soc. London* B 248:379–435.

Farlow, James A., ed. 1989. "Paleobiology of the Dinosaurs." *Geol. Soc. Amer.
Special Paper* 238.

Gillette, David D. 1986. "A New Place for Old Bones." *Ghost Ranch Jour.* 1:2–6.

Gillette, David D. and Martin G. Lockley, eds. 1989. *Dinosaur Tracks and Traces*.
Cambridge: Cambridge University Press.

Gottesfeld, Allen S. 1972. "Paleoecology of the Lower Part of the Chinle Formation in the Petrified Forest." *Mus. Northern Arizona, Bulletin Series* 47:59–73.

Gregory, Joseph T. 1945. "Osteology and Relationships of *Trilophosaurus*." *Univ. Texas Publ.* 4401:273–359, pls. 18–33.

Hallam, A. 1974. *A Revolution in the Earth Sciences*. Oxford: Clarendon Press.

Harshbarger, J. W., C. A. Repenning, and J. H. Irwin. 1957. "Stratigraphy of the Uppermost Triassic and the Jurassic Rocks of the Navajo Country." *U.S. Geol. Surv. Prof. Paper 291, with Bureau of Indian Affairs.*

Hay, Oliver Perry. 1930. *Second Bibliography and Catalogue of the Fossil Vertebrates of North America*. Washington: Carnegie Inst. Washington, Publication 390, II.

Hopson, James A. 1980. "Relative Brain Size in Dinosaurs. Implications for Dinosaurian Endothermy." In D. K. Thomas and Everett C. Olson, eds., *A Cold Look at the Warm Blooded Dinosaurs*, 287–310. Boulder, Colo.: Westview Press.

Horner, John R. 1982. "Evidence of Colonial Nesting and 'Site Fidelity' among Ornithischian Dinosaurs." *Nature* 297:675–76.

———. 1984. "The Nesting Behavior of Dinosaurs." *Scientific American* 250:130–37.

Horner, J. R. and R. Makela. 1979. "Nest of Juveniles Provides Evidence of Family Structure among Dinosaurs." *Nature* 282:296–98.

von Huene, Friedrich. 1906. "Über die Dinosaurier der ausser-europäischen Trias." *Geologische und Palaeontologische Abhandlungen*. Berlin; Jena (n.s.) 8:97–156, pls. 8–23.

———. 1915. "On Reptiles of the New Mexican Trias in the Cope Collection." *Bull. Amer. Mus. Nat. Hist.* 34:485–507.

Hunt, Adrian P. 1989. "A New ?Ornithischian Dinosaur from the Bull Canyon Formation (Upper Triassic) of East-Central New Mexico." In S. G. Lucas and A. P. Hunt, eds., *Dawn of the Age of Dinosaurs in the American Southwest*, pp. 355–58, pls. 8–9. Albuquerque: New Mexico Mus. Hat. Hist.

Hunt, Adrian P. and Spencer G. Lucas. 1991. "*Rioarribasaurus:* A New name for a Late Triassic Dinosaur from New Mexico (USA)." *Paläontologische Zeitschrift* 65:191–98.

———. 1993. "Comments on a Proposed Neotype for *Coelophysis bauri* (Cope 1887) (Reptilia, Saurischia) Case 2840." *Bull. Zool. Nomenclature* 50:147–50.

Irby, Grace. 1993a. "Paleoichnology of the Cameron Dinosaur Tracksite, Lower Jurassic Dinosaur Canyon Member, Moenave Formation, Northeastern Arizona." Master's thesis, Northern Arizona University, Flagstaff.

———. 1993b. "Early Jurassic Dinosaur Tracksites, Northeastern Arizona."

Mesa, Arizona, Southwest Paleontological Society, *Proceedings First Annual Symposium Fossils of Arizona:* 15–25, figs. 1–8.

Irby, Grace and M. Morales. 1993. "Rare Occurrence of Running Dinosaurs in a Mass Tracksite, Lower Jurassic Dinosaur Canyon Member, Moenave Formation, Ward Terrace, Northeastern Arizona." *Geol. Soc. Amer.,* Abstracts 25(5): 56A.

Jenkins, Farish A., Jr., A. W. Crompton, and William R. Downs. 1983. "Mesozoic Mammals from Arizona: New Evidence of Mammalian Evolution."*Science* 222:1233–35.

Linnaeus, C. 1758. *Systema Naturae.* 10th ed. Stockholm: Laurentii salvii.

Lockley, Martin. 1991. *Tracking Dinosaurs: A New Look at an Ancient World.* Cambridge: Cambridge University Press.

Long, R. A. and Rose Houk. 1988. *Dawn of the Dinosaurs: The Triassic in Petrified Forest.* Petrified Forest, Ariz.: Petrified Forest Museum Association.

Long, R. A. and Kevin Padian. 1986. "Vertebrate Biostratigraphy of the Late Chinle Formation, Petrified Forest National Park, Arizona: Preliminary Results." In Padian, ed., *The Beginning of the Age of Dinosaurs,* 161–69. Cambridge: Cambridge University Press.

Lucas, Spencer G. 1993. "The Chinle Group; Revised Stratigraphy and Biochronology of Upper Triassic Nonmarine Strata in the Western United States. In Michael Morales, ed. "Aspects of Mesozoic Geology and Paleontology of the Colorado Plateau." *Museum of Northern Arizona, Bulletin Series* 59:27–50.

Lucas, Spencer G. and Adrian P. Hunt, eds. 1989. *Dawn of the Age of Dinosaurs in the American Southwest.* Albuquerque: New Mexico Mus. Nat. Hist.

Lull, Richard Swann. 1953. "Triassic Life of the Connecticut Valley (Revised Edition)." *Conn. Geol. Nat. Hist. Survey Bull* 81:1–331.

McGowan, Christopher. 1991. *Dinosaurs, Spitfires, and Sea Dragons.* Cambridge: Harvard University Press.

Mantell, Gideon Algernon. 1825. "Notice on the *Iguanodon,* a Newly Discovered Fossil Reptile, from the Sandstone of Tilgate Forest, in Sussex." *Phil. Trans. Roy. Soc. London* 115:179–86, plate 14.

Mayr, Ernst and Peter D. Ashlock. 1991. *Principles of Systematic Zoology.* 2d ed. New York: McGraw-Hill.

Miller, Russell, and the editors of Time-Life Books. 1983. *Continents in Collision.* Alexandria, Va.: Time-Life Books.

Norman, David. 1985. *The Illustrated Encyclopedia of Dinosaurs.* New York: Crescent Books.

——. 1991. *Dinosaur!* London: Boxtree Limited.

O'Keeffe, Georgia. 1976. *Georgia O'Keeffe: Text and 108 Color Plates.* New York: Viking.

Osborn, Henry Fairfield. 1917. "Skeletal Adaptations of *Ornitholestes, Struthiomimus, Tyrannosaurus.*" *Bull. Amer. Mus. Nat. Hist.* 35:733–71, pls. 24–27.

Ostrom, John H. 1969. "Osteology of *Deinonychus antirrhopus,* an Unusual Theropod from the Lower Cretaceous of Montana." *Peabody Mus. Nat. Hist. Yale Univ. Bull.* 30:1–165.

———. 1978. "The Osteology of *Compsognathus longipes* Wagner." *Zitteliana* 4:73–118.

———. 1980. "The Evidence for Endothermy in Dinosaurs." In Roger D. K. Thomas and Everett C. Olson, eds., *A Cold Look at the Warm-Blooded Dinosaurs,* 15–54. Boulder, Colo: Westview Press.

O'Sullivan, Robert B. 1974. "The Upper Triassic Chinle Formation in North-Central New Mexico." In C. T. Siemers, ed., *New Mexico Geol. Soc. Twenty-Fifth Field Conf. Guidebook. Ghost Ranch,* (Cent.-North N.M.):171–74.

———. 1977. "Triassic Rocks in the San Juan Basin of New Mexico and Adjacent Areas." *New Mexico Geol. Soc., Twenty-Eighth Field Conf. Guidebook, San Juan Basin:* 139–45.

Owen, Richard. 1842. "Report on British Fossil Reptiles, Part III." *Report of the British Association for the Advancement of Science, Eleventh Meeting, Plymouth* (July 1841): 60–204.

Pack, Arthur N. 1960. "The Ghost Ranch Story." *Board of Christian Education of the United Presbyterian Church in the U.S.A.* Philadelphia: W. L. Jenkins.

Padian, Kevin. 1984. "Pterosaur Remains from the Kayenta Formation (?Early Jurassic) of Arizona." *Palaeontology* 27:407–13.

———. 1986. "On the Type Material of *Coelophysis* Cope (Saurischia: Theropoda) and a New Specimen from the Petrified Forest of Arizona (Late Triassic; Chinle Formation)." In Kevin Padian, ed., *The Beginning of the Age of Dinosaurs,* 45–60. Cambridge: Cambridge University Press.

———. 1990. "The Ornithischian Form Genus *Revueltosaurus* from the Petrified Forest of Arizona (Late Triassic: Norian; Chinle Formation)." *Jour. Vert. Paleont.* 10:268–69.

Paul, Gregory S. 1988. *Predatory Dinosaurs of the World: A Complete Illustrated Guide.* New York: Simon and Schuster. A New York Academy of Sciences Book.

Raath, M. A. 1969. "A New Coelurosaurian Dinosaur from the Forest Sandstone of Rhodesia." *Arnoldia* 4:1–25.

———. 1980. "The Theropod Dinosaur *Syntarsus* (Saurischia: Podokesauridae) Discovered in South Africa." *S. Afr. Jour. Sci.* 76:375–76.

Repenning, C. A., M. E. Cooley, and J. P. Akers. 1969. "Stratigraphy of the Chinle and Moenkopi Formations, Navajo and Hopi Indian Reservations Arizona, New Mexico, and Utah." *U.S. Geol. Surv. Prof. Paper* 521–B.

Richardson, William H. 1849. *Journal of William H. Richardson, a Private soldier in the Campaign of New and Old Mexico, Under the Command of Colonel Doniphan, of Missouri.* 3d ed. New York, p. 34.

Ricqlès, Armand J., de. 1980. "Tissue Structures of Dinosaur Bone: Functional Significance and Possible Relation to Dinosaur Physiology." In Roger D. K. Thomas and Everett C. Olson, eds., *A Cold Look at the Warm-Blooded Dinosaurs*, 103–39. Boulder, Colo.: Westview Press.

——. 1983. "Cyclical Growth in the Long Limb Bones of a Sauropod Dinosaur." *Palaeontologica* 28:225–32, pls. 7–9.

Ride, W.D.L. (chairman) et al. 1985. *International Code of Zoological Nomenclature, Third Edition, adopted by the XX General Assembly of the International Union of Biological Sciences.* London: International Trust for Zoological Nomenclature in association with British Museum (Natural History).

Rogers, Raymond R., Carl C. Swisher III, Paul C. Sereno, Alfredo M. Monetta, Catherine A. Forster, and Ricardo N. Martinez. 1993. "The Ischigualasto Tetrapod Assemblage (Late Triassic, Argentina) and ^{40}Ar/^{39}Ar Dating of Dinosaur Origins." *Science* 260:794–97.

Rowe, Timothy. 1989. "A New Species of the Theropod Dinosaur *Syntarsus* from the Early Jurassic Kayenta Formation of Arizona." *Jour. Vert. Paleont.* 9:125–36.

Rowe, Timothy and Jacques Gauthier. 1990. "Ceratosauria." In David B. Weishampel, Peter Dodson, and Halszka Osmólska, eds., *The Dinosauria*, 151–68. Berkeley: University of California Press.

Schaeffer, Bobb. 1967. "Late Triassic Fishes from the Western United States." *Bull. Amer. Mus. Nat. Hist.* 135:285–342, pls. 8–30.

Schuchert, Charles and Clara Mae LeVene. 1940. *O. C. Marsh: Pioneer in Paleontology.* New Haven: Yale University Press.

Schwartz, Hilde L. and David D. Gillette. 1994. "Geology and Taphonomy of the *Coelophysis* Quarry, Upper Triassic Chinle Formation, Ghost Ranch, New Mexico." *Jour. Paleont.* 68:1118–30.

Seeley, Harry Govier. 1887. "On the Classification of the Fossil Animals Commonly Named Dinosauria." *Proc. Roy. Soc. London* 43:165–71.

Sereno, Paul C. and Fernando E. Novas. 1992. "The Complete Skull and Skeleton of an Early Dinosaur." *Science* 258:1137–40.

Sereno, Paul C., Catherine A. Forster, Raymond R. Rogers, and Alfredo M. Monetta. 1993. "Primitive Dinosaur Skeleton from Argentina and the Early Evolution of Dinosauria." *Nature* 361:64–66.

Simpson, George Gaylord. 1945. "The Principles of Classification and a Classification of Mammals." *Bull. Amer. Mus. Nat. Hist.* 85: (part 1, pp. 1–33, devoted to the "Principles of Taxonomy").

——. 1961. *Principles of Animal Taxonomy.* New York: Columbia University Press.

Smiley, Terah L. 1985. "The Geology and Climate of the Indigenous Forest, Petrified Forest National Park, Arizona." In Edwin H. Colbert and R. Roy Johnson, eds., *The Petrified Forest Through the Ages. Mus. Northern Arizona, Bulletin Series* 54.

Smith, David. 1992. "The Type Specimen of *Oviraptor philoceratops*, a Theropod Dinosaur from the Upper Cretaceous of Mongolia." *N. Jb. Geol. Paläont. Abh.* 186:365–88.

Sternberg, Charles H. 1932. *Hunting Dinosaurs in the Badlands of the Red Deer River, Alberta, Canada.* San Diego: Jensen. (Reprint of 1917, same title, Lawrence, Kansas: World Company Press.)

Stewart, J. H., F. G. Poole, and R. F. Wilson. 1972. "Stratigraphy and Origin of the Chinle Formation and Related Upper Triassic Strata in the Colorado Plateau Region." *U.S. Geol. Surv. Prof. Paper* 690.

Storer, Tracy I. 1951. *General Zoology.* 2nd ed. New York, London: McGraw-Hill.

Sullivan, Walter. 1974. *Continents in Motion: The New Earth Debate.* New York: McGraw-Hill.

Talbot, Mignon. 1911. "*Podokesaurus holyokensis:* A New Dinosaur from the Triassic of the Connecticut Valley," *Amer. Jour. Sci.* series 4, vol. 31: 469–79, pl. iv.

Tarling, D. H. and M. P. Tarling. 1971. *Continental Drift: A Study of the Earth's Moving Surface.* London: G. Bell.

Thomas, D. K. and Everett C. Olson, eds. 1980. *A Cold Look at the Warm-Blooded Dinosaurs.* Boulder, Colo.: Westview Press.

Thulborn, Tony. 1990. *Dinosaur Tracks.* London: Chapman and Hall.

Thulborn, Richard A. and Mary Wade. 1979. "Dinosaur Stampede in the Cretaceous of Queensland." *Lethaia* 12:275–79.

Wegener, Alfred. 1966. *The Origin of Continents and Oceans.* (Translation from the 4th rev. German ed., by John Biram.) New York: Dover.

Weishampel, David, Peter Dodson, and Halszka Osmólska, eds. 1990. *The Dinosauria.* Berkeley: University of California Press.

Welles, Samuel P. 1984. "*Dilophosaurus wetherilli* (Dinosauria, Theropoda) Osteology and Comparisons." *Palaeontographica*, Abt. A, 185:85–180.

Wild, R. 1984. "Flugsaurier aus der Obertrias von Italien." *Naturwissenschaften* 71:1–11.

Wiman, Carl. 1913. "Über die paläontologische Bedeutung des Massensterbens unter den Tieren." *Paleont. Zeitschr.* 1:145–54.

Whitaker, George O. and Joan Meyers. 1965. *Dinosaur Hunt.* New York: Harcourt, Brace.

INDEX

mission of David D. Gillette, Ron Behrman, and Kathryn Matthew, former director of the New Mexico Museum of Natural History.

Figures 19, 28, 29, 32, 33, 34, 35, 36, 37, 38, 39, 40, 41, 42, and 43 were drawn by the late Lois Darling under the direction of the author and originally published in *Bulletin* 57 (1989) of the Museum of Northern Arizona. These figures are the property of the American Museum of Natural History, New York, and are published by permission of Richard H. Tedford of that museum, and by permission of the Museum of Northern Arizona.

Figures 18, 22, 23, 24, 32, and 46 are published by permission of Richard H. Tedford of the American Museum of Natural History.

Figure 31 was drawn by Louise Waller under the direction of the author and was first published in *Bulletin* 57 (1989) of the Museum of Northern Arizona, and is used by permission of that museum.

Figure 17 was originally prepared for *Bulletin* 57 (1989) of the Museum of Northern Arizona. In its present amended form, prepared under the direction of the author, it is published by permission of the Museum of Northern Arizona.

Figure 26 was presented to the author specifically for use in this book by Kenneth Carpenter of the Denver Museum. It is published by permission of Dr. Carpenter and the Denver Museum.

Figure 20 is published by permission of John H. Ostrom of Yale University and by the Yale Peabody Museum.

Figure 48 is a portion of a mural painted by Margaret Colbert for the Petrified Forest National Park and is published by permission of the superintendent of Petrified Forest National Park.

Figure 49 is from a painting by Margaret Colbert, now the property of the Museum of Northern Arizona, and is published by permission of the museum.

Figure 51 is amended from a map originally prepared by the author and published in *A Fossil Hunter's Notebook* by Edwin H. Colbert (E. P. Dutton, New York, 1980). The copyright has reverted to the author, and the amended figure is here published by permission of the author.